D0212501

T.M
✓
/

The Philosophy in Christianity

ROYAL INSTITUTE OF PHILOSOPHY LECTURE SERIES: 25
SUPPLEMENT TO *PHILOSOPHY* 1989

EDITED BY

Godfrey Vesey

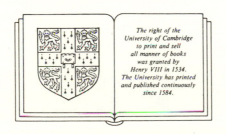

The right of the
University of Cambridge
to print and sell
all manner of books
was granted by
Henry VIII in 1534.
The University has printed
and published continuously
since 1584.

CAMBRIDGE UNIVERSITY PRESS

CAMBRIDGE
NEW YORK PORT CHESTER MELBOURNE SYDNEY

Randall Library UNC-W

Published by the Press Syndicate of the University of Cambridge
The Pitt Building, Trumpington Street, Cambridge, CB2 1RP
40 West 20th Street, New York, NY 10011, USA
10 Stamford Road, Oakleigh, Melbourne 3166, Australia

© The Royal Institute of Philosophy 1989

British Library Cataloguing in Publication Data

Vesey, Godfrey
Philosophy in Christianity.
1. Christian theology. Influence of European philosophy
I. Title
230'.01
ISBN 0 521 37578 9 (paperback)

Library of Congress Cataloguing in Publication Data

Philosophy in Christianity/edited by Godfrey Vesey,
p. cm. – (Royal Institute of Philosophy lecture series: 25)
ISBN 0 521 37578 9
1. Philosophy and religion – History of doctrines.
2. Christianity – Philosophy – History of doctrines.
I. Vesey, Godfrey Norman Agmondisham. II. Series:
Royal Institute of Philosophy lectures: v. 25.
BR100, P537   1989
261.6'1 – dc20

Origination by PPC Limited, Leatherhead, Surrey
Printed in Great Britain by the University Press, Cambridge

Contents

BR
100
·P537
1989

Foreword

GODFREY VESEY

The growth of controversy in the early centuries of the Church obliged Christian thinkers to construct a theology. In developing this theology they were aware of their debt to the scriptures, but perhaps not so deeply aware of their debt to contemporary Platonist philosophy. They drew quite heavily on a world-view that we do not share. Thinking about this, I decided to invite the 1988/89 Royal Institute of Philosophy lecturers to lecture on 'The Philosophy in Christianity'.

The lecturers have tended to assume that the audience, and readership, would be acquainted with at least the broad outlines of Platonism. What I am going to say first is addressed to those for whom this assumption is false.

Platonism

In the *Phaedo* Plato makes Socrates describe his experiences in natural science. Socrates 'thought it would be marvellous to know the causes for which each thing comes, and ceases, and continues, to be'. He had heard someone reading from a book, said to be by Anaxagoras, 'asserting that it is mind that produces order and is the cause of everything', and this explanation pleased him:

> Somehow it seemed right that mind should be the cause of everything, and I reflected that if this is so, mind . . . arranges each individual thing in the way that is best for it. . . . These reflections made me suppose, to my delight, that in Anaxagoras I had found an authority on causation who was after my own heart. I assumed that he would begin by informing us whether the earth is flat or round, and would then proceed to explain in detail the reason and logical necessity for this by stating how and why it was better that it should be so . . . I thought that by assigning a cause to each phenomenon separately and to the universe as a whole he would make perfectly clear what is best for each and what is the universal good (*Phaedo*, 97c–98b).

Socrates' hopes were quickly dashed when he bought the books by Anaxagoras. Like most people, Anaxagoras evidently regarded such things as air and æther and water as causes. He neither looked for, nor believed in, 'a power which keeps things disposed at any given moment in the best possible way'.

Socrates' description of his experiences in natural science concludes with his saying that he would be delighted to learn about the workings of such a cause from anyone, but that since he has been unable either to discover it himself, or to learn about it from another, he has worked out his own makeshift approach to the problem of causation.

What Socrates calls his 'makeshift approach to the problem of causation' is what has become known as 'Plato's Theory of Forms' (or, in an older terminology, 'Plato's Theory of Ideas'). Suppose we have to give the reason why a given object is beautiful. What we ought to say, Plato suggests, is that 'the one thing that makes that object beautiful is the presence in it, or association with it, in whatever way the relation comes about, of absolute beauty' (*Phaedo,* 100d). 'Absolute beauty' is the 'Form' of beauty.

It is not at all clear, from what Plato goes on to say in the *Phaedo*, what he is getting at. What does he mean by 'absolute beauty', 'absolute equality', 'absolute tallness'? In short, what are 'Forms'? And what is the relationship of the Forms of beauty, equality, tallness to the beautiful, equal, tall things we see around us?

The first part of an answer is suggested in another dialogue, the *Republic*. It involves a distinction between 'the visible' and 'the intelligible'. Plato introduces the distinction with what he says about 'opposites'. Opposites are things like thick and thin, tall and short, great and small, beautiful and ugly, just and unjust, holy and unholy, wise and stupid, one and many, equal and unequal. In one dialogue (*Greater Hippias,* 289a–d) Plato quotes Heraclitus. Man is both wise, by comparison with an ape, and stupid, by comparison with a god. He is both wise and stupid. Wisdom and stupidity are together, confounded, in man. In Book VII of the *Republic* (523b–524d) Plato contrasts seeing that something is a finger with seeing how big it is. Vision seems adequate for the judgment that the object is a finger, but not for how big it is. The finger next to the thumb is large by comparison with the outside, or 'little' finger, but small by comparison with the middle finger. 'The great and the small are confounded' in the finger. So it cannot be by vision that one is aware of largeness or smallness. It must be in some other way. It is, Plato says, 'by intelligence':

> Intelligence is compelled to contemplate the great and the small, not thus confounded but as distinct entities, in the opposite way from sensation. . . . And this is the origin of the designation *intelligible* for the one and *visible* for the other (*Republic*, 524c).

His idea seems to be that one can be aware, by vision, of a finger as large only because one can be aware, by intelligence, of largeness itself, a distinct entity that he calls 'the great'. And the same for all the other opposites, such as beautiful and ugly, tall and short. In visible things the opposites are always 'confounded'. We apprehend the largeness, confounded with smallness, in the finger, through its reminding us of the absolute largeness we have previously apprehended by intelligence.

If we go along with Plato in this, to us, strange line of thinking, then we are faced with two questions. First, *when* did we apprehend absolute largeness, absolute beauty, absolute tallness, etc.? Secondly, what is meant by saying that these absolute things are *intelligible*?

Plato deals with the first of these two questions in the *Phaedo*, 65d–66a, 74a–75d. This time the opposites he considers are equality and inequality. Socrates asks 'Do they (the things we see) seem to us to be equal in the sense of absolute equality, or do they fall short of it in so far as they only approximate to equality?', receives the answer that they fall a long way short, and continues as follows:

> . . . it must be through the senses that we obtained the notion that all sensible equals are striving after absolute equality but falling short of it. . . . So before we began to see and hear and use our other senses we must somewhere have acquired the knowledge that there is such a thing as absolute equality. Otherwise we could never have realized, by using it as a standard of comparison, that all equal objects of sense are desirous of being like it, but are only imperfect copies. Did we not begin to see and hear and possess our other senses from the moment of birth? But we admitted that we must have obtained our knowledge of equality before we obtained them. So we must have obtained it before birth (*Phaedo*, 75a–c).

Plato is committed, by this argument, to the view that we exist before birth, but in a non-bodily state so that the soul is not impeded, by the senses, from 'applying its pure and unadulterated thought to the pure and unadulterated object' (*Phaedo*, 66a). He evidently thinks of the pre-birth soul as existing in the same intelligible world as the Forms. Incidentally, much of the argument in the *Phaedo* is directed to proving that some of us return to this intelligible world after death.

Secondly, what does Plato mean by saying that absolute largeness, absolute beauty, absolute tallness, absolute equality are intelligible? He means that we can, in theory at least, know and say what they are. We can, in theory, define them. Plato does not represent discovering the definition as being at all easy. It is not simply a matter of finding out how the word is used, to what sort of things it is applied, or what the conventions are for its use. Plato had inherited Socrates' distaste for the conventionalism and relativism of the Sophists. This comes out in the way he formulates his questions. If it is about holiness, for instance, his question is: 'What is the essential form of holiness which makes all holy actions holy?' (*Euthyphro*, 6d). It is a question about the eternal, unchanging thing, holiness, not about our possibly changing use of the word 'holy'. Plato was a firm believer in there being two worlds with two different modes of existence: the Forms have Being, but visible things are for ever changing; they are in a world of Becoming. The realm of Becoming is dependent on the realm of Being.

Socrates called all this his 'makeshift approach to the problem of causation'. It strikes us as strange to call it a causal explanation. Moreover, Plato himself did not seem very happy with it. First, unlike the sort of explanation for which Socrates longed, it makes no mention of 'what is best for each and what is the universal good'. Secondly, while absolute beauty, the Form of beauty, may be said, in some very wide sense of 'cause', to be the cause of beautiful things being beautiful, it cannot be said to be the cause of beautiful things existing.

Plato dealt with the first of these two deficiencies in his theory by giving a special status to the Form of the good. He gave it a role in the apprehension of the other Forms comparable to that of the sun in the apprehension of visible things. It 'gives their truth to the objects of knowledge and the power of knowing to the knower', and so is 'the cause of knowledge, and of truth in so far as known' (*Republic*, VI, 508c). Although Plato calls the Form of the good a Form it is not like other Forms. Just as 'the sun not only furnishes to visibles the power of visibility but also provides for their generation and growth and nurture though it is not itself generation' so 'the objects of knowledge not only receive from the presence of the good their being known, but their very existence and essence is derived to them from it, though the good itself is not essence but still transcends essence in dignity and surpassing power' (509b). The ultimate aim of the philosopher is to attain the apprehension of this supreme reality. When the philosopher 'attempts through discourse of reason and apart from all perceptions of sense to find his way to the very essence of each thing and does not desist till he apprehends by thought itself the nature of the good in itself, he arrives at the limit of the intelligible' (VII, 532a–b).

Plato deals with the second deficiency in the *Timaeus*. The Forms are 'copied' in the sensible world. This requires there to be a 'receptacle' for the copies, a 'being which receives all things and in some mysterious way partakes of the intelligible' (51a). Plato suggests that it requires, also, a being that does the copying, a craftsman-like God ('Demiurge'). Now, something cannot partake of the intelligible and be devoid of soul. So the sensible world is 'a living creature truly endowed with soul and intelligence by the providence of God' (30b). That is, there is a 'World Soul' at work. Plato says he is here 'using the language of probability'. He may have been trying to find a place, in his creation hypothesis, for Anaxagoras' view 'that it is mind that produces order and is the cause of everything' (*Phaedo* 97c).

Christian philosophers did not simply take over where Plato left off. They drew on what is now called 'School Platonism', a tradition inaugurated by Plato's successor Xenocrates, who attempted to bring together Plato's disconnected suggestions to form a coherent system. For some two centuries this system was overshadowed by other developments in Greek philosophy that had less permanent influence on Christian thought. But in the first century BC Platonism came back into fashion. This was for two reasons: the literary excellence of Plato's own writings, and a revival of interest in religion and in the thought of a better and more orderly world.

The attraction of Platonism for religious thinkers can be seen in the writings of the Greek-speaking Jewish aristocrat Philo of Alexandria. Philo took over Plato's concept of an intelligible world, and amalgamated it with the biblical notion of a heavenly realm in which God dwells. He used Plato's creation narrative to confirm the biblical account given in Genesis. The Demiurge of Plato's *Timaeus* was assimilated to the Form of the Good; and a personal, active deity was now seen as the supreme principle of explanation. Philo conceived God as completely simple and immutable; but also as a wise and beneficent world ruler. A Platonist philosophy of this type was adopted by most thoughtful Christians in the first few centuries.

The Lectures and the Lecturers

I can now make a start on saying something about the lectures in this collection, and the lecturers.

The lectures are not printed in the order in which they were given. I have re-ordered them into four groups, as follows:

(i)   Lectures relevant to the Trinity and the Incarnation:

'Logos and Trinity: Patterns of Platonist Influence on Early Christianity', by John Dillon, Regius Professor of Greek at Trinity College, Dublin;

'Reason in Mystery' by Norman Kretzmann, Susan Linn Sage Professor of Philosophy at Cornell University;

'The Philosophy in Christianity: Arius and Athanasius', by the Reverend Maurice Wiles, Regius Professor of Divinity at Oxford University;

'Could God Become Man?', by Richard Swinburne, Nolloth Professor of the Philosophy of the Christian Religion at Oxford University.

(ii)   Lectures on God and his creation, including the problem of predestination and freewill:

'Augustine's Philosophy of Being', by the Reverend Christopher Stead, formerly Ely Professor of Divinity at Cambridge University;

'Predestination and Freedom in Augustine's Ethics', by Gerard O'Daly, Lecturer in Classical and Archaeological Studies at the University of Nottingham;

'God as Creator', by the Reverend Keith Ward, Professor of the History and Philosophy of Religion at King's College, London;

'Foreknowledge and the Vulnerability of God', by J. R. Lucas, Fellow of Merton College, Oxford.

(iii) Lectures on man's approach to God:

'On Not Knowing Too Much About God', by A. H. Armstrong, formerly Gladstone Professor of Greek at Liverpool University;

'"When Two Are to Become One": Mysticism and Monism', by Grace Jantzen, Lecturer in the History and Philosophy of Religion at King's College, London;

'Faith and Goodness', by Eleonore Stump, Professor of Philosophy at Virginia Polytechnic Institute and State University;

'Hope', by Stewart Sutherland, Vice-Chancellor of London University.

(iv) Lectures on philosophy, religion and truth:

'Christian Averroism, Fideism and the "Two-fold Truth"', by Stuart Brown, Professor of Philosophy at the Open University;

'Does Philosophy "Leave Everything as it is"? Even Theology?', by Renford Bambrough, Sidgwick Lecturer in Philosophy at Cambridge University.

The Trinity and the Incarnation

Dillon takes it as being 'generally agreed that Christian thinkers were profoundly influenced in the development of their theology by their growing acquaintance with contemporary Greek philosophy, and in particular with Platonism'. The two issues he addresses are (i) the need for, and the nature of, a mediator between God and Man, and (ii) the internal structure of the supreme principle itself, a structure which sacrificed absolute unity and simplicity in the interest of developing the relationship, within deity, of essence, potency and activity. On each of these questions Platonism had much to offer, specifically by providing models for relationships between a supreme god and a secondary, creator god, or alternatively a supreme god and his creative reason-principle (*logos*). (Admittedly these models were ultimately rejected by orthodox Christianity.) Platonism offered models, too, for the various aspects of the supreme divinity itself—or, more exactly, its three possible aspects, whether they be denominated Being, Life and Mind, or Essence, Potency and Activity.

This is what Kretzmann calls the 'inert' philosophy in Christianity. Christianity would be unrecognizable without the later Greek metaphysics around which Christian doctrine first developed, he says, but it is inert. It is active philosophy, philosophical theology, that is 'the only philosophy of more than historical interest . . . in Christianity.'

Philosophical theology is broader than natural theology. It admits doctrinal propositions, not accessible to observation and reason, such as the doctrines of the Trinity and Incarnation. Its ongoing project is that of supporting, elucidating, extending and connecting these propositions by means of analysis and argument. Medieval philosophical theologians, especially in the thirteenth century, were attempting to follow Augustine in enhancing faith based on authority, with understanding based on reason.

Kretzmann defends Bonaventure's defence of philosophical theology against Gregory the Great's charge that it is destructive of faith as a theological virtue, and against Peter Lombard's warning that mysteries of faith cannot be investigated in a way conducive to salvation. Christian doctrine includes mysteries, but the Church takes them to be ridiculous and impossible only *prima facie*, not *per se*. It is possible to clarify and defend them. Genuine philosophical theology is out to discover reason in mystery, not to turn reason against mystery. An illustration of this is Aquinas' confirmation of the doctrine of the Trinity by uncovering connections between it and other doctrines, and thereby aiding one's understanding of creation and salvation.

Wiles' lecture is about the heresy of Arius. I looked this up in my favourite book on the philosophy of religion, A. Seth Pringle-Pattison, *Studies in the Philosophy of Religion* (Oxford, 1930).

> In the beginning of the fourth century an acute crisis was provoked by Arius, who definitely taught that the Son, or the Logos, is not co-eternal with the Father, but a creaturely being, created by the Father out of nothing, to be the mediator of further creation. Arius propounded this theory apparently in the interest of monotheism; but the Arian Christ, a demigod called into existence to create the world, is a purely mythological figure, neither god nor man, but standing midway between the two. As against Arianism, the Church at the Council of Nicaea (AD 325) declared its belief in the deity of Jesus Christ in the fullest sense: 'God of God, Light of Light, Very God of Very God, Begotten not made, Being of one substance with the Father'. And the position of Athanasius, though on the face of it more incredible than the heresy it combated, lent itself in the sequel more readily to philosophical interpretation (pp. 244–245).

Wiles indicates a more sympathetic approach to the thought of Arius on the part of contemporary scholars. He sees Athanasius and Arius as engaged in essentially the same task of making sense of their scriptural faith and doing so in a way which gives to philosophy a less straightforward and less external role than has often been suggested in the past. He picks out as crucial to the debate the question of how the Christian can participate in the divine. The Athanasian Christ can mediate this participation because, as truly divine and also incarnate, his very nature constitutes the bridge which makes participation in the divine, salvation, a possibility for us.

Whereas Wiles is concerned with the Son being co-eternal with the Father, his Oxford colleague, Swinburne, is concerned with the Son becoming, at a certain moment in human history, human. The Council of Chalcedon assumed that an individual, God, could become human, or cease to be human, while remaining the same individual. Is this internally consistent? Is it consistent with the picture of Christ in the New Testament?

In answer to the second of these questions Swinburne says that many readers of the New Testament feel that it pictures a Jesus rather more like ourselves than the Christ of the traditional exposition of the Chalcedonian definition; and that this is required by the Christian doctrine of atonement. He advances a new interpretation, utilizing the Freudian doctrine of the divided mind. The consciousness of God includes the consciousness of God incarnate, but not conversely. This enables us to say that God could become man in a rather fuller sense than the traditional interpretation allowed. This is consistent with the Chalcedonian definition, which did not affirm total interpenetration of two natures.

God and His Creation; Predestination and Freewill

Much of Stead's lecture is about the Platonism of Augustine. But he mentions, in passing, the moral problems raised by God's knowledge of his creation. He writes:

> It might appear that if God foreknows that X will sin, then it is inevitable that X will sin; and if it is inevitable, then X is not free and cannot be blamed. Augustine replies that God does not cause X to sin by foreknowing it; what God foreknows is that X will freely choose to sin, and his foreknowledge depends on X's choice. In two later works he takes a different line, suggesting that God does indeed contrive that some individuals shall sin, and sin of their own free choice; he does this by omitting to supply the grace to overcome temptation. I do not think this in the least acceptable as a way to vindicate God's goodness. Nor do I think Augustine gives an adequate account of human freedom.

O'Daly goes into Augustine's position on predestination and freewill in considerable detail. He critically examines Augustine's concept of the will. He comes to much the same conclusion as Stead. 'A philosophical defence of Augustine's notion of the freedom of the will seems impossible: it remains a glorious and influential failure.'   Similarly, Ward questions the legitimacy of Augustine's idea of a will that may justly be punished for its choice, given his belief that the whole world flows from the immutable and necessary being of God. He thinks that most present-day theologians would reject what follows from this: that God determines a will to make a choice which is then punished eternally. He contrasts the concept of the wholly immutable God, which the classical tradition developed, with the concept of God to be found in the Bible. 'The prophetic call is for repentance and trust in God. That implies a stress on choice, on acceptance of responsibility for one's actions, and on a belief that one should, and therefore could, have done otherwise . . . God himself is spoken of as responding to human choices. . . . The natural way to take all this is to say that some of God's actions, in judgment and mercy, are dependent on human choices.'

Lucas starts his lecture with passages from the Bible in which, he says, 'the clear picture is of a God who can change his mind':

> Such a view accords with the natural reading of the Bible, preserves free will, and fits the higher, human view of God that Jesus enjoins us to adopt. But is has been discountenanced by most theologians, partly on logical, partly on theological grounds. Logically, it has seemed impossible for an omniscient being not to know all truths, including those about future contingents; theologically, it has been felt to derogate from the perfection of God that He should change his mind.

Lucas argues that both these grounds for rejecting the Biblical view of God are mistaken, and that 'once we cease imputing to the suffering God of the Christian religion the supposed perfection of the God of the philosophers, we can see how it is that God can be God without thereby depriving us of freedom and responsibility'. God is not only fallible, but vulnerable, and the vulnerability of God is the peculiar characteristic of Christian teaching. The symbol of Christianity is the cross.

A human father is certainly vulnerable to his offspring making a mess of things. Whether God is, similarly, vulnerable, I do not know. Despite what is said in the Bible, my tendency is to distrust applying to God the terms we apply to our fellow humans.

Man's Approach to God

Armstrong's lecture has the lovely title, 'On Not Knowing Too Much About God'.

He thinks that Christianity's willingness to make extremely precise dogmatic statements about God is largely due to the influence of

Godfrey Vesey

Hellenic philosophy on Christian thinking. But there is a great deal in Plato's dialogues 'the reading of which can strengthen the tendency to diffidence and encourage the reader to develop it in various ways'. Armstrong's lecture is about two developments from this original diffidence: the Apophatic Way, or *Via Negativa*, of the Neoplatonists, and the ancient traditions of Scepticism, the Pyrrhonian and the Academic; and about how Scepticism and the Negative Way help one another 'in leading towards a salutary and liberating ignorance'.

Armstrong avoids the use of the word 'mystic' to describe Plotinus' intense experience of the presence of that which he knew he could not think or speak of. Jantzen avoids neither that term, nor the term 'monism'. She is concerned with the question whether 'mysticism requires monism as its underlying metaphysic, a unity of substance or essence between God and the soul'. Her answer is that it does not. The Creator-creature distinction is preserved in the mystical experience. The union is not a unity of substance; it is a union, or concurrence, of wills.

The role of the will, inspired by the agent's apprehension of goodness, in faith, is the subject of Stump's lecture. Current work in the philosophy of religion on the subject of faith has tended to concentrate on the connection of faith to evidence and rationality. She turns to Aquinas for an account which recognizes the place of the will in faith. For him the will is a natural appetite for goodness in general. The intellect can represent certain things as good, and move the will as a final cause does, but there can be considerations sufficient to move the will but not the intellect. It is then that we talk of faith. Faith is an intellectual assent to a proposition when the object of the intellect is not sufficient to move the intellect by itself. In faith assent is generated by the will, which is moved by the object of faith sufficiently to command the intellect to assent. Faith differs from opinion in holding to its object with certitude. In this respect it is like knowledge. The ultimate object of the will can be thought of in either of two ways. It is the happiness of the willer. It is God, who is the true good, and thus the perfect happiness of the willer. The propositions of faith, entertained by the intellect, describe the combination of these ultimate goods, eternal life in union with God, and present it as available to the believer by virtue of Christ's atonement for our sins on the cross.

Stump deals with three possible objections to this account of faith. Whether she would object to Jantzen's saying that union with God is a union of wills, I am not sure. Can it be said of God that he has a natural appetite for goodness? Are not his being and his goodness the same thing? I do not know how one is to deal with questions like this.

Stump contrasts Aquinas' view of the will as an appetite for goodness with the view of it 'as the neutral steering capacity of a person's psyche'.

Sutherland contrasts the hope that has a place in the Pauline trinity of faith, hope and charity, with the concept of hope developed by three empirically orientated English philosophers, H. H. Price, Jonathan Harrison and J. P. Day. The philosphers agree that hope is not simply a feeling of desire, or wish; it also contains elements of belief. They disagree about the belief content. Is what I hope for 'probable' (Day), or simply 'neither inevitable nor impossible' (Harrison), or both 'logically and causally possible' (Price)? Sutherland prefers Harrison's view, but has reservations. What interests the French philosopher, Gabriel Marcel, on the topic of hope, is that it has 'roots in the very depth of what I am'. This, for Sutherland, is a matter of a 'moral vision': 'the essential content of hope is a moral vision of what might be'. He lists four implications of the characterization of the content of religious hope as vision: one is dealing in pictures rather than in empirical predictions; hope founded on vision pays due regard to uncertainty; hope focused by vision is discussable (one can examine, defend, moderate, develop the moral vision); vision expressed in hope helps redirect our minds from total preoccupation with this immanent world, and provides a standard against which the particular and immanent may be measured.

The most distinctive object of religious hope is the hope for heaven, whether in this life or in a life to come. I am reminded, by some of the things Sutherland says about the religious hope for heaven, of something Dietrich Bonhoeffer said about salvation, in his *Letters and Papers from Prison* (27 June 1944):

> Salvation means salvation from cares and needs, from fears and longing, from sin and death into a better world beyond the grave. But is this really the distinctive feature of Christianity as proclaimed in the Gospels and St Paul? I am sure it is not. The difference between the Christian hope of resurrection and a mythological hope is that the Christian hope sends a man back to his life on earth in a wholly new way which is even more sharply defined than it is in the Old Testament.

Philosophy, Religion and Truth

It is all very well when Christians are in sympathy with the ideas of philosophers, and can even make use of them in formulating their doctrines. But what happens when religion and philosophy are at odds? Plato seems to have believed in the possibility of an individual surviving death. But not Aristotle. Should one attempt to interpret what Aristotle says so as to make it compatible with the Christian faith? Or can there be two truths: one of philosophy and one of religion?

In the 1270s, Brown says, the Bishop of Paris attacked the Averroists for saying that something could be 'true in philosophy, but not according to the Catholic faith, as if there were two truths'. Brown raises three issues for discussion. The one to which he devotes most attention is the controversy about the nature of faith:

> There is a controversy about the nature of faith, with the Averroists presenting it for the most part as non-rational, as quite different from rational belief, as not requiring the support of rational belief and indeed as, perhaps unlike other kinds of belief, a matter of what we resolve.

Brown comes down on the side of saying that faith has to involve beliefs of the kind that call for reasons. Does this mean that he disagrees with Stump, who holds that in faith assent is generated by the will? I think it does. He certainly disagrees with the twentieth-century philosopher Ludwig Wittgenstein. He says that Wittgenstein's later philosophy offers more support to the Averroists than to their opponents.

In the final lecture in the volume Bambrough considers whether philosophy, if it is purely descriptive, 'leaves everything as it is'. Does it leave theology as it is? He distinguishes three different understandings of God's question to Job: 'Where wast thou when I laid the foundations of the earth?' One can take the account of the conversation between God and Job 'in a way that one might call *literal*, and is sometimes called fundamentalist'. A second group of believers 'would put more emphasis than the first group on the pictorial and analogical character of the formulations of their faith . . . yet the members of this group will reasonably take themselves to be serious in their commitment to the absolute truths of their religion'. The members of the third group read the Book of Job 'as literature'. This is 'to dispense with, or at least to regard as inessential, the doctrinal basis'. Does giving this sketch of believers and unbelievers 'leave everything as it is'?

Bambrough's answer to this question, in the context of what else he says, seems to me to be a defence of Wittgenstein against Brown's charge that on three important issues he is on the Averroist side. It makes me wonder what Bambrough thought of John Cook's paper on 'Wittgenstein on Religious Belief' in *Philosophy* **63** (1988). Perhaps this will emerge in the course of discussion after the 1989/90 lectures. They are to be on Wittgenstein, who was born in 1889.

I am grateful to the lecturers not only for their lectures, but also for their comments on an early draft of this foreword. I am especially grateful to the Revd Professor Christopher Stead and to the Rector of St Peter's, Bedford, the Revd John Schild.

Logos and Trinity: Patterns of Platonist Influence on Early Christianity

JOHN DILLON

I

I think it would be generally agreed that the two surest ways of getting into serious trouble in Christian circles in the first three or four centuries of the Church's existence were to engage in speculation either on the nature of Christ the Son and his relation to his Father, or on the mutual relations of the members of the Trinity. While passions have cooled somewhat in the intervening centuries, these are still now subjects which a Classical scholar must approach with trepidation—partly, at least, because the two disciplines of Classical Philology and Patristics, which were for so long so intimately connected, in the persons of a series of great scholars,[1] are now so far removed from one another. I propose on this occasion to stick mainly to what I profess to know something about, that is the development of Platonic doctrine over the first few centuries AD, but I will inevitably be led from time to time into more dangerous speculations, and I trust I will receive due tolerance, as well as proper correction, where it is necessary.

I take it as being generally agreed that Christian thinkers were profoundly influenced in the development of their theology by their growing acquaintance with contemporary Greek philosophy, and in particular with Platonism.[2] It is with two features of this contemporary Platonism that I wish to deal, the development of a doctrine of a second god or principle subordinate to the supreme principle, and the (rather more gradual) growth of a system of three principles, either hierarchically arranged or mutually entailed on the same level, since it is

---

[1] I think of such names as Erasmus, Robert Estienne, Lachmann, Friedrich Blass, and even of Dr S. T. Bloomfield, Fellow of Sidney Sussex College, Cambridge, early in the last century—though their contributions were largely philological.

[2] Stoicism was influential as well, of course, and Christian polemicists also derived benefit from Epicurean and Sceptical arguments against traditional Greek mythology and religion, unsympathetic though they otherwise were with those philosophical schools.

1

plain that each of these features of Platonism had important repercussions on Christianity.

Plato bequeathed to his successors, not so much a closed and well-rounded philosophical system, as an immensely stimulating and fruitful set of problems. Of course one can derive positive principles from the dialogues (and his successors also had the benefit of his 'unwritten' doctrines, as we to some extent do as well), but these principles, such as the doctrine of two levels of reality, Being and Becoming, the benevolence of the Deity and the purposiveness of the universe, the Theory of Forms, or the immortality of the soul, all bring with them inherent problems, which later, more scholastic thinkers, beginning with Xenocrates, third head of the Academy (from 339 to 314 BC) and the real founder, I should say, of Platonism as a system, never ceased striving to resolve.

One major problem which we have to deal with in the present context is that of the relationship between the Good, the supreme principle of *Republic*, Books *VI–VII* (in particular, the Sun Simile of *Rep. VI*, 508–509), and the Demiurge of the *Timaeus*. The Good is certainly an ultimate principle, which confers not only 'goodness', in the sense of order and structure, but also existence (*epekeina tes ousias*). The Demiurge, however, though he has no other principle above him, is not so clearly supreme. For one thing, the 'Paradigm' or model which he contemplates to guide him in his creation of the physical world is not presented as being either created by him or as part of him (as the contents of his mind); for another thing, he is confronted by an intractable substratum, the 'Receptacle', or the 'wandering cause', which is only partly subject to his control, so that he can only create an imperfect image of the model.

Plato, unfortunately, makes no move to relate these two entities, since he does not comment on the relationships between his various dialogues. The Demiurge, at least, in contrast to the Good, does not have to be taken literally, and most Platonists in ancient times (with the conspicuous exceptions of Plutarch and Atticus, in the first and second centuries AD) accepted the position of Speusippus and Xenocrates that the description of the creation of the world in time is a myth, presented in this way only in the interests of clarity of instruction.[3]

However, many of those who accepted that the creation myth of the *Timaeus* was not to be taken literally did not, it seems, take the further step of concluding that this really puts the Demiurge, as such, out of business. If he is not a creator in the manner presented in the dialogue, he becomes no more than the creative aspect of the divine Intellect, the

---

[3] Speusippus, Fr. 61 Taran; Xenocrates, Frs. 154–158 Isnardi Parente/Fr. 54 Heinze.

model which he contemplates becoming simply the contents of that Intellect in its transcendent aspect. What is peculiar, in the circumstances, is that the Demiurge survives in the Platonic tradition as a divine entity, even though he is involved in a very troublesome demarcation dispute with another basic element of Platonist metaphysics (of which in the *Timaeus* myth he is the creator), the World Soul.

However, even if one depersonalizes the Demiurge, as some Platonists, under the influence of the Stoic theory of the *Logos*, plainly did, one is still left with a secondary and subordinate divine entity, whose relationship with the first principle must be defined. Philo of Alexandria is not, of course, himself a Platonist, but he is well attuned to contemporary Platonism, and constitutes good evidence, I think, for trends in Platonist theory around the dawn of the Christian era, as well as being himself a stimulus to the theologizing of the Alexandrian Christian Fathers, Clement and Origen. Philo may be more concerned than would a contemporary Platonist to preserve the unity of the deity, but not *that* much more, I think. At any rate, we find in him the demiurgic aspect of divinity assimilated to the Stoic *Logos*, and thoroughly subordinated to the Supreme God. In the *De Opificio Mundi* it is unequivocally God, the supreme God, who creates both the intelligible world (the Paradigm of the *Timaeus*) and the physical world:

> Having resolved to create this visible world of ours, he fashioned first the intelligible world, in order that in fashioning the physical world he might be able to use an immaterial and most godlike model, producing from this elder model a younger imitation which would contain within itself as many sensible classes of being as there were intelligible ones in the original (*Opif.* 16).

This intelligible world is presented as none other than the *Logos*, viewed statically (cf. *Opif.* 20), while viewed dynamically, the *Logos* is the sum-total of the spermatic reason-principles which permeate the physical world and give it form. This system is thoroughly Stoic, except for the important fact that God Himself is immaterial and transcendent. That makes it Platonist, and it is such a Platonized *Logos* that St John adopts in his Gospel.

Despite depersonalizing the Demiurge, Philo is prepared on occasion to use personal, and indeed familial, terms when talking of the Logos. In the treatise *On Flight and Finding*, for example (*Fug.* 109), *à propos* an exegesis of the figure of the High Priest in *Numbers* 35:12, we find the Logos described as the 'son' of God and Sophia. Earlier (ibid. 101) he has been called the 'image' (*eikon*) of God, chief of all the intelligibles, and nearest to the truly existing One. Again, at *De Agricultura* 51, we find God portrayed as 'King and Shepherd', setting over his flock 'his true *logos* and firstborn Son', in language strangely anticipatory of that of the Gospels. Such language is pregnant with both promise and problems for Christian theologians of the second and third centuries. Elsewhere, in the treatise *On the Immutability of God* (*Deus* 31–32), Philo produces a more elaborate familial image, by characterizing the *Logos* (or strictly, the noetic cosmos) as the 'elder son' of God, to whom he accords the honours of primogeniture (*presbeia*), and whom he plans should stay with him, while the physical cosmos is described as the *younger* son, who goes forth on his travels, rather like the Prodigal Son, in the process generating Time, very much as does the Plotinian hypostasis of Soul later. This tendency to personification is perhaps only a feature of Philo's love of high-flown and elaborate imagery, but it could have interesting consequences if taken more literally than he intended.

Only one real Platonist before Plotinus can be identified as making use of the concept of the Logos, and that is Plutarch, though this may be a function of the inadequate evidence we possess for the period. Even with Plutarch, the evidence is somewhat controversial, since a Logos-figure only appears in one treatise, that *On Isis and Osiris*, in the guise of the Egyptian god Osiris. At 372EF, Plutarch presents Isis, 'the female principle of Nature', whom Plutarch regards both as the Receptacle of the *Timaeus* and an irrational world-soul, as fired by love for the Good as first principle, and desirous of being impregnated by it. What in fact she is impregnated by is 'effluxes and likenesses' (*aporrhoiai kai homoiotetes*) from the Good, in other words, spermatic *logoi*, the totality of which is Osiris, the Logos.

Plutarch then makes a distinction between the 'soul' of Osiris, which remains transcendently 'above', as the intelligible world, and his 'body', which is the reason-principles which descend into Matter, and are 'torn apart' by this process, in that they are distributed into sensible individuals. Plutarch is less than specific here, but it is plain that even the soul of Osiris is not identical with the Supreme Principle, but rather is the hypostatized sum-total of its 'thoughts'. It is troublesome that Plutarch does not speak of Osiris as a Logos in this passage, though he does refer to the components of his body as '*logoi* and forms'. In fact, it is another figure, Hermes (Thoth), whom Plutarch here (373B) presents as Logos, but this should not disturb us unduly, I think, as the role of Thoth as witness in the trial of Horus (the physical world) for illegitimacy is an integral part of the Egyptian myth, and Thoth, *qua* Hermes, is traditionally allegorized as the Logos of God. For our purposes, at any rate, it is no matter, since a Logos-figure is certainly envisaged here by Plutarch, performing demiurgic functions. The fact that Hermes, at least, is a son of Zeus makes the relationship to the Supreme Principle plainer.

Logos-theology, then, has at least a foothold in Platonism in the Middle Platonic period, but it is not, perhaps, the dominant pattern. The alternative is the contrast between a First God and a Second God, the latter descended from a more literal interpretation of the Demiurge of the *Timaeus*, and more directly concerned with creation, while the First God remains aloof, wrapped in his own thoughts, rather in the manner of Aristotle's Unmoved Mover.

Some such distinction is adumbrated, I think, in Albinus (or Alcinous), in Ch. 10 of his *Didaskalikos*, where a distinction is made between a Primal God (*protos theos*), and Intellect (*nous*) of the whole heaven (that is, the cosmos). 'The former', says Albinus, 'being motionless himself, directs his activity towards this latter, even as the sun towards vision, when someone looks at it [a reference, presumably, to the Sun simile of the *Republic*] and as an object of desire sets desire in motion, while remaining itself motionless [a reference to Aristotle's theory of the Unmoved Mover in *Metaphysics* XII]; even thus will this Intellect move the Intellect of the whole heaven.'

This 'Intellect of the Whole Heaven' (*nous tou sympantos ouranou*) is plainly a demiurgic entity, being responsible for creation through its guidance of the Soul of the World (*psychê tou kosmou*), while being itself guided by the First God, whom Albinus now terms 'Father'. Their relationship is described as follows (ibid. 164, 35ff. Hermann).

> God is 'Father' by reason of the fact that he is cause of all things and orders the heavenly Intellect and Soul of the World to conform with (*pros*), himself and his own thoughts (*noeseis*); for by his own will (*boulesis*) he has filled all things with himself, raising up the Soul of the World and turning it towards himself, as being the cause of its Intellect. And this latter, being set in order (*kosmêtheis*) by the Father (or 'its father') itself sets in order the whole of nature within this world.

Albinus' God the Father, then, comes across as a relatively active entity; though acting on creation at one remove, or even two, through Soul and Intellect. The 'heavenly Intellect', in turn, is a rather dim figure, though plainly crucial in its way. Its relation to the World Soul is interesting; it is on the one hand presented as the Intellect *of* the World-Soul, and so not its creator, as in the *Timaeus* myth, but also as dominating it, and using it to organize the world. This encapsulates the rather uneasy relationship which a demiurge-figure has with the World Soul in later Platonism.

The Demiurge really comes into his own, though, in the thought of Albinus' junior contemporary, the Neopythagorean Numenius (fr. *c.* AD 140). Numenius makes a strong distinction between the 'Father' and the 'Creator' (*poiêtês*), basing his distinction on the famous passage of the *Timaeus*, 28C ('Now to discover the Maker and Father of this Universe were a task indeed; and having discovered, to declare unto all men were a thing impossible')—or rather, perhaps, making use of this passage to support a doctrine he had already arrived at! Proclus (*In Tim.* I, 303, 27ff.=Fr. 21 Des Places) described his theological scheme, rather impatiently, as follows:

> Numenius proclaims three gods, calling the first 'Father', the second 'Creator', and the third 'Creation' (*poiema*); for the cosmos, according to him, is the third god. So, according to him, the Demiurge is double, being both the first god and the second, and the third is the object of his demiurgic activity—it is better to use this terminology than to use the sort of dramatic bombast that he employs, naming them respectively Grandfather, Offspring and Descendant (*pappos, engonos, apogonos*).

This is not, I think, an entirely accurate (and certainly not an unbiased) account of Numenius' doctrine, but it is worth quoting for the terminology it preserves, especially the last three terms. Numenius would seem to be influenced, not just by the *Timaeus*, but by that mysterious passage of the pseudo-Platonic *Second Letter* (312E), that so fascinated later Platonists, which presents a succession of three 'kings', and levels of reality attached to them. His Third God, the *poiema*, is in fact a sort of projection of the Second, as we can see from a passage of Numenius' dialogue *On The Good* quoted verbatim by Eusebius (Fr. 11 Des Places):

> The First God, existing in his own place, is simple and, consorting as he does with himself alone, can never be divisible. The Second and Third Gods, however, are in fact one; but in the process of coming into contact with Matter, which is the Dyad, he gives unity to it, but is himself divided by it, since Matter has a character prone to desire and is in flux.

It is clear from this that for Numenius it is the second god that is the Demiurge in any active sense, and his demiurgic activity causes him to at least project an image of himself which is divided about the material realm as an immanent world soul (though Numenius actually speaks of the Demiurge himself being divided). The First God sits in splendour above all this activity, being a creator only in the sense that he is the father of the creator god (as we learn in Fr. 12 Des Places).

This relation between Numenius' first and second gods has considerable relevance, it seems to me, for the Christology of such a thinker as Origen, or even of Justin before him. Origen, at least, knew Numenius, as his various references to him in the *Contra Celsum* (I, 15; IV, 51; V, 38; V, 57) attest. A particularly significant detail, I think, almost certainly borrowed from Numenius and one that got him into bad trouble, at least posthumously, is his distinguishing, in the *De Principiis* (*I*, 2, 13, cf. Fr. 6) between God the Father as *autoagathon* or *agathotes* ('The Good') and Christ as merely *agathos* ('good'), a distinction Numenius makes pointedly in Fr. 16. As we have seen, such a distinction arises from the juxtaposition of *Republic VI*, 508–509, and *Timaeus* 29E ('*agathos en*'), but no one before Numenius seems to have made it the basis for setting the Demiurge at a lower level of dignity than the Primal God. Origen seems to adopt this formulation gratefully as expressing just what he feels to be the distinction between the Father and the Son, grounding his position, as he is always careful to do, firmly in Scripture, by quoting *Mk* 10:18 and *Luc* 18:99: 'No one is good but God alone'—although that passage does not in fact make the distinction he wants to draw from it.

II

Enough has now been said, perhaps, for the present purpose about the influence of the Middle Platonic Logos/Demiurge on early Christian theology. Let us turn now to consider that other very troublesome doctrine, the Trinity.

Now, as I have suggested at the outset, there was always within Platonism a tendency to triadic schemata, but most of them are irrelevant to our present purpose. Let us consider some of these briefly, before setting them aside, as they are all relevant to the basic tendency to think triadically.

1. First, and most irrelevant, is the triad of God–Ideas–Matter, often presented in doxographic sources, actually, with 'Idea' in the singular.[4] All, I think, that is relevant here is the postulating of the 'middle term' of the triad, that is, Idea or Form, as a creative link between the two extremes of God and Matter. This seeing of an intermediate between any two terms is a tendency basic to later Platonism which is important for the formulation of the Trinity which really concerns us.

2. Somewhat less irrelevant is the triad of creative, immaterial principles which take shape, not explicitly in Plato himself, but progressively in later Platonism,[5] consisting of a first intellectual principle or

[4] Ps.-Plut. *Epit.* I, 3; Stobaeus, *Ecl.* I, 10, 16=Aetius, *Placita* I, 3 (Diels, *Dox. Gr.,* 287–288).

[5] As I have mentioned earlier, the influence of the 'three kings' passage of the pseudo-Platonic Second Letter (312E) is either a stimulus to, or itself a symptom of, this development, as is, later, the metaphysical interpretation of the latter part of the *Parmenides*.

Father-God, a secondary intellectual principle, Creator-God or Logos, and a World-Soul (*pater-demiourgos/logos-psyche*). This we have already seen manifesting itself variously in Plutarch, Albinus, and Numenius, while Philo contributes an allied, but distinct (and distinctively interesting) triad of God–Sophia–Logos, where Sophia has a higher rank and more intimate relation to God than the properly Platonic World-Soul (a concept for which Philo has no use, finding no sanction for it in the Pentateuch), but yet exhibits the attributes of that multi-level Platonic female principle, the Indefinite Dyad/World-Soul/Matter.[6] This triad receives its most developed form in the three hypostases first propounded by Plotinus, who placed pure unity, the One, prior to Intellect, and distinguished Intellect clearly from Soul. Once again, this is not what we want, but it is closer, in that all the principles are on the same side, so to speak, engaged in the creation of an ordered universe. The degree of overlapping in function in Middle Platonic systems between Demiurge/Logos and World-Soul is also significant for our purpose.

3. More relevant still is a triad which appears first in that curious theosophical compilation of the late second century AD, the *Chaldaean Oracles*. Here we find what later Platonists, at least, from Porphyry on, saw as a trinity composed of the 'Father', the 'power' (*dynamis*) of the Father, and Intellect (*nous*). This schema appears particularly clearly in Fr. 4 of Des Places' edition:[7]

For his Power remains with him (sc. the Father), while his Intellect proceeds from him.

From this verse Platonist philosophers from Porphyry on derived a trinity of Father (or Existence, *hyparxis*), Power, Intellect, which they equated with a triad of principles, Being–Life–Intellect (*on–zoe–nous*) derived from a notable passage of Plato's *Sophist* (248E), where the Eleatic Stranger asserts that true Being cannot be conceived as not also possessing life and intellection.

4. What the composer of the *Oracles* really had in mind here we can no longer be sure, but he has brought us to the threshold of the trinity we are in search of. This is the triad of 'moments' within the hypostasis of Nous (Being–Life–Intellect proper) first formulated as such by Porphyry (though Plotinus certainly recognized the existence of a Life-aspect, as well as a Being-aspect, in Nous[8]). For Porphyry, if not

---

[6] I have written on this principle more extensively elsewhere, in 'Female Principles in Platonism', *Itaca: Quaderns Catalans de Cultura Classica*, I (1985), 107–123.

[7] *Oracles Chaldaiques*, ed. E. Des Places (Bude ed.) (Paris, 1971).

[8] Cf. e.g. *Enn.* V, 4, 2; V, 5, 1; V, 6, 6; VI, 6, 8; and Pierre Hadot, 'Etre, Vie, Pensee chez Plotin et avant Plotin', in *Les Sources de Plotin* (*Entretiens Fondation Hardt V*) (Vandoeuvres-Genève, 1960), 107–157.

already for Plotinus, such a triadic schema as this was necessary for the proper elucidation of the genesis and structure of the hypostasis of Nous.[9] Nous constitutes itself from the One as a result of a process which involves, first, an outflowing from the One of an indefinite life-force, which can be characterized as a potency (*dynamis*); and then a turning-back of the life-force on its source and contemplation of that source by which it constitutes itself as Intellect. That which it now contemplates is not exactly the One in its true simplicity, but a reflected image of it, which becomes the 'object of intellection' (*noeton*), Being (*on*) in the strictest sense. The relationship between Intellect and Being, which actually generates the multiplicity of the Forms, is the Life of the intellectual realm. Each moment of the trinity is thus the condition for the existence of the others *as such*. Intellect would not be intellect if it had not an object of contemplation; that aspect of the One which becomes the intelligible object would not exist as such if that which flowed forth did not also revert; and the life which was at first indefinite, as the flowing-forth, would not now be defined, were it not for the existence of these two interacting poles.

This intellectual trinity, then, makes logical sense, and it is relevant to the Christian trinity in a way that other models are not, in that its members are not arranged in a hierarchy, but are co-ordinate, though Being does occupy a place of seniority, as being in effect the manifestation of the One. An objection might here be raised, however, since, both in Plotinus and in later Platonists such as Proclus, this is a triadic division of the hypostasis of Intellect, not directly involving the One, and so not providing an exact model for the Christian Trinity, which does, obviously, involve the Father.

We must here, however, take account of a feature of Porphyry's metaphysics on which a certain amount of confusion persists, even among Platonists.[10] For Porphyry (we are told by Damascius[11]), the First Principle is the Father of the intelligible triad. This betokens a significant simplification even of Plotinus' metaphysical scheme, and is certainly in stark contrast to the much greater elaboration of those of Lamblichus and his successors, with whom, in fact, Damascius is contrasting Porphyry in this passage. Porphyry also, however, main-

---

[9] A notable passage illustrating Porphyry's use of this schema occurs in his *Timaeus Commentary*, Fr. 79 Sodano (=Procl. *In Tim.* III, 64, 8ff. Diehl). But cf. also *Anon. Comm. in Parm.* XIV, 16ff. Hadot (probably Porphyry; certainly doctrinally concordant with him), and Marius Victorinus, *Adv. Arium*. I, 57, 9ff. (certainly dependent on Porphyry).

[10] See, however, the good discussion by Pierre Hadot, 'La metaphysique de Porphyre', in *Porphyre (Entretiens Fondation Hardt XII)* (Vandoeuvres-Genève, 1966), 127–163.

[11] *De Princ.* I, 86, 9ff. Ruelle.

tained the absolute transcendence of the first God, as we learn from a fragment of his *History of Philosophy* (Fr. 18 Nauck)—and there are many similar utterances in the *Parmenides Commentary* (e.g. III, 7; ἀσύμβλητος ὑπεροχὴ πρὸς πᾶν ὁποῦν; VI, 19)—but we find similar statements in the *Chaldaean Oracles*, on which Porphyry is basing himself (e.g. Fr. 3: 'the Father snatched himself up, not even enclosing within his intellectual Power the fire proper to him', which is actually quoted in the *Anon. In Parm. IX*, 1ff.), so we need see no contradiction here with the evidence of Damascius. For Porphyry, it would seem, the first principle, the Father, while maintaining his 'incomparable superiority', also presides over a triad made up of Potency or Life, and Activity (*energeia*) or Intellect. The fact that Intellect contemplates the Father, in so far as it can (and we may suppose that Porphyry maintained the distinction made by Plotinus between the One in itself and the One as object of intellection), does not compromise the Father's non-co-ordination with anything else.

Now it was Porphyry, despite his notoriety as an enemy of Christianity, not Plotinus, nor yet Iamblichus, who exercised the greatest influence over Christian thinkers both East and West in the fourth and fifth centuries, so that it is his form of 'trinitarian' doctrine that it is of prime importance to understand. I am not competent, I am afraid, to discuss in any detail the theology of the Cappadocian Fathers[12], but I

---

[12] I leave out of account the remarkable figure of Marius Victorinus, though he is actually the best evidence for Porphyry's trinitarian doctrine (cf. e.g. *Adv. Ar.* I, 56–60; IV, 19–29), since he cannot be regarded as a 'mainline' Christian theologian, useful though he was to St Augustine in many respects. Augustine, I think, actually recognizes this Porphyrian Trinity, though he pretends, at least, not to grasp its significance, in an important passage in the *City of God* (X, 23), where he is quoting from Porphyry's *Philosophy from Oracles* on the question of what are the proper agents of purification. Porphyry, it seems, declared these to be, not the Sun or the Moon, but the *archai*, or 'first principles'. 'We know', says Augustine, 'what Porphyry, as a Platonist, means by the "principles". He refers to God the Father, and God the Son, whom he calls in Greek the Intellect or Mind of the Father (i.e the *nous tou patros* or *patrikos nous*). About the Holy Spirit he says nothing, or at least nothing clear; although I do not understand what other being he refers to as holding the middle position between the two. If, like Plotinus in his discussion of the three "principal substances" (i.e. *Enn.* V, 1), he had intended it to be inferred that this third entity was soul, he would certainly not have said that this held the middle place between the two others, the Father and the Son' (trans. Henry Bettenson). One might be forgiven for regarding Augustine here as indulging in deliberate obtuseness. Porphyry is plainly, in giving an exegesis of the *Oracles*, presenting a trinity of Father, Power of the Father (or Life), and Intellect of the Father. His system is not to be assimilated to the three hypostases of Plotinian metaphysics (though he also accepted them). If

have been most impressed by reading Gregory of Nazianzus' *Third Theological Oration* (Oration 29),[13] in which he is concerned with refuting the Eunomians, who asserted a strong version of Arianism, to the effect that the Son is of a quite different nature to the Father (not even 'like' him). Eunomius is thus, if anything, reflecting Middle Platonic doctrine about the distinction between the first and second Gods. Gregory, in turn, seems, in countering him, to make use of the Porphyrian doctrine of the relationship between the Father, his Power, and Intellect.

In Ch. 2 of the *Oration* Gregory begins his exposition with a striking phrase: 'For this reason, (God), initially a monad, and moving into a dyad, comes to a stand as a triad (μονὰς ἀπ ἀϱχῆς, εις δυαδα κινηθεῖσα, μεχϱὶ τϱιάδος ἔστη). He goes on to gloss this remarkable statement by saying, 'that is, on our terms, the Father, the Son and the Holy Spirit'. This in turn would be troublesome, if this order were taken strictly, since it is properly the Holy Spirit that should be the dyadic, processive element in the triad, but this in fact it turns out to be just below, where the Monas is described as "sire" (*gennetor*) of the Son, but "sender-forth" (*proboleus*) of the Holy Spirit.'

What we have here, then, is the Plotinian–Porphyrian process of *mone*, *proodos* and *epistrophe* (widely adopted by all the Cappodocian fathers), applied to the relationship between the three moments with the noetic triad—The Son, as *nous*, brings the indefinite, 'dyadic', procession of Potency to a halt by reverting on the source which, by virtue of being reverted upon, becomes the Father. Gregory is particularly insistent, in view of his particular opposition, that Son-ship (and indeed Spirit-ship) involves no inferiority, temporal or otherwise.[14] The only aspect in which he seeks to distance himself from the Neoplatonic tradition is in the matter of the *intentionality* of this process of outflowing from the Father. 'I will not venture', he says (p. 76, I Mason), 'to speak of an "overflowing of goodness" (*hyperkhusis agathotetos*), which one of the Greek philosophers has dared to talk of, like a mixing-bowl (*krater*) overflowing, stating this quite clearly in these terms where he is speaking of the first and second Cause', making an explicit reference here, as Henry and Schwyzer have discerned, to *Enn. V*, 2, 1, where Plotinus says:

[13] I use the edition, *The Five Theological Orations of Gregory of Nazianzus*, A. J. Mason (ed.) (Cambridge, 1899).
[14] Cf. also *Theol Orat.* V, 9–10, where this is emphasized.

Augustine had cared to enquire more deeply, instead of indulging in polemics (as he does again below, at X, 29), he might have learned something to his advantage, but he is incurious, as he plainly was also about the higher theological flights of Marius Victorinus, preferring to believe that the Platonists have only dim reflections of the Truth.

The One, perfect because it seeks nothing, has nothing, and needs nothing, overflows, as it were (οἷον ὑπερερρύη), and its superabundance makes it something other than itself. This, when it has come into being, turns back upon the One and is filled, and becomes Intellect by working toward it. Its halt and turning towards the One constitutes Being, its gaze upon the One Intellect.

Gregory repudiates the *automatic* aspect of this outpouring, as being improper for the personal God of Christianity—he wishes to postulate an act of will here—but the overall schema he accepts gratefully. However, though this is a fairly direct reference to Plotinus, and shows Gregory's acquaintance with the *Enneads* in some form, it must be seen, I think, through the filter of Porphyry's metaphysics, which suited Gregory much better. The Plotinian One does, after all, clearly transcend Nous, and Plotinus does not really develop the notion of *dynamis* as the intermediary stage of outpouring which culminates in Nous (except, it should be said, in his interesting exposition of 'Intelligible Matter', which is assimilated to the Indefinite Dyad, in *Enn. II, 4,* 1–5).[15] Porphyry, on the other hand, as we have seen, telescopes the first and second Plotinian hypostases, and at the same time formalizes the three moments within what is for him the supreme hypostasis.

Plotinian metaphysics, therefore, in its Porphyrian form, seems to provide the basis for the philosophical Christian doctrine of the Trinity from Gregory on, since Gregory's formulation seems to have become authoritative, at least in the Eastern Church. Such men as John of Damascus, John of Scythopolis and Maximus the Confessor seem merely to build on Gregory in this matter, Maximus seeing the triad of *ousia*, *dynamis* and *energeia* manifested everywhere in the intelligible world.[16]

This has been a rather tentative and inadequate excursion into the complexities of Christian Theology, but I have been mainly concerned here to sort out a continuing confusion, especially among Christian theologians, as to just what the relevant Neoplatonic doctrine about the nature of God is that was available for philosophically literate Christians to draw on. It is emphatically not the basic Plotinian triad of One, Intellect, and Soul. That is irrelevant to a Trinity of co-ordinate 'persons'. Nor yet is it really the Plotinian form of the doctrine of the relationship between the One and the Intellect, since the One is still on a higher plane from Intellect. Only in Porphyry's version of the doctrine, itself a creative development on *Chaldaean Oracles*, do we

[15] See J. M. Rist, 'The Identified Dyad and Intelligible Matter in Plotinus', *CQ* n.s., **12** (1962), 99–107.

[16] See I. P. Sheldon-Williams's useful chapter on Maximus in *The Cambridge History of Later Greek and Early Mediaeval Philosophy*, 492–505.

find what we want, and even in Porphyry there are subtleties which most Christians missed, or chose to miss. Porphyry does seem to distinguish between the One (a term he still maintained), or Father, viewed 'in himself', and the One as object of intellection (*noeton*), in which capacity he is properly 'Father of the noetic triad'. He was thus able to accept all of Plotinus' characterizations of the One, while still 'telescoping' it into what in later Neoplatonism, certainly (from Iamblichus on), was seen as a quite distinct level of reality, the Intelligible, or One-Being.

But in the transferral from philosophy to theology, as we know, confusions and distortions do occur. Early Christian thinkers, in 'despoiling the Egyptians', were looking for what was useful to them. What I have tried to show is that the basic parameters of discourse on these two very troublesome central questions of theology, the relation of the Father and the Son, and the mutual relations of the Trinity, were already available in contemporary Platonism.

Reason in Mystery

NORMAN KRETZMANN

Philosophical Theology and Natural Theology

The philosophy in Christianity is both inert and active. The late Greek metaphysics around which Christian doctrine first developed is Christianity's inert philosophical skeleton. Even if the dehellenizers could succeed in their efforts to remove it, Christianity itself would be unrecognizable without it. But the philosophy that is in Christianity actively, the enterprise of philosophical theology, is in it insecurely and only intermittently because it seems vulnerable to important religious and philosophical objections. As I see it, philosophical theology can be and actually has been successfully defended against those objections, and it is, I believe, incomparably the most interesting and important philosophy in Christianity—in fact, the *only* philosophy of more than historical interest there really is in Christianity.

I'm using the term 'philosophical theology' in a sense that seems to be at least on its way to becoming standard,[1] a sense in which it is to be distinguished from natural theology, the other sort of theology that has been practised by philosophers. Natural theology may be broad or strict in its criteria for admissible premises and acceptable forms of argument, but its specifying characteristic is its refusal to admit as premises any doctrinal propositions that are not also accessible to observation and reason.[2] Supporters of natural theology would explain that it imposes those strictures in order to be able to claim that it can offer proof. Philosophical theology shares the methods of natural theology broadly conceived—i.e. analysis and argumentation of all the sorts accepted in philosophy and the sciences—but it lifts natural theology's restriction on premises. In particular, philosophical theology accepts as premises doctrinal propositions that are not also initially accessible to

---

[1] See Scott MacDonald's article 'Theologia naturalis/Theodicy' in the forthcoming *Handbook of Ontology and Metaphysics*, Burkhardt and Smith (eds) (Munich: Philosophia Verlag). I am grateful to Professor MacDonald for letting me see an advance copy of his article.

[2] See MacDonald, op. cit. As MacDonald describes it, broad natural theology might countenance accepting a doctrinal proposition expressed in Scripture as justifiably believed although not, of course, as divinely revealed. Philosophical theology, by contrast, may be unconcerned with the proposition's initial justification, treating it as an assumption.

observation and reason. From a philosophical point of view, it takes up such premises as assumptions. Argumentation based on such premises may be (and historically has been) as rigorous as any, but the status of its premises of course precludes its satisfying the peculiarly stringent criteria of Aristotelian demonstration. A philosophical theologian engaged in such reasoning tests the coherence of doctrinal propositions, develops their implications, attempts explanations of them, discovers their connections with other doctrinal propositions, and so on, with no pretence at offering proofs of the sort putatively available in natural theology.

So the subject matter of philosophical theology is broader than that of natural theology. It includes such doctrines as trinity and incarnation, which natural theology must exclude, though it also covers the doctrines to which natural theology confines its attention, such generally monotheistic doctrines as God's existence and unity. But, of course, trinity and incarnation are among the doctrinally distinguishing characteristics of Christianity; in fact, all the distinctively Christian doctrines are, I think, like those two in being initially inaccessible to observation and reason. And so, because the strictures of natural theology preclude its considering the doctrines that are the very differentiae of Christianity, the philosophy that is natural theology is at best adjacent to Christianity, not in it. Philosophical theology, the ongoing project of supporting, elucidating, extending, and connecting propositions of Christian doctrine by the standard philosophical means of analysis and argument, is now and always has been the active philosophy in Christianity, when Christianity has tolerated its presence at all.

The Goals of Philosophical Theology

During the Middle Ages, the golden age of philosophical theology, the vast majority of Christian philosophers contributed to this enterprise. They were trying to accomplish at least two things, both of which are or ought still to be the principal goals of philosophical theology. In the first place, a Christian philosopher recognizing that many people, perhaps including herself, view certain Christian doctrines as *prima facie* absurd, incoherent, or incompatible with other Christian doctrines may employ analysis and argument in order to defend those doctrines against such charges. In the second place, a Christian philosopher may engage in extending those doctrines and exploring their implications in order to bear out her conviction that the doctrines themselves are eminently understandable and acceptable, that their seeming absurd, incoherent, or incompatible with others is only a feature of our point of view. The first of these goals is more apparent in

Aquinas's *Summa contra gentiles*, for instance, the second in his *Summa theologiae*. Natural theology and philosophical theology are both suited for apologetics, the first goal, but it is only philosophical theology in which doctrinal exploration and development can be carried out. Since apologetics is far more likely to be effective if it is an outgrowth of doctrinal clarification, both general and detailed, the first of these goals is subsidiary to the second.

Philosophical Theology and Reformed Epistemology

The people who are now contributing to philosophical theology are more likely to be philosophers than theologians by profession. They are or ought to be particularly interested in the unsurpassably thorough and often penetrating contributions made by medieval philosophical theologians in their summas, in their hundreds of Sentences-commentaries, and in their thousands of disputed questions. Their principles, methods, and achievements, especially in the thirteenth century, provide the best available sources and models for philosophical theology, though most of them are still known only to a few historians of philosophy. But some influential work now being done in philosophy of religion might easily lead someone interested in philosophical theology to revert to deliberately ignoring the field's most valuable historical resources just as they are beginning to emerge from centuries of neglect by philosophers.

Nicholas Wolterstorff and Alvin Plantinga, the founders of 'Reformed epistemology', take the repudiation of classical foundationalism as their point of departure in opposing an evidentialist approach to the basic propositions of the Christian faith. As they see it, classical foundationalism characterizes many developments in the history of philosophy, including, very prominently, Aquinas's work on Christian doctrine, which they classify as 'natural theology'.[3] The grounds they have for describing Aquinas's work as natural theology or as classical foundationalism would suffice for characterizing the work of medieval philosophical theologians generally in those terms,[4] and so

[3] See, e.g., Plantinga, 'Reason and Belief in God', in Plantinga and Wolterstorff (eds), *Faith and Rationality: Reason and Belief in God* (Notre Dame, Ind.: University of Notre Dame Press, 1983, 16–93), 40: 'Thomas Aquinas, of course, is the natural theologian *par excellence*'.

[4] Wolterstorff indicates this clearly in his Introduction to *Faith and Rationality* (see n. 3 above), where in explaining the neologism '"Calvinist epistemology" or "Reformed epistemology"' he says, 'Characteristic of the Continental Calvinist tradition has been a revulsion against arguments in favour of theism or Christianity. Of course, at its beginnings this tradition was not appraising the giving of such arguments in the context of the Enlightenment insistence on the importance of Reason. It was instead appraising it in the context of the long medieval tradition of natural theology' (7–8).

Reformed epistemology may very well lead one to think that medieval philosophers should continue to be ignored, even, or *especially*, when they apply their philosophy to Christian doctrine. Wolterstorff and Plantinga themselves pretty clearly think no such thing, and each of them is an important contributor to philosophical theology. Still, Wolterstorff is likely to be read as giving the work of medieval philosophical theologians a moribundity certificate: 'Aquinas offers one classic version of foundationalism. . . . But . . . within the community of those working in philosophy of knowledge and philosophy of science foundationalism has suffered a series of deadly blows in the last twenty-five years. To many of those acquainted with the history of the development it now looks all but dead. So it looks to me.'[5] And Plantinga appears to declare it ruined: 'we can get a better understanding of Aquinas and the evidentialist objector if we see them as accepting some version of *classical foundationalism*. . . . It is evident, however, that classical foundationalism is bankrupt.'[6]

I am not now interested in arguing the merits of their case against foundationalism. But even if foundationalism has gone bankrupt and died, only a small part of the work of medieval philosophical theologians can be made to fit the Reformed epistemologists' characterization of classical foundationalism. And that small (though important) part of it is just the part that counts as natural theology in the sense in which I'm using that term.[7] In all their work they were attempting to follow

[5] *Reason Within the Bounds of Religion* (Grand Rapids, Mich.: William B. Eerdmanns, 1976), 26, 29.

[6] Op. cit., 48, 62.

[7] Plantinga sometimes restricts natural theology along these lines—e.g. 'Suppose we think of natural theology as the attempt to prove or demonstrate the existence of God' (op. cit., 63), but as a target for criticism on the basis of Reformed epistemology it is typically characterized more broadly. See, e.g., this passage from Wolterstoff, in which he is describing 'the practice of natural theology among the medievals': 'We may take Anselm and Aquinas as typical—Anselm's goal in constructing the ontological argument, *as [in]* the remainder of the *Proslogion*, was to bring it about that what already he believed he now would know. In his view an essential component in this process of transmuting belief (faith) into knowledge (understanding) was constructing proofs. Aquinas was *no different* on these matters. . . . the goal of natural theology for Aquinas was exactly the same as for Anselm: to transmute what already one believed into something known. *Demonstration* was seen as *indispensable* to this transmutation project' ('Can Belief in God Be Rational?', 135–186 in Plantinga and Wolterstorff, op. cit., 140–141; emphasis added). The goal and the method picked out here do belong to natural theology strictly construed, which is perhaps more prominent in Anselm than in Aquinas, but the clear suggestion of this passage is that that goal and method belong to Anselm's and Aquinas's applications of reason to revelation quite generally. As

their leader, Augustine, in the enterprise of enhancing faith based on authority with understanding based on reason as far as feasible.[8] But it was only in their work on such propositions as 'God exists' and 'God is one' that they applied natural theology's strictures, insisting on naturally accessible premises and demonstrative arguments in order to attempt proofs of doctrinal propositions they considered susceptible of proof. In the vast bulk of their work, however, in all of it that is concerned with Christian doctrine specifically, they applied the broader standards of philosophical theology. And so even if the negative aspect of Reformed epistemology were altogether successful, it would provide no basis for a negative assessment of most of the work medieval philosophers carried out on Christian doctrine.

With the aim of defending and furthering philosophical theology, I have so far distinguished it from natural theology, set out two connected goals of philosophical theology, and claimed that the Reformed epistemologists' misleading attitude towards the work of medieval philosophers in theology is based on a misapprehension of the nature of their work. I want now to consider some of the most formidable objections against philosophical theology as carried out in the Middle Ages, and some of the ways in which those objections were dealt with.

Tertullian's Wholesale Repudiation[9]

Everyone with any knowledge of the history of Christianity or, for that matter, anyone who reads the newspapers knows that Christianity is sometimes associated with a principled anti-intellectualism. In the Patristic period this familiar strain in Christianity manifested itself as specifically anti-philosophical, partly because of St Paul's warnings against the misuse of worldly wisdom, the most pertinent of which is 'Beware lest any man spoil you through philosophy and vain deceit . . .' (Col. 2:8), and perhaps more urgently because the attempt to combine pagan philosophy (the only kind there was) with Christian doctrine was justifiably considered to be a source of heresies. As Tertullian put it,

[8] I discuss Augustine in this connection in my article 'Faith Seeks, Understanding Finds: Augustine's Charter for Christian Philosophy' in Thomas Flint (ed.), *Christian Philosophy* (Notre Dame, Ind.: University of Notre Dame Press, 1989).

[9] The treatment of Tertullian in the following paragraphs is adapted from my article cited in n. 8 above.

we will see, that suggestion is misleading, at least in the case of Aquinas and other thirteenth-century philosophical theologians. (I criticize Plantinga's anti-evidentialism on non-historical grounds in 'Evidence Against Anti-Evidentialism', forthcoming in a volume edited by Kelly Clark).

'philosophy is the core of worldly wisdom, the rash interpreter of God's nature and plan. In fact, the heresies themselves are secretly nourished by philosophy.'[10]

Like Augustine two hundred years after him, Tertullian discussed at length the interrelations of authority, faith, reason, and understanding. But, in vehement opposition to the project for which Augustine eventually won a place of honour, Tertullian viewed the application of reasoning to religious truth as denigrating or at best a waste of time: 'After Christ Jesus, we have no need of curiosity; after the Gospel, no need of inquiry'.[11]

This sort of wholesale repudiation could be and was silenced effectively by elaborating on Jesus' own injunction in the Gospel, 'Seek, and ye shall find', and by citing such other Scriptural authority as I Peter 3:15: 'be ready always to give an answer to every man that asketh you a reason of the hope that is in you'. Augustine of course made good use of such passages in his successful efforts to establish philosophical theology's right to operate in Christianity, but he also appealed more fundamentally, and, I think, persuasively, to a consideration of human nature: 'Let no one think that God hates in us that in respect of which he made us superior to all other living beings. Let no one think, I say, that we should believe in such a way as not to accept or seek reason, since we could not even believe if we did not have rational souls.'[12] By the thirteenth century, or even by the time of Anselm, Augustine's work in and on behalf of philosophical theology had rendered this sort of wholesale repudiation altogether ineffectual, although it is, I think, still occasionally attempted by Christians today.

The Objection of the Two Gregories

Once Augustine had provided Christian philosophical theology with its charter, arguing for and building on a view of the relationship between faith and understanding which made philosophical theology not just a permissible project but a conditional duty for Christians,[13] Tertullian's party was put out of power for a thousand years. But that doesn't mean it went altogether unrepresented during the golden age of philosophical theology. Another sort of principled anti-intellectualist objection was forcefully presented by Gregory the Great almost two hundred years

[10] *De praescriptione haereticorum*, vii, 2–3 (ed. R. F. Refoule, *Corpus Christianorum* Series Latina [CC], Vol. I, 92.4–7).

[11] *De praescriptione haereticorum*, vii, 12 (ed. cit., 193.37–39).

[12] *Epistula CXX*, i, 3. See my article 'Faith Seeks . . .' (n. 8 above) for further discussion.

[13] I defend this interpretation in 'Faith Seeks . . .'.

after Augustine, when he preached that philosophical theology was destructive of faith as a theological virtue: 'Faith for which human reason provides evidence (*experimentum*) is without merit'.[14] And the great Gregory's pronouncement was reinforced for thirteenth-century philosophical theologians in a letter Pope Gregory IX addressed to the theology faculty at the University of Paris in the generation before Aquinas and Bonaventure joined it (on the same day): 'And when [some among you] presume to furnish faith unduly with natural reason, do they not render it in one respect useless and empty? For "faith for which human reason provides evidence is without merit".'[15]

For a reply to this objection of the two Gregories I turn to Bonaventure, who addressed it directly in a passage that also provides a glimpse of his conception of philosophical theology.[16] (In this passage he uses some then standard but now potentially misleading teminology: 'probable reasoning' to indicate reasoning whose premises are not self-evident or known to have been derived from self-evident propositions, and 'opinion' to indicate the conclusion of such reasoning.) 'Gregory [the Great]', Bonaventure explains, 'means this to apply to cases in which faith's believing (*credulitas*) rests entirely on the evidence of probable reasoning. Genuine faith does not ... rest on opinion as its foundation.' The fact that Bonaventure is talking about probable reasoning rather than demonstration, and about opinion, based on probable reasoning, rather than knowledge (*scientia*), based on demonstration, shows that he is assessing this objection against the background of philosophical rather than natural theology.[17] 'On the

---

[14] *XL Homilia in evangelia*, II, hom. 26, n. 1: 'Sed sciendum nobis est quod divina operatio si ratione comprehenditur, non est admirabilis; nec fides habet meritum, cui humana ratio praebet experimentum' (PL 76.1197C).

[15] *Ep. 'Ab Aegyptiis argentea' ad theologos Paris., 7 Iul. 1228* ('Denzinger', ed. xxxvi (1976), 824).

[16] III Sent., d. 24, a. 2, q. 2c, and ad 2 (edn. III, 521). See also Prooemium, q. 2, obj. 6, and ad 6 (edn. I, 10–11); and *Quaestiones disputatae de mysterio trinitatis* q. 1, a. 2, s.c. 3, and ad 3 (edn. V, 53, 57).

[17] For Bonaventure's assessment of the relationship between faith and the sort of knowledge it is possible to have of such theological propositions as 'God exists' and 'God is one', see III Sent., d. 24, a. 2, q. 3 (edn. III, 521–524), where his conclusion is that while faith is not compatible with the knowledge characterized by free and open comprehension that is an aspect of the beatific vision (which of course involves comprehension of all truths about God and not just those theoretically accessible to natural theology), it is not only compatible with but dominant over the highest degree of knowledge available in this life, the sort obtained by the use of demonstrative reason, the sort especially associated with natural theology. On this last point Bonaventure clearly differs from Augustine (see 'Faith Seeks ...', cited in n. 8 above) and

contrary', he continues, 'that probable conclusion of which we have spoken, which can be called opinion, drawn from the arguments, rests on faith itself as on a firmer [foundation] . . . and yet it does so in such a way that it supports and gratifies faith.' 'Indeed, the generated conclusion does not strive against faith but rather subjects itself to faith and becomes its servant. For the weak, it is the nourishment of faith; for those who have matured in faith, it is a delight.'[18]

What I have quoted so far from this passage strikes me as expressing a characterization that would fit thirteenth-century philosophical theology generally quite well. But in this same passage Bonaventure makes an observation that is, I think, unusual and worrisome, alluding to a philosophical criticism in the midst of his reply to the religious objection: 'One indication of this [dependence of probable conclusions on faith] is the fact that many arguments that strike us as probable and quite reasonable regarding the faith seem to unbelievers to be misuses [of reason]'. This perceived misuse of reason cannot be the perpetration of invalid arguments, which Bonaventure would tolerate no more than any unbeliever would, and which has nothing to do with dependence on premises drawn from faith. He seems much more likely to mean that arguments of philosophical theology offend the thoughtful unbeliever because they depend on premises supported only by an authority the acceptance of which would beg the central question. If that is the only basis for the charge of the misuse of reason, this same passage provides material for a reassuring reply by the philosophical theologian. Bonaventure could point out that these arguments, if successful, will uncover support other than authority for the adopted premise, just as working out the implications of any assumption may contribute to its support. But, as we will see, such a reply might be too narrow for Bonaventure's version of philosophical theology.

Peter Lombard's Warning

As I've already suggested, many of the medieval commentaries on the twelfth-century *Sentences* of Peter Lombard are among the paradigms of philosophical theology, and so the persistence of religious objections to the project long after Augustine had established it could hardly be illustrated more pointedly than by an ominous passage quoted approvingly by the Master of the Sentences himself. In his discussion of

---

[18] Cf. Prooemium, q. 2c.

Aquinas (see *Summa theologiae* [ST] IIaIIae q. 1, a. 5, and Ia q. 2, a. 2, ad 1, where he distinguishes as 'preambles' to faith the doctrinal propositions he takes to have been proved).

transubstantiation Peter might easily be read as warning off his unforeseen hundreds of commentators when he says, 'A mystery of the faith can be *believed* in a way conducive to salvation (*salubriter*); it cannot be *investigated* in a way conducive to salvation'.[19]

Bonaventure's way of dealing with this objection is thoughtful and plausible, but is focuses on apologetics, the subsidiary one of the two goals of philosophical theology I mentioned earlier. As we will see (and might have supposed), apologetics is not the main concern of his own philosophical theology.

> In this part the text gives rise to some problems, and the first one concerns this remark of the Master's: 'A mystery of the faith can be believed in a way conducive to salvation; it cannot be investigated in a way conducive to salvation'. For on this basis it seems that all who carry on disputations regarding matters of the faith are gravely sinning. I reply that we have to say that the force [of this remark] must depend as much on the phrase 'a mystery of the faith' as on the verb 'investigate'. For a mystery is something concealed, and it is not to be investigated as if a human being wanted to *comprehend* by reason what the Lord wanted to hide. Anyone who does otherwise does sin and is being presumptuous in raising himself up to something he cannot attain. On the other hand, whoever engages in disputation about the faith not [merely] in order to investigate a mystery but in order to *defend* it does not act contrary to what Augustine and the Master say.[20]

---

[19] *Sententiae*, IV, d. 11, c. 2, n. 2 (Editio Tertia; Grottaferrata (Romae): Editiones Collegii S. Bonaventurae ad Claras Aquas, 1981). Peter attributes the passage to Augustine 'in libro Sententiarum Prosperi', but the editors correct the reference to Lanfranc [1010–89], *De corpore et sanguine Christi*, c. 10 (PL 150.421D).

[20] IV Sent., d. 11, p. 1, a. un., q. 6, dub. 1 (edn. IV, 252). For the allusion to Augustine here, see n. 19 above. Aquinas takes much the same tack with this objection. IV Sent., d. 11, q. 3, a. 4, expositio textus: '[A mystery] "cannot be investigated in a way conducive to salvation"—i.e. if someone is investigating in order to try to *comprehend* it. For it is presumptuous and dangerous when a person does not want to believe more than can be seen by reason. Investigating for purposes of *defending* the faith is useful, however.' But Richard of Middleton, writing a few years later, shows more concern with the structure of philosophical theology than with its application in apologetics. IV Sent., d. 11, q. 6, circa litteram: 'As for the passage "it cannot be investigated in a way conducive to salvation", it is to be understood as alluding to a prying (*curiosa*) investigation that goes beyond appropriate limits, or to an investigation that is not founded on faith'. On the medieval attitude toward illegitimate *curiositas* see Jan A. Aertsen, *Nature and Creature: Thomas Aquinas's Way of Thought* (Leiden: E. J. Brill, 1988), 33–40.

Norman Kretzmann

Philosophical Objections to Philosophical Theology

The focus on a *mystery* of the faith in this last example of a religious objection provides a natural bridge to some crucial philosophical objections that can be raised in a consideration of what is perhaps the most famous passage in Tertullian (even though it is usually crudely paraphrased as 'I believe it because it is absurd'): 'The Son of God died. This is believable, because it is ridiculous. And after having been buried he rose again. This is certain, because it is impossible.'[21] Tertullian here takes some of the central doctrines of Christianity to be not only inaccessible but even repugnant to reason. He clearly thinks his epithets 'ridiculous' and 'impossible' apply to these doctrines themselves and not just to the first impressions they make. If he's right in thinking so, then reasoning applied to such doctrines *cannot* show them to be coherent or produce a correct understanding of them, nor can they even be adopted as premises in non-trivial argumentation. And in that case a genuinely philosophical theology is impossible, as he in fact believed. Tertullian says these things about doctrinal mysteries because he considers philosophy to be an abomination in Christianity, but the things he says can be used just as well by non-Christian philosophers who appraise the combination just as negatively. Since some propositions central to Christian doctrine are mysteries, inaccessible to reason, no enterprise purporting to accept any and every doctrinal proposition as a premise can count as philosophical. I'll call this the objection against mystery.

But the Tertullian passage provides grounds for another philosophical objection as well. In this passage he tries to banish active philosophy from Christianity in such a way as to leave the Christian *faith* not only undiminished but strengthened. Of course he takes these doctrinal mysteries to have been divinely revealed, but in declaring them 'believable' and, to the believer, 'certain' he doesn't cite divine authority but points instead to the fact that they are inaccessible and repugnant to reason. Non-Christian philosophers might well complain about philosophical theology's acceptance of question-beggingly authoritative propositions as premises, as Bonaventure's reply to the objection of the two Gregories suggests. But there are much stronger grounds for a philosophical objection against the starting-points of philosophical theology if, as Tertullian suggests, Christianity is committed to the perverse canon of credibility that considers the very inaccessibility and repugnance to reason exhibited by doctrinal mysteries to be an important consideration in support of believing them.

[21] *De carne Christi*, v, 4 (ed. E. Kroymann, CC Vol. II; 881.27–29).

The Objection Against Mystery

The objection against mystery is the simpler of these two philosophical objections, and I will consider it first. Tertullian's view that Christian doctrine includes mysteries, propositions that are inaccessible to reason and that must be believed by Christians, became and remained part of orthodox Christian doctrine through the Middle Ages and beyond. Here, for instance, are some of the official pronouncements on faith and reason from the session devoted to those topics at the first Vatican Council, in 1870: 'The unchanging consensus of the Catholic Church has maintained and does maintain that the organization of cognition is not only twofold in source but also distinct in object. It is twofold in source because on the one hand we acquire cognition by natural reason, on the other by divine faith. It is distinct in object because, beyond the things to which natural reason can attain, mysteries concealed in God are propounded to us as things that are to believed, mysteries that cannot enter into the process of becoming known (*innotescere*) unless they have been divinely revealed. . . . If anyone should say that divine revelation contains no genuine mysteries in the strict sense, but that by means of correctly developed reason all the dogmas of the faith could be understood and demonstrated on the basis of natural principles, let him be anathema.'[22] I think this nineteenth-century pronouncement does fairly represent 'the unchanging consensus of the Catholic Church'. In any case, for my present purposes it certainly can be taken as depicting thirteenth-century orthodoxy.

In order to understand how philosophical theology could flourish within that orthodoxy, as it surely did, it is important to notice two features of the Church's attitude towards mysteries. In the first place, the claim is not simply that mysteries cannot be known, but rather that they 'cannot enter into the process of becoming known unless they have been divinely revealed'. And that claim is altogether consonant with the principles and practices of philosophical theology, which acknowledges that a doctrinal mystery is a proposition no serious rational person could have come up with on his own, and which adopts that proposition as an assumption in order to apply to it the standard techniques of philosophy with the possible consequence of being able to clarify and defend it. The Church's position on mysteries, unlike Tertullian's, takes them to be ridiculous and impossible only *prima facie*, not *per se*. Though they are held not to be thoroughly understandable (in this life), they are definitely not presented as impervious to reason. And so the philosophical objection against mystery does not apply to orthodoxy as it does to Tertullian's position.

[22] Concilium Vaticanum I: sessio III: Constitutio de fide catholica, Cap. 4. De fide et ratione ('Denzinger', ed. cit., 3015, 3041).

In the second place, notice that what this orthodoxy condemns is generalized natural theology, which, quite unlike philosophical theology, does presuppose 'that by means of correctly developed reason *all* the dogmas of the faith could be understood and *demonstrated* on the basis of *natural* principles'. Genuine philosophical theology is out to discover reason in mystery, not to turn reason against mystery, and so is in no way threatened by this orthodox Christian position on mystery.

Aquinas's Philosophical Theology Applied to Trinity

The way in which medieval philosophical theology operates on mystery without running afoul of the Church's position or philosophy's objection can be outlined in a sketch of Aquinas's approach to trinity.[23]

Trinity, the quintessential Christian doctrine, is also officially classified as a genuine mystery in the strict sense, and I will focus on it in the remainder of this investigation. Obviously nothing could count as Christian philosophical theology that had to treat trinity as *per se* 'ridiculous' or 'impossible', or as officially protected against philosophical investigation. Just as obviously, trinity is outside the scope of natural theology, as Aquinas indicates when he says that 'It is impossible to arrive at a cognition of the Trinity of the divine Persons by means of natural reason'.[24] But Aquinas says this in the twenty-second of a series of seventy-seven articles of *Summa theologiae* devoted to analysing and arguing about the details of this mystery—i.e. in the midst of subjecting trinity to philosophical theology. The existence and the oneness of God, he says, can be proved; they fall within the scope of natural theology. The existence of the three Persons, the threeness of God, not only cannot be proved but even seems inconsistent with some of what Aquinas claims can be proved. For these reasons trinity is a genuine mystery, subject not to proof but rather to clarification within philosophical theology.

Aquinas takes his stand on the unprovability of trinity not because all attempts at such a proof have failed, and not simply because it is officially classified as a mystery, but because he believes he can *prove* that we cannot prove that there are three Persons. All rational proof regarding the existence and attributes of God proceeds by reasoning

[23] I treat Aquinas's approach to trinity much more fully and somewhat differently in my article 'Trinity and Transcendentals', forthcoming in Ronald J. Feenstra and Cornelius Plantinga, Jr (eds), *Trinity, Incarnation, and Atonement* (Notre Dame, Ind.: University of Notre Dame Press, 1989).

[24] ST Ia q. 32, a. 1c.

from nature to nature's creator, he maintains, but 'the creative force of God is common to the whole Trinity and so pertains to the unity of the [divine] essence and not to the distinction of the Persons'.[25] That is why Aquinas thinks the existence of the three Persons cannot be proved, why it does not fall within the scope of natural theology.

Although we cannot by means of natural reason find out that *there are* three Persons, if we accept their existence as a datum, we can in principle make a great deal of progress in *understanding* the Trinity through natural reason, unpacking the basic concepts and drawing conclusions from the fundamental doctrinal claims—i.e. treating the doctrine within philosophical theology. As Aquinas explains in the very article in which he rules out the possibility of acquiring cognition of the Trinity through natural reason,

> there are *two* ways in which reason is employed regarding any matter. It is employed in one way to provide sufficient proof of something fundamental. . . . In the other way reason is employed . . . to show that consequent effects are suited to something fundamental that has already been posited. . . . It is in the first way, then, that reason can be employed to prove that God is one, and things of that sort. But it is in the second way that reason is employed in the clarification of the Trinity. For once the Trinity has been posited, reasonings of that sort are suitable, although not so as to provide a sufficient proof of the Trinity of Persons by those reasonings.[26]

On the basis of everything I've been saying so far it should be evident that I take natural theology to include only Aquinas's first way of employing reason on Christian doctrine, and philosophical theology to include both ways. And, as Aquinas says here, it is only philosophical theology's distinctive operation, clarification based on posited doctrinal propositions, that applies to trinity.[27] In the light of Peter Lombard's

---

[25] ST Ia q. 32, a. 1c.

[26] ST Ia q. 32, a. 1, ad 2. For some detailed applications of philosophical theology to trinity besides ST Ia qq. 27–43 see, e.g., *Summa contra gentiles,* IV, 2–26; *Quaestiones disputatae de potentia,* qq. 8–10; *Compendium theologiae,* Chs. 36–67.

[27] See also the Prooemium of Aquinas's Commentary on Boethius's *De trinitate*: 'Now the method of treating of the Trinity is two-fold, as Augustine says in *De trinitate* I (ii, 3–4)—viz. on the basis of authorities and on the basis of reasonings. Augustine combined these two methods, as he himself says [ibid.]. But some of the holy Fathers, Ambrose and Hilary, for example, used only the one based on authorities. Boethius, on the other hand, decided to pursue the other method, the one based on reasonings, *presupposing* what other men had tracked down on the basis of authorities.' Notice that Aquinas's full description of Boethius's approach to trinity shows it to be, like

warning about the investigation of the mysteries, it's interesting that Aquinas carefully points out that it isn't mere intellectual curiosity or even a defence of the faith that is served by the rational clarification of trinity. In his view this application of philosophical theology, confirming trinity by uncovering connections between it and other doctrines, aids one's understanding of creation and salvation.[28]

Canons of Credibility

The last objection against philosophical theology I can consider on this occasion is the second one I introduced in connection with Tertullian's perverse canon of credibility. As we have seen, Christianity is not committed to any such anti-intellectualism as Tertullian proclaims. But there certainly is room for other objections or critical questions about the epistemic status of mysteries as the starting-points of philosophical theology.

The philosophically safest position is that doctrinal mysteries are introduced into philosophical theology as no more than assumptions, postulates whose coherence, credibility, and compatibility with other doctrinal propositions are to be determined by the analysis and argumentation to which they will be subjected. And although no Christian philosophical theologian would say *only* that much about them, he might well say that sort of thing and treat them in that way when he is attending not to the propositions themselves but to his job of clarifying them within philosophical theology. For instance, we have seen Aquinas in such circumstances refer to trinity simply as having been 'posited'.[29] Treating mysteries methodologically as mere assumptions is a sensible course of action available even to a Christian philosophical

[28] ST Ia q. 32, a. 1, ad 3.

[29] Clement of Alexandria seems to have gone much further—too far—in this direction. 'His main concern is to meet the pagan critic who scorns faith as an unreasoning opinion formed without proper consideration ... Clement replies, first, that all argument has to take something for granted, and faith in religious knowledge is analogous to those initial postulates which make subsequent discussion possible' (Henry Chadwick, *Early Christian Thought and the Classical Tradition: Studies in Justin, Clement, and Origen* (Oxford: Clarendon Press, 1966), 52). Chadwick cites Clement's *Strōmateis,* ii, 13, 4; vii, 95; viii, 6–7; and *Ek tōn prophētikōn eklogai,* 4, 2.

Augustine's and Aquinas's, the approach of philosophical theology. Armand Maurer's translation of this passage is on pp. 5–6 of his *Thomas Aquinas: Faith, Reason, and Theology* (Toronto: Pontifical Institute of Mediaeval Studies, 1987). I am grateful to Scott MacDonald for calling my attention to the passage.

theologian whose religious commitment to those doctrines remains intact before, during, and after his work on them.[30]

All the same, it may seem that a Christian philosophical theologian cannot altogether avoid the question of initial credibility. Mysteries look *incredible*, and yet he is willing to try to find reason in *those* propositions, as distinct from infinitely many other apparently incredible propositions, just because, despite the look of them, he believes them to be true. What is it about those propositions that can elicit such a commitment from a philosopher? Or does he view them as initially credible only because he is also a Christian? If his explanation of their initial credibility terminates in his claim that they rest on divine authority, he has only religious grounds for taking these apparently incredible propositions seriously. The work of philosophical theology can of course begin on just that basis, but the possibility of more widely accessible, trans-authoritative explanations of initial credibility is certainly worth considering.

Augustine, effectively the founder of the field, can occasionally be taken as claiming that initial credibility is based simply on a subjective assurance of divine authority. Regarding his disputation with Evodius in *De libero arbitrio*, for instance, he says 'we argued in such a way that, if we could manage it, our carefully considered, well worked out reasoning would bring to our understanding what we believed about this matter on the basis of the available divine authority'.[31] But in fact his discussions of initial credibility show that he takes one's assurance of divine authority to be, at least ideally, explainable on objective, rational grounds: 'Necessarily we are led to learn in two ways: by authority and by reason. Authority is temporally prior, but reason is prior in reality'.[32] 'Authority demands faith, and prepares a person for reason. Reason leads to understanding and knowledge. Reason does not entirely desert authority, however, when we consider who is to be believed.'[33] And here is an illustration of his idea of a trans-authoritative explanation of initial credibility: 'In this matter [of Christ's existence and teachings]... I believed a report that had the strength of numbers, agreement, and antiquity. And everyone knows that you [heretics], so few in

[30] For a classic presentation of this attitude, see Augustine, *Epistula CXX*, ii, 12: 'And if ... the human, rational, intellectual soul, which was made in God's image, does not elude our thought and understanding, if by mind and understanding we can grasp its excellence, ... it may not be absurd for us to try to raise our soul to understanding its creator as well, with his help. But if it fails in this and falls back on itself, let it be content with devout faith as long as it is wandering, absent from the Lord.'

[31] *Retractationes* I, ix, 1.

[32] *De ordine* II, ix, 26.

[33] *De vera religione*, xxiv, 45.

number, so confused, and so recent, offer nothing that has the dignity of authority.'[34]

Although Augustine wrote voluminously on authority and reason, I don't think he gets much more detailed than that in his account of trans-authoritative canons of initial credibility. And I believe that almost all his medieval successors in philosophical theology followed his lead in this matter when they considered the question of initial credibility at all. But in several important respects their situation was different from that of contemporary philosophical theologians regarding the question of initial credibility. Every philosophical theologian in the thirteenth century was contributing to an enterprise universally acknowledged to be full of accomplishments, and each new contributor was aware of the enhanced credibility achieved for doctrinal mysteries by the clarification of them his predecessors had effected. With not only Augustine's charter but also their discipline's tradition behind them, it would not be surprising if they had long since stopped worrying about initial credibility. What is more, they were, understandably, intent on the outcome of their enterprise rather than on its starting-points, which they could more readily neglect because they were, after all, typically addressing only other believers.[35]

But at least one thirteenth-century philosopher took a different approach. I will conclude with a critical sketch of Bonaventure's attempt to show that the mystery of the Trinity is credible even before it has been clarified by the full effect of philosophical theology.

Bonaventure on the Initial Credibility of a Mystery

Bonaventure's *Disputed Questions on the Mystery of the Trinity*[36] consists in eight questions. Each of the seven questions after the first is

[34] *De utilitate credendi,* xiv, 31.

[35] Augustine's remonstrations with Consentius provide an illustration of this attitude: 'you say that you have laid down a principle for yourself that truth must be perceived on the basis of faith rather than on the basis of reason. . . . See, then, whether in accordance with those words of yours you should not follow only the authority of the saints in this matter [the doctrine of the Trinity] on which our faith is chiefly founded, rather than asking me to make it understandable to you by reason. For when I begin to lead you into the understanding of so great a mystery in any way at all (something I will be able to do only if God helps from within), all I will be doing in discussing it is giving you such reasons as I can' (*Epistula CXX* i, 2).

[36] *Quaestiones disputatae de mysterio trinitatis* (Quaracchi edn. V, 45–115) was written probably around 1256, near Bonaventure's departure from the University of Paris to take up his duties as General of the Franciscan Order. It

concerned with one divine attribute: unity, simplicity, infinity, eternality, immutability, necessity, and primacy. Questions 2–7 contain two articles apiece. In each case the first article is intended to establish that the attribute in question is indeed correctly ascribed to God, while the second article undertakes to show that trinity is compatible with the ascription of that attribute. Thus, for instance, the Thesis of the first article of Question 2, on divine unity, is 'That God is one is a truth not only credible but also understandable', and the Thesis of its second article is 'In God trinity and supreme unity have no incompatibility, but a remarkable agreement and harmony'. The single article of q. 8 is the counterpart of the second articles in qq. 2–7, and its Thesis is 'Primacy not only does not exclude trinity, but even includes it'.[37] In the compatibility arguments in qq. 2–8 trinity itself is not argued for but treated as a datum; in qq. 2–7 the arguments in favour of ascribing this or that attribute to God always include arguments that purport to be independent of any authoritative support. And so, as far as I can see, Bonaventure might well intend all the Theses in these questions to be accessible to unaided reason, and thus consider these Disputed Questions to be offering *proofs* of the *compatibility* of trinity with other doctrines and thus confirmation for trinity, though not, of course, a proof of that doctrine itself. Obviously the material in qq. 2–8 deserves study and appraisal, but my interest now is in q. 1, where Bonaventure does what he thinks enables him to treat trinity in qq. 2–8 as more than a mere postulate.

God's existence and God's being three Persons are the topics of q. 1, but not directly. Its immediate concern is with the epistemic status of

[37] Here are the Theses of the other articles. Q. 3, a. 1: 'The divine being (*esse*) is supremely simple'; a. 2: 'The Trinity of the Persons does not do away with supreme simplicity, nor does supreme simplicity exclude trinity'; q. 4, a. 1: 'Because the divine being and capability (*posse*) is supremely simple it is infinite (in so far as "infinite" rules out a limit to the quantity of power [*virtus*])'; a. 2: 'In God supreme infinity is compatible with the Trinity of the Persons'; q. 5, a. 1: 'The divine being is eternal because it is simple, all at once, and infinite'; a. 2: 'Necessarily, the Trinity of the Persons is compatible with eternality'; q. 6, a. 1: 'The divine being is altogether immutable'; a. 2: 'The Trinity of the Persons is compatible with supreme immutability'; q. 7, a. 1: 'The divine being is necessary with the absolutely perfect necessity of immutability'; a. 2: 'The necessary and supremely free divine being is compatible with the Trinity of the Persons'.

has been translated by Zachary Hayes, OFM, *Saint Bonaventure's Disputed Questions on the Mystery of the Trinity: An Introduction and Translation* (St Bonaventure, NY: The Franciscan Institute, 1979). For historical data, the place of this treatise in Bonaventure's work, and a good deal of valuable background information, see Hayes's detailed Introduction.

those doctrines, as is indicated by its title: 'Concerning the certainty with which the existence of God is known and the faith with which the trinity of God is believed'. The question asked in the first article of q. 1 is 'Is it an indubitable truth that God exists?', and Bonaventure's answer is summarized in the Thesis: 'That God exists is not dubitable if "dubitable" is understood [as applying to] a truth that lacks evidentness (*ratio evidentiae*) in itself, in relation to the basis for proving it, or in relation to intellect apprehending it; nevertheless, there can be doubt about it on the part of a knower in virtue of some defect in that knower's acts of apprehending, considering, or analysing it'. So, on Bonaventure's view the proposition 'God exists' is, considered in itself, an indubitable truth.

Trinity's Initial Credibility Extrinsically Considered

My present interest is in the contrasting second article of q. 1, where Bonaventure addresses the question of initial credibility:

> Supposing that it is an indubitable truth that God exists [as has just been argued], the next question is whether it is a credible truth that God is three (*Deum esse trinum*)[38]

—a question that Bonaventure of course answers affirmatively. That the issue is initial credibility is fairly clear simply because he is raising this question at the outset, before the philosophical theology carried out in these disputed questions could be said to have enhanced its credibility, and his treatment of the proposition in this article bears out that impression. The proposition 'God is three' is not in itself obviously a doctrinal mystery, but the arguments for God's existence in the first article are pretty clearly monotheistic, and 'God is one' is to be argued for in the first article of the next question. In any case, 'God is three' is considered throughout q. 1, a. 2, on the assumption that God is *also* one, and it should thus be taken to represent the *mystery* of the Trinity. So the proposition Bonaventure is concerned with is really 'God is three and one', a proposition I will refer to simply as trinity. The fact that Bonaventure takes trinity's *truth* for granted does not beg any questions important to the issue of its *credibility*.

The work of a. 2 begins with Bonaventure's introductory analysis of credibility: 'What is [a] suitable and [b] obligatory to be believed is

---

[38] Q. 1, a. 2, occupies pp. 51–58 of Vol. V of the Quaracchi edition. My references to short, numbered units of the article will be clear without further detail. In other cases I will attach page and line numbers to the quoted passages.

what I call credible' (51a47–48). Bonaventure's 'suitable' (*congruum*) does seem to represent a standard canon of credibility; what is credible is not merely what it is logically possible to believe. His inclusion of 'obligatory' (*debitum*), on the other hand, is clearly not standard. What leads Bonaventure to take belief in trinity to be obligatory is the familiar divine injunctions to believe, and the divine establishment of belief as a necessary condition of salvation.[39] Thus his taking it to be obligatory entails his taking it to have divine authority, and in this way Bonaventure's including 'obligatory to be believed' in his analysis of 'credible' makes sense epistemologically. But since he simply takes the divine authority for granted here, nothing in his arguments in support of one's being obliged to believe trinity supplies any trans-authoritative explanation of trinity's initial credibility.

Of the twenty-seven opening arguments of this article, fourteen are affirmative (the A-arguments, I'll call them), intended to show that trinity *is* initially credible, as Bonaventure maintains, and thirteen are negative (the N-arguments), opposing his position. Of the A-arguments, A1–A8 support trinity's being considered *obligatory*, and A9–A14 support its being considered *suitable* to be believed.[40] On the other side, arguments N1–N8 oppose trinity's being considered *suitable*, N9–N12 oppose its being considered *obligatory* to be believed, and N13 raises a general critical question regarding a Christian's motive for believing trinity even if it is a credible truth. For reasons already given, my interest is in non-authoritative grounds for initial credibility, and so I am setting aside the arguments having to do with obligatoriness.[41]

The *suitability* of believing a proposition, P, becomes an issue only when P is presented to someone to whom it looks unsuitable to be

[39] Arguments A1–A8, those in support of characterizing trinity as a proposition one is obliged to believe, are all based primarily on authoritive pronouncements on requirements for salvation, each of which is said to imply believing trinity. Perhaps the clearest example is A1, which combines the trinitarian formula of baptism in Matthew 28:19 with Mark 16:16, 'He that believeth and is baptized shall be saved; but he that believeth not shall be damned'.

[40] It is worth noting that in A9, as occasionally elsewhere in q. 1, a. 2, the proposition explicitly at issue is not merely 'God is three', but 'God is three *and one*'.

[41] The only evidence of trinity's credibility offered in these arguments besides the claim that belief in trinity is a necessary condition for salvation is added in A3, which also points out 'the danger in going wrong' in an inquiry into trinity. That could look like an argument for remaining content with mere belief if it were not tied to a quotation from Augustine's *De trinitate* I, iii, 5: 'When one inquires into the unity of the Trinity—of the Father, the Son, and the Holy Spirit—nowhere is it more dangerous to go wrong, more difficult to inquire, *or more rewarding to discover something*'.

believed. Let P be a proposition of quantum mechanics, and suppose that to me P looks initially incredible—not just astonishing, but ridiculous and impossible. A knowledgeable friend who wants to educate me would be unlikely to make much progress if she began by focusing on P itself, which affronts my reason. She could more easily make P initially credible for me by establishing certain relevant considerations *extrinsic* to P, such as its being believed by people whose minds I respect. A consideration of that sort would be particularly effective if it led me to think that the reason I found P unsuitable to be believed was that my understanding of it was different from the physicists' understanding of it, even though we used the same words. I would in that way have been put in a position to appreciate a detailed clarification of P, based on considerations *intrinsic* to it.

In his article, Bonaventure's approach to suitability of belief is that of the knowledgeable friend. It begins with arguments A9–A14, all of which point to extrinsic considerations in favour of taking trinity as suitable to be believed.[42] Arguments that deal with a proposition extrinsically cannot in any way enhance the proposition's *intelligibility*, only its initial *credibility*; but that is all that Bonaventure claims for these arguments.

We might expect that the opening arguments opposed to trinity's suitability to be believed, arguments N1–N8, would depend on considerations intrinsic to trinity. After all, it is the *content* of trinity that makes it seem *un*suitable to be believed. But in fact his approach in these arguments, too, is almost exclusively extrinsic, depending on considerations against trinity's *credibility*, postponing considerations of its *intelligibility*.[43]

---

[42] Briefly, the extrinsic considerations cited are these. A9 and A10 point out that trinity is the *fundamental* proposition put forward for belief (a status that will become clear later); A11 and A12 claim that trinity is believed by the wise and by an innumerable multitude; A13 cites the authority of Scripture along with trans-authoritative considerations of its antiquity, miracles, and prophecies. A14, the most interesting of the lot, cites Augustine's threefold classification of credible things (*De diversis quaestionibus LXXXIII*, q. 48), in which historical propositions are described as merely credible but never understandable, and theological propositions are described as understandable if they are first believed. Bonaventure's line is that propositions of the latter sort, the eventually understandable ones, are 'more credible' than the former, and so trinity is even more credible than 'Abraham begot Isaac', which is 'very credible indeed'.

[43] Beyond such simple claims as 'all reason dictates the contrary of the proposition that one is really three' (N1), there is no attention in these arguments to the content of trinity except this in N2: 'All created nature displays the contrary of the [trinitarian] proposition that what is one in a form

In their uniformly extrinsic concern with trinity the opening arguments for and against the suitability of believing it cannot contribute to clarifying the proposition. These arguments, then, are not the sort that characterize philosophical theology, but they may constitute a helpful preparation for it, establishing trinity's rational respectability along with initial credibility.

Bonaventure's Survey of the Sources and Arguments

After the opening arguments, the body of the article begins with Bonaventure's Thesis: 'That God is three is a credible truth, because it is [a] suitable, [b] obligatory, and [c] worthy to be believed[44] (54b14–15). As an introduction to Bonaventure's Reply, the Thesis looks like a forecast of more of the same; even the addition of 'worthy' (*dignum*) to the canons of credibility seems not much more than a variation on 'suitable'. But in fact the character of his article alters radically with the beginning of the Reply. 'Worthy' turns out to be a significant addition to 'suitable' and 'obligatory', and even those two familiar canons are interpreted differently. More importantly, the previous approach to trinity via only extrinsic considerations is replaced by direct attention to this content of the proposition.[45]

Bonaventure's Reply in this article is too broad and impressionistic to count as a paradigm of philosophical theology, but it provides a very interesting survey of the kinds of evidence appropriate for natural, biblical, and philosophical theology, and an intriguing sketch of a line of argument that might be developed in the detailed philosophical clarification of trinity.

In his initial explanation of the Thesis, Bonaventure says regarding trinity:

[44] I have translated Bonaventure's active infinitive here as if it were passive in order to accommodate 'worthy'.

[45] Perhaps the noteworthy differences between the opening arguments and the Reply reflect the practice common among thirteenth-century masters of assigning the development of those arguments to one's students.

---

that is not made many is made many in entities that have that form, since in connection with every created nature, when the entities that have the form are made many, the form is made many' (*contrarium huius quod est, unum in forma non multiplicata multiplicari in suppositis, praetendit omnis natura creata; in qualibet enim natura creata, supposito multiplicato, multiplicatur forma*). And even in N2 the main thrust of the argument is extrinsic to trinity: 'Everything whose contrary is displayed by created nature is incredible to reason'. Arguments N1–N4 deny that trinity is *rationally* suitable to be believed, N5–N7 deny that it is *religiously* suitable, and N8 denies that it is in *any* way suitable to be believed.

since that credible truth is the foundation of the whole Christian faith, it has three kinds of evidence (*triplex habet testimonium*[46]), so that the foundation may remain unshaken (54b19–22).

By calling trinity 'the foundation of the whole Chrisitan faith' he means more than that it distinguishes Christianity from Judaism and Islam; he thinks it is possible to construct an argument in which all the principal doctrines of Christianity are derived from 'God is three and one' (56a16–30). But my interest now is not in derivations from trinity but in the three kinds of evidence Bonaventure thinks there are for trinity itself. He presents them as three 'Books': the Book of Nature (or the Book of the Creature) (54b28–55a36), the Book of Scripture (55a36–b30), and the Book of Life (55b31–56a30). As I see them, they could be helpfully subtitled the Book of Natural Theology, the Book of Biblical Theology, and the Book of Philosophical Theology.

The evidence provided by the Book of Nature is of two sorts: *vestiges* of the Trinity in corporeal nature, and the *image* of the Trinity in the human soul. By this evidence we are *led* to believe trinity, which on this basis is made *suitable* to be believed. Like Aquinas, Bonaventure would deny that anyone could derive trinity from the contemplation of nature alone, but 'the twofold evidence of the Book of Nature *was* efficacious [in that respect] in the state of nature as it was created', before the Fall (55a30–36), and the present obscurity of this Book is a function only of the reader's darkened vision.[47]

The evidence provided by the Book of Scripture is of two sorts: *implicit* in the Old Testament, and *explicit* in the New. By this evidence we are *constrained* to believe trinity, which on this basis is made *obligatory* to be believed.

I have been brutally brief about these first two Books in order to get on to the third. Besides, what Bonaventure says about the first is derivative from Augustine's well-known discussions in *De trinitate*, and what he says about the second is familiar to anyone who has taken the slightest interest in Scriptural evidence for trinity. His treatment of the third is less familiar. Furthermore, he evaluates the evidence in

[46] Bonaventure's use of '*testimonium*' here is an unmistakable allusion to I John 5:7, '*Tres sunt, qui testimonium dant in caelo, Pater, Verbum, et Spiritus sanctus, et hi tres unum sunt*', a passage he discusses later in his Reply (55b22–30). Although 'testimony' (as KJV has it) is clearly preferable to 'evidence' as a translation of '*testimonium*' in I John, the line Bonaventure develops in the remainder of his Reply seems to call for 'evidence' here.

[47] Strictly speaking, the evidence presented in Bonaventure's Book of Nature constituted a basis for natural theology only before the Fall. The evidence is still there, but post-Fall human beings can make only diminished use of it, and only after they have found out otherwise what to look for.

each of the three Books as (1) efficacious (formerly), (2) more efficacious, and (3) most efficacious. But notice, before closing these first two Books, that in this portion of Article 2 what makes trinity *suitable* to be believed is not considerations extrinsic to it, but observations of human and non-human nature that are supposed to provide confirmation of trinity itself; and what now makes trinity *obligatory* to be believed is not divine or ecclesiastical authority that salvation depends on believing it, but Scriptural passages in which trinity itself is expressed or thought to be implied.

Bonaventure's designations for the first two Books are apt and altogether unsurprising, but 'Book of Life' strikes me as odd.[48] As I see it, 'Book of Light' would be better suited to the sort of evidence he considers under this designation (and to its connection with philosophical theology). Like the first two, this third Book has two sorts of evidence for trinity: *the innate light* of reason (*lumen inditum*) and *the infused light* of divine revelation and illumination (*lumen infusum*). By the combination of these two sorts of evidence we are *raised* to believe trinity, which on this basis is made *worthy* to be believed.[49] Bonaventure's claims for the Book of Life are at least as sweeping as any Augustine made in founding philosophical theology:

> From the combination of these two lights the habit of faith is elicited [in a person] as evidence for believing that God is three *and* [to believe], as a consequence, *every* truth that pertains to the practice of the Christian religion (55b43–47).[50]

[48] Bonaventure pretty clearly derives the designation from John 1:4, 'In him was life; and the life was the light of men', which he cites in this connection (55b39–40). Still, in his own terminology it is light, not life, with which the evidence in this Book is directly associated. For a thorough presentation of thirteenth-century considerations of the concept of the Book of Life and its association with the second Person of the Trinity, see Aquinas's disputed question *De libro vitae (Quaestiones disputatae de veritate*, q. 7).

[49] Bonaventure also characterizes the cognitive aspect of the beatific vision as the Book of Life (55b34–37), but what this Book provides after this life is not really *evidence*, as Bonaventure suggests by the adverbs he uses in his characterization of the celestial version: *per se, in se, explicite, expresse*. I confine my attention to the Book of Life in this life.

[50] '... *ex quorum luminum concursu habitus fidei tanquam argumentum elicitur ad credendum, Deum esse trinum, et consequenter omne verum, quod pertinet ad christianae religionis cultum*.' The crucial phrase 'the habit of faith is elicited [in a person] as evidence for believing' strikes me as particularly difficult. (I feel warranted in translating '*argumentum*' as 'evidence' largely because the Vulgate has '*argumentum*' where KJV has 'evidence' in Hebrews 11:1—'Faith is ... the evidence of things not seen'.) Scott MacDonald has called my attention to a remarkable passage in Aquinas that can be read almost as if written in an attempt to explain this difficult passage in Bonaventure—i.e. *In librum Boethii De trinitate* q. 3, a. 1, ad 4.)

This passage is difficult as well as surprising, and Bonaventure goes on at once to offer an explanation, though not of everything in it that needs explaining. What he says does show unmistakably, however, that 'the combination of these two lights', the 'most efficacious' Book of evidence, results in philosophical theology.

His elucidation of his sweeping claim consists in a sketch of an argument that begins with premises on which, he says, 'Christians, Jews, Saracens, and even heretics agree' (56a2–3) because they are accessible to unaided reason, 'the innate light'. He then proceeds with minimal (but carefully acknowledged) assistance from revelation or illumination, 'the infused light' (needing to borrow only the premise 'God is love', I think), and reaches a subconclusion that is a version of the doctrine of the Trinity—'He generates [one] and spirates one, coequal and consubstantial with himself' (56a13–14)—before pressing on to derive the rest of Christian doctrine from that subconclusion—the creation, incarnation, passion, last judgment, punishment, and rewards.

Yes, I think he goes too far, or at least too fast. But it would be instructive and rewarding to try constructing the long argument he briefly sketches in order to see just where its shortcomings are. What is important for my present purposes, however, is not the argument itself but his allusion to this sort of enterprise in his rejoinder to the last of the opening arguments, N13, the importance of which he signals by taking it up before rebutting the other negative arguments, N1–N12, in the order in which they were offered.

N13 takes the form of a question: even if trinity is a credible truth (in spite of everything brought out in the twelve preceding negative arguments), 'what moves a Christian to *believe* that truth?' (54a33–34). The question is not idle. One certainly can acknowledge the credibility of a proposition without believing it. In Bonaventure's answer he mentions motives he might be expected to mention: 'the authentic testimony of Scripture', 'the examples and witnessings of the Saints', 'the arguments of the Doctors', 'the judgment of the universal Church', and 'irrefutable miracles'. But all these he describes as 'auxiliary motives' (*moventia adminiculantia*) (56b18–19).

> What moves us *principally* is the illumination that is born in the innate light [of reason] and consummated in the infused light [of revelation] (56b7–10).

Although this description of the principal motive for believing appears to emphasize the relative importance of revelation, it is worth noticing that beginning with innate light and ending by drawing on the infused light is also simply the order of his argument sketch. It begins with what 'one's own reason dictates to everyone' (55b50) and then makes a transition which, Bonaventure acknowledges, 'is not dictated by the innate light on its own, but by the infused light, from which, *together with* the innate light, one gathers that God must be thought of' in the way that advances the argument (56a11–13). So I think it is fair to characterize Bonaventure's description of the principal motivation to believe as an apt description of philosophical theology as carried on successfully by an open-minded philosopher. And, interpretations of medieval philosophers aside, that account of the principal motivation for believing is the one I subscribe to.[51]

[51] I am grateful to Scott MacDonald and to Eleonore Stump, each of whom prepared detailed, helpful comments on an earlier draft of this paper.

The Philosophy in Christianity: Arius and Athanasius[1]

MAURICE WILES

Cui bono? Cherchez la femme! These ancient maxims offer counsel to the investigator of an unsolved murder or some inexplicable pattern of behaviour. They advise the pursuit of what has come more recently to be known as a form of lateral thinking. The puzzle may not best be solved by an intensification of the examination of the immediate data. The primary clue may lie out of sight somewhere further back. Financial advantage or sexual attraction, which does not show up as a feature of the immediate situation, may be the hidden motive of the traditionally male agent's actions. When that is recognized, the otherwise inexplicable phenomena may become intelligible.

The early Church, particularly under the influence of the third-century writer Hippolytus, had a somewhat similar view of how to achieve an understanding of heresy. Orthodox belief was generally regarded as so clearly the correct embodiment of God-given revealed truth that the emergence of heresy was a puzzle in need of explanation. Evil motives, such as private antagonism or personal ambition, were often alleged. But more intellectual explanations were also called for. Why should the heretic's hatred of the truth have taken the particular form that it did? The key to answering that question, they maintained, often lay in the heretic's undue dependence on the teachings of philosophy. It was there that one needed to look to account for the particular form that the heretic's distortion of Christian truth had taken. The epistle to the Colossians (2:8) had warned the Church of the danger of being taken prey by philosophy, and heresy was the outcome of failing to heed that warning.

In the light of this general theory the roots of Arianism have often been ascribed to Aristotelian philosophy. Arius, who was a presbyter in the church of Alexandria at the time of the outbreak of the controversy, is described by one of the early Church historians, Sozomen (*HE* 4:5), as διαλεκτικώτατος—an acute reasoner, a highly dialectical man. This has, sometimes, been understood to imply a deep commitment to the precise forms of Aristotelian logic and their application to Christian

---

[1] I am grateful to Dr Rebecca Lyman for helpful comments on an earlier draft of this paper.

theology. Moreover adherence to a specifically Aristotelian under-standing of οὐσία (substance) has been seen as a source of confusion in the interpretation of the credal term ὁμοούσιος (of one substance) and of the Arian refusal to accept it as defining the relation between the Father and Son. But a more careful examination of the evidence does not bear out an explanation along these lines. Although different philosophical schools still existed, there had been a good deal of cross-influence between them. There is scant sign in the case of the Arian controversy of any strictly Aristotelian influence at work, of the sort that such a theory presupposes. Arius and Athanasius, his chief orthodox opponent, shared a common background of a broadly eclectic Platonist kind. Moreover it is clear that the introduction of substance language into the debate, and thereby into the Nicene creed, was not done with any precise philosophical connotation in mind. Neither differing philosophical allegiance nor differing evaluation of the importance of philosophical reasoning was a crucial factor in the split between Athanasius and the Arians. The role of philosophy in that essentially Christian debate was of a less straightforward and less external kind.

Arius is not only described by the Church historians as an acute reasoner; he is also described as an expositor of scripture (Theodoret *HE* 1:1). Although we have very little of his work on which to base our judgment, it is clear enough that he draws thoughtfully and extensively on the teaching of scripture. On that score there is again no significant difference between him and Athanasius. Neither has any doubt that Christ is Son of God in a unique sense. But the ways in which scripture speaks about Christ as Son of God are immensely varied. It is as Son that Jesus prays to his Father in Gethsemane, struggling to align his will with that of the Father in an act of filial obedience (Mk. 14:36). But it is also the Son who is spoken of as in the bosom of the Father and thus alone able to reveal him (Jn. 1:18). He and his Father are one (Jn. 10:30); yet the Father is greater than he (Jn. 14:28). Such language cries out for further elucidation and clarification. Arius and Athanasius were at one in believing that scripture, rightly understood, conveyed a single, uniform saving truth about God. Any attempt to show that it does so in the face of its apparently diverse teaching requires some kind of overall framework of understanding. And was that not precisely what the philosophers of the time were already seeking to provide in relation to the equally diverse and puzzling phenomena of human life as a whole?

In using the insights of philosophy to present a coherent account of the scriptural witness, Arius and Athanasius were not pioneers in the fourth century. Christians of the second and third centuries had been doing it already. Philosophy was not, therefore, something wholly external, a feature exclusively of the surrounding pagan world. It also came to Arius and Athanasius embedded within the Christian tradition that they inherited, and to which they both sought to be loyal as well as being faithful interpreters of scripture.

Philosophy was certainly an important element in the Alexandrian scene to which both Arius and Athanasius belonged. There is no way of telling whether either of them had very close contact with the philosophical school at Alexandria. It is not very likely that they did, but it is reasonable to suppose that they would have had some general idea of the issues being discussed there. In any event we have little knowledge of the Alexandrian school at that time. 'It is', says A. C. Lloyd, 'clouded in obscurity from the time Plotinus was there [c. 233–244] till about 400.' In trying to assess the philosophical climate to which they would have been exposed, we need therefore to draw more generally on the philosophical literature available to us from the immediately preceding centuries.

I have already spoken of that general philosophical tradition as Platonist in basic character, but affected by the influence of both Aristotelian and Stoic thought. It was not a static tradition but a living, changing one. Looking back on it as historians, we classify it into distinct periods with their distinct titles: Middle Platonism and Neoplatonism. But it is important that we don't think of them as discrete entities, replacing one another at a particular moment like frames in a slide-show. The most distinctive characteristics of Neoplatonism with its increased emphasis on transcendence were already recognizable tendencies in the later Middle Platonic period. Recent discussion of the philosophical background to the thought of Arius has laid a good deal of stress on whether or not he knew the work of Plotinus, the founding father of Neoplatonism. Plotinus, as we have already observed, had been in Alexandria some seventy-five years before the outbreak of the Arian controversy, but it was some time before his work began to be at all widely disseminated. It is questionable whether the issue can be settled with any confidence, one way or the other. But it is perhaps not as important as is sometimes claimed. It is the nature of the issues that were being debated at the time that is crucial for our purpose. And these included many of the most problematic features of Platonism, especially ones that related to the contemporary emergence of Neoplatonic thought. Moreover many of these questions which philosophers were subjecting to careful critical scrutiny and for which a variety of solutions were being put forward, had important points of affinity with the issues which were troubling Christian theologians at that time. What is the relation between unity and the multiplicity of experience, between the eternally changeless and the phenomenal realms? Is there some mediation between the two, and if so what is the nature and status of any such mediatorial entities? And how does the Demiurge of Plato's *Timaeus* relate to Plato's account of the ideal forms? As background to any attempt to assess the place of philosophy within the Arian debate, I propose to outline five areas of philosophical discussion, current at the time, which are, even if only indirectly, significant for the understanding of the issues involved in that debate.[2]

(1) Perhaps the most fundamental problem for a Platonist philosophy is the relation between the ideal forms and the phenomenal world. The logic of the basic Platonist position requires a sharp contrast between the timeless and the temporal, the changeless and the changing, the immutable and the mutable. Yet for all the directness of the contrast, the chasm between the two cannot be unbridgeable. For the ideal world is the ground of the existence of the phenomenal. There must be some positive relation between the two. How is that relation to be described? Is our world simply a copy of the ideal world—or does the relation go deeper so that the lower can be spoken of as participating in the higher? When the notion of transcendence is most strongly affirmed, the relation of the this-worldly to the higher reality will be spoken of primarily in the negative terms we have been using. That higher reality can be defined only in terms of what it is not—it is time*less*, change*less, im*mutable. In religious terms a conception of that kind finds its expression in mystical or apophatic ways. God is to be defined by what he is not. Where, on the other hand, perhaps under Stoic influence, more weight is given to the presence of an immanent logos or rationality within our world, a more positive relation can be affirmed. God is intellect or goodness itself, in which we as rational beings can in some measure participate. The way is then open for a more positive use of language applied analogically to God and for a more sacramental apprehension of the world. But the dominant tendency of the time, which was to find its culmination in Neoplatonism, was to lay increasing emphasis on the transcendent or negative pole.

(2) In the *Timaeus* (28c) Plato had spoken of God as 'Father and Creator of all'. Was that phrase to be taken, as would seem most natural, as referring to the same single reality? Some philosophers, like Atticus, understood it in that way. There was a single divine, creative reality, who was both Father and Creator. But others, like Numenius, took Plato's words as referring to two distinct realities—a first God who is Father and a second God who is Creator. Thereby a greater distance was maintained between the supreme reality and the world that derives from it. So the divine is conceived as existing in the form of more than

[2] For a much more detailed account of the most relevant features of this second- and third-century philosophical discussion, see John Dillon, 'Logos and Trinity: Patterns of Platonist Influence on Early Christianity', above.

one entity, ordered in a hierarchical sequence. Such hierarchies were often threefold, as with Plato himself and also with Plotinus' conception of the One, the world mind and world soul. There was a gradual progression from pure unity to the realm of the ideas and then to the animating power of the world. Such hierarchies were variously named and variously understood. But there was much discussion of a mediating process between the highest reality and the created world. The issue was one of increasing significance in the philosophical thought of the time.

(3) Various names were given to these higher levels of divine reality—unity (τὸ ἕν), being (οὐσία), intellect (νοῦς), the good (τὸ ἀγαθον). In psychology and ethics, which were important features in the teaching of the philosophical schools, much attention was also given to the concept of the will. As is to be expected in a scheme of thought in which the divine is not conceived in personal terms, will is not a concept much used in relation to the supreme divine reality. But it is not wholly absent. Platonists were concerned not merely to give some account of the emergence of a world, but also to affirm some form of providence clearly distinguishable from Stoic conceptions of fate or other prevalent forms of fatalist teaching. That concern with cosmology, and still more with providence, led to the occasional introduction of the idea of will into philosophical discussion of the divine. The relation of will to intellect or being with reference to God was an emerging issue of concern.

(4) The contrast between the divine as eternal and changeless and the world as temporal and changing poses a problem about the temporality of the world. If we say that the world itself is eternal, do we not deny its fundamental character as temporal and contingent? But if we affirm its creation to be in time, do we not deny the eternal and changeless character of the divine, which must at some time have changed and begun to give rise to a world? Some, like Plotinus, saw no objection to the idea of an eternal process of emanation, an eternal dependence of the world on the changeless One. But for others, both before and after him, the act of creation, the bringing of order out of formless matter, could not be reckoned eternal—whatever might be true of the formless matter itself. So careful discussion was called for about the different senses of 'creation', and still more about the different senses of 'time'. The creation of the world could not be unequivocally affirmed either as timeless or as within time. As an illustration of the type of distinction being proposed, one can take the words of Atticus that 'there was time before the creation of the world, but there was not measured (τεταγμένος) time'.

(5) Philosophy concerned itself not only with the origin of things but also with the goal of human life. Plato had spoken of the ideal of

'likeness to God', and that goal was espoused not only by Platonists but by some Stoics also. Both saw it as something that could only be attained by moral training and endeavour. But there were differences between them, particularly concerning the role of the emotions in the moral life. Moreover for the Platonist, for whom God was clearly distinct from nature and yet for whom some form of participation in the divine was possible, such a formulation of the goal in terms of likeness to God served to link ethical progress with a religiously conceived participation in God—at least, as Albinus is careful to add, with the second if not the supreme God.

These contemporary issues in all their diversity provided the intellectual and religious climate in which Christian reflection was being carried on. Whether or not Christian authors can be shown to hold particular opinions on specific issues of philosophical debate, their own reflections bear the imprint of contemporary philosophical vocabulary and perspectives. In the case of Arius and Athanasius, that philosophical environment certainly contributed to the ways in which they responded to the central theological issue of their day. But that is a far cry from seeing them as philosophers or direct participants in a specifically philosophical debate. A contemporary scholar's approach to his subject today, for example, can be much influenced by the concepts and vocabulary of evolution without him or her having had any direct involvement in either biology or the philosophy of science. It is in this generalized, but none the less highly significant way, that we need to envisage the role of philosophy in the great theological controversy of the early fourth century.

What then was the nature of the theological issue at the heart of that controversy? The evidence available to us does not enable us to offer a confident answer to that question, which is much debated among historians of theology at the present time. I shall begin by giving a very brief survey of the way in which the Church's thought about the person of the Son had been developing up to that time. Both scripture and the worshipping practice of the Church pointed to the existence of one who was the divine source of revelation and salvation, but who could not be simply identified with God, the one whom he himself called Father. So Christians spoke of a second divine being, whom they called not only Son (with the risk of crude misunderstanding in a world of Greek myths) but also Word and Wisdom. Those latter designations had firm roots in the Old Testament, but for educated Christian apologists deliberately seeking points of contact between their Christian faith and the surrounding culture, they were also strongly suggestive of that second divine reality in philosophical thought, where the pure transcendent unity gives rise to rationality and to the realm of the ideas. This second divine being was clearly derivative from God—even if, as in

Origen's view, eternally derivative as was the world from the One in the Plotinian scheme. Understood within such a context, the existence of a second divine being was not felt to constitute any threat to monotheistic faith, for the Father remained the one source of all else. Furthermore, such an approach did not only help to make sense of the idea of the Word or Son as the agent of God's providence in creation and history; it was also of help in enabling Christians to conceive and speak of him as actually embodied in a full and unique manner in the person of Jesus Christ. At the same time his perfect reflection of the Father's rationality and goodness and also the devotion offered to him in the worship of the Church led Christians to speak of him and to address him in language almost as exalted as that used of the Father. A framework might have been provided for containing the tension that we referred to earlier as inherent in the language of the New Testament, but the tension itself was still there. Such a tension was a perpetual invitation to crisis and dispute.

Meanwhile Christian teaching about the creation of the world was moving in a direction that took it further away from that of the philosophical schools, and at the same time exacerbated the tension inherent in Christian teaching about the Son. Earlier Christian teachers had not clearly differentiated their view of creation from the characteristic Platonic view of creation as the ordering of formless matter. Moreover for Origen human souls had an eternal kinship with the divine Word, which while not undermining their dependent created status, enabled him to conceive the Word as a bond or mediating nature between God and the lower level of the created, yet kindred, spiritual order. But increasingly the stress came to be laid on the absoluteness of God's creative work as creation out of nothing. The great divide was not between the spiritual realm (God, the Word, angels, human souls) and the phenomenal; it was between God and the created order, between God and everything else. The tension always inherent in Christian understanding of the Son was being stretched to breaking point. How in such an altered framework was the person of the Son to be understood?

In trying to see how Arius and Athanasius responded to this issue, I shall base my account of Arius somewhat narrowly on the two short letters of his, that have come down to us from the earliest period of the debate—the one a confession of faith to his bishop, Alexander of Alexandria, with whom he was in conflict and the other a request for support from his most powerful ally outside Alexandria, Eusebius of Nicomedia.[3] The letters have a clear polemical purpose and may not

---

[3] The text of these two letters in English translation is most readily accessible in J. Stevenson, *A New Eusebius*, revised edn (SPCK, 1987), Extracts 283 and 284 (pp. 324–327).

necessarily give a balanced account of Arius' overall position. But there is no reason to doubt that they do express beliefs that he felt to be important and to be under threat in the dispute with his bishop.

If we analyse the contents of those two letters, they can be summarized as embodying seven affirmations or points of teaching:

(1) God, more specifically God the Father, is uniquely transcendent.
(2) The Son is the product of God's will.
(3) The Son is 'from what is not', because the only conceivable alternatives (that there are two ultimates; that he is a part of the Father; that he is from some lower essence) are all unacceptable.
(4) He is a creature, but unlike any other creature since he is God's agent in the creation of all other creatures.
(5) His existence is pre-temporal, but he is not without beginning, as the Father is.
(6) He is unchangeable.
(7) He is god (θεός).

The centrality of these issues to the initial debate is further witnessed by the fact that nos. 3–6 are all directly contradicted in the anathemas attached to the creed accepted at the Council of Nicaea, and nos. 2 and 7 are clearly repudiated or shown to be inadequate in the text of the creed itself.

Our task then is to try to gain from their fragmentary evidence a coherent picture of Arius's answer to the aporia with which Christian theology was faced, and to determine how philosophy has entered into the construction of that answer.

One of the Church historians, Socrates, tells us that it was Alexander's insistence on the full coeternity of the Son with the Father that so offended Arius as to provide the igniting spark for the bitter controversy. Intelligible though such a concept might have been within an Origenist view of an eternal spiritual world, in the changed climate of thought of Arius's day it appeared to Arius to carry drastic and unacceptable implications. To place the Son coequally alongside the Father, particularly if that was expressed in terms of sharing the οὐσία or being of the Father, must, it appeared to him, involve either the denial of the oneness of God as supreme reality or the denial of the distinct existence of the divine Son. The tension inherent in Christian tradition had been lost.

Arius's alternative account begins with an insistence on the unique transcendence of God. The developed Christian understanding of creation combined with the more radically transcendent strain in Platonism to convince him that no other reality could exist as derived from God, except on the basis of God's will. Any other relation would be an unacceptable qualification of the unity of God and of the absoluteness of his creative work. So it must be that the Son is the product of God's will. Such a stress on the will derives primarily from the more personalist Christian tradition, but it had also, as we have seen, its precedent within the philosophical tradition. But Arius has no desire or intention to play down the unique mediatorial role of the Son, as the divine agent in creation, revelation and incarnation. That was an integral element in the traditional faith to which he was fully committed. The question was how such a unique status was to be defined, if the Son's existence was understood to be, like all other creatures, dependent wholly on God's will. And here the philosophical discussions about different senses of 'creation' and 'time' in relation to the world offered a useful guide. In affirming that the Son was a 'creature but not like any other of the creatures' and that his creation was outside time but not without beginning, Arius was not simply indulging in tortuous equivocation. However difficult the concepts, they stood within a tradition of philosophical reflection on the relation of the cosmos to God. That tradition could well appear to Arius as one that offered a way of giving reasoned expression to the ambivalence inherent in scripture and traditional language about the Son.

At first hearing Arius's two final propositions—that the Son is changeless and that he is θεός—may seem to involve some going back on his earlier insistence on the radical uniqueness of the Father and the created status of the Son. It is not easy to determine just from the letters themselves how they are to be understood in relation to the earlier propositions. A contemporary letter of his bishop, Alexander, provides a clue. In it he complains that Arius inconsistently shifts his ground under pressure of argument, sometimes acknowledging the Son to be unchangeable while at others affirming him to be changeable. It seems pretty clear that the unchangeableness which Arius affirms is not to be identified with the unchangeableness that applies to the Father. It is a moral rather than a metaphysical unchangeableness, an unchangeableness sustained by the Son's freely chosen will and obedience rather than an unchangeableness inherent in his nature as such—as is the case with the Father. And it is that too that constitutes him θεός—his perfect moral likeness to and unity with the Father.

These final constituents of the outline position that emerges from these two brief letters of Arius are not merely consistent with what has gone before; nor do they simply give positive content to the uniqueness of the Son, justifying the Christian acknowledgment of him as divine. Set them in the context of philosophical discussions of ethics, and they add a dimension to Arius's position which is probably more important than would appear from the texts at first reading. For both Platonist and Stoic in their different ways a likeness to God that needed to be learned the hard way through moral endeavour and progress was the true goal of human life. A Son, whose unchangeable divinity was the fruit of his own consistent moral choosing was thus not merely a Son who could be intelligibly envisaged as the subject of the life of Jesus. He was a potential savour whose 'learned obedience' (Heb. 5:8) could be a source of salvation, intelligible both in terms of Christian discipleship and of that growth in 'likeness to God' which philosophy aspired to teach.

Why then did Athanasius react so violently to such a vision? What part did philosophy play in determining his contrasting response to the theological problem before the Church? I have already insisted that there was no major difference of philosophical approach between them. But there were differences of philosophical emphasis, which contributed to the different theological positions they embraced. Two such differences are particularly significant.

Free will is a difficult and contentious issue, even in its application to human persons without the added complication of its reference to God. Its relation to necessity was, as it still is, a matter for dispute. In Athanasius' eyes the concept of will as Arius used it, both in relation to the Father in his work of creation and in relation to the Son, was an unsatisfactory one. He was wrong philosophically to separate it so sharply from being. By doing so he had unnecessarily and damagingly separated the Son from the Father, and introduced an element of arbitrariness, and therefore of unreliability, into the ways of the God on whom we rely for our salvation.

Arius had used the category of will to bridge the gap between the transcendent God and the created order which was radically other than God in being. Athanasius' rejection of the dichotomy between will and being goes hand in hand with a more sympathetic attitude towards the old Platonic notion of the created order's participation in the divine. Although God is radically other than his creation, that does not cut him off from his creation. It is God, and not some lower order of created divine being, with whom Christians have to do in revelation and the life of the Church. More significantly still the goal of 'likeness to God' is not just a matter of moral likeness, though that it certainly is; it is participation in the divine, something that can even be spoken of as θεοποίησις (divinization), which is the destiny of the Christian. And Christ can convey it, because as truly divine and also incarnate, his very nature constitutes the bridge which makes participation in the divine a possibility for us. The Arian Christ could not be the source of a salvation thus conceived. His status as creature but not like any other of the creatures and as outside time yet not without beginning is, in Athanasius' eyes, religiously inadequate, and also intellectually equivocal and incoherent. But Athanasius' alternative vision deriving much of its framework and plausibility fron an older, less transcendental Platonism, had its own *prima facie* incoherences to face. How can Father and Son be coequal and distinct, and still constitute the one transcendent God? And how can the supreme, transcendent God be incarnate as the person of Jesus Christ? There is no sign that Athanasius used his philosophical resources in any very specific way to illuminate either of those questions. The implications of the word 'homoousios' (of one substance) were later explored in some detail in the search for philosophical illumination of the problem, but the term in itself brought no such illumination at the outset. Its introduction into the creed at Nicaea seems to have been designed more to exclude Arius and his most determined supporters than to provide clarification of an alternative orthodox view. It was only many years after the Council that Athanasius began to use it for the expression of his own theological convictions. So too the union of the fully divine and the fully human in the person of the incarnate Christ was later illuminated by analogy with philosophical explorations of the mysterious relation between the immaterial soul and the physical body. But that also was something that was to come only later.

So different philosophical emphases within the same overall philosophical view gave expression to conflicting configurations of Christian belief. But significant though those distinguishable philosophical affiliations are, they do not seem to me to be the primary determinant of either position or to be the main cause of the division between them. That role is probably better ascribed to differing styles of piety and differing understandings of salvation. But even to say that is probably to offer a false contrast. For conceptions of piety and salvation are not wholly independent of philosophical considerations. They involve giving differing weight to different aspects of Christian faith and experience. And those different religious judgments may themselves be, in part at least, caused by already existing philosophical preferences, and may also help to determine what philosophical option a religious thinker will choose to adopt for the elaboration of his or her beliefs.

In short, the role of philosophy in this fourth-century debate is to be seen primarily in the way in which the debate as a whole was couched rather than in its influence on the particular answers given. It is in the posing of the questions about the person of the Son and about human salvation in the terms of a Platonic ontology that the most lasting contribution of philosophy is to be found. And a lasting one it has certainly been. Its effect is still very much with us, because the Nicene creed which embodies answers to that particular way of putting the questions now stands as a normative statement of Christian truth. Part, but admittedly only part, of the difficulty that many people today find in such traditional statements of faith coming down to us from the past is that our contemporary questions and frameworks of understanding are likely to have been formed by very different styles of philosophical thought from those which underlay and permeated all forms of fourth-century Christian belief, orthodox and heretical alike.

Could God Become Man?

RICHARD SWINBURNE

I

The central doctrine of Christianity is that God intervened in human history in the person of Jesus Christ in a unique way; and that quickly became understood as the doctrine that in Jesus Christ God became man. In AD 451 the Council of Chalcedon formulated that doctrine in a precise way utilizing the current philosophical terminology, which provided a standard for the orthodoxy of subsequent thought on this issue. It affirmed its belief in 'our Lord Jesus Christ, . . . truly God and truly man, . . . in two natures . . . the distinction of natures being in no way annulled by the union, but rather the characteristics of each nature being preserved and coming together to form one person'.[1] One individual, one thing that is; and being a rational individual, one person. An individual's nature are those general properties which make it the sort of individual it is. The nature of my desk is to be a solid material object of a certain shape; the nature of the oak tree in the wood is to take in water and light, and to grow into a characteristic shape with characteristic leaves and give off oxygen. Chalcedon affirmed that the one individual Jesus Christ had a divine nature, was God that is; and it assumed that the divine nature was an essential nature. That is, any individual who is God cannot cease to be God and become something else instead, and could not ever have been anything else instead. If you lose your essential nature you cease to be. The desk's nature is essential. If you chop it up for firewood or vaporize it, so that there is no longer the material of a certain shape, then there is no longer the desk. Chalcedon assumed that human nature is not (or not invariably) an essential nature. That is, just occasionally, an individual could become human or cease to be human while remaining the same individual. It then affirmed that the one individual, Jesus Christ, who was eternally God, became also (at a certain moment of human history, about 1 AD) human (i.e. man). He acquired the characteristics of man in addition to those of God.

Let us call this claim of the Council of Chalcedon the Chalcedonian definition. My object in this paper is to investigate first whether the

[1] Translated in H. Bettenson, *Documents of the Christian Church*, 2nd edn, (Oxford University Press, 1967), 51.

Chalcedonian definition is internally consistent (i.e. coherent), and secondly whether it is consistent with the picture of Christ in the New Testament, utilized in theories of the Atonement, and summarized in another affirmation of the Council of Chalcedon that Christ was 'like us, in all respects, apart from sin'. Is the Chalcedonian definition, that is, consistent with a wider spectrum of Christian teaching? The doctrine with which I am concerned is embedded so deep within the Christian theological system that it is not possible to discuss it at the length of a paper without making important philosophical assumptions (ones for which I have argued elsewhere); and without avoiding entirely many neighbouring theological doctrines. I shall, for example of the latter, ignore the assumption of Chalcedon that Jesus Christ is not the only divine person but is the second of three such within the unity of the Trinity.[2] I believe however that the issues of consistency which are our concern can be discussed without bringing in that consideration.

II

I shall assume that to be a God (i.e. divine), an individual must be a person who is omnipotent, omniscient, and perfectly free, perfectly good, a source of moral obligation, omnipresent, creator of any universe there may be, eternal and necessary. Traditional theism has always insisted that God is characterized by these divine properties, though there have been some very different ideas within Christian theism as to what some of them involve.[3]

What is it to be human? It is sufficient if you have a human body animated by a human soul. To be a human body a body must be largely

---

[2] For discussion of the doctrine of the Trinity, see my 'Could There Be More Than One God?' *Faith and Philosophy* **5** (1988), 225–241.

[3] I have spelled out my account of the divine properties, the sense in which they belong necessarily to the individual who is God, and how his having them necessarily would make God supremely worthy of worship in *The Coherence of Theism* (Oxford: Clarendon Press, 1977). I have given my grounds for believing that the God best evidenced by argument has the divine properties necessarily in *The Existence of God* (Oxford: Clarendon Press, 1979), Ch. 5. If it be allowed that the individual who is God is not so necessarily then there would seem to be little problem in God becoming man; the individual who is God could temporarily abandon his divine properties and acquire human properties instead. Something akin to this was involved in the 'kenotic' Christology developed in the nineteeth century. For a modern exposition by a philosopher of a semi-kenotic view see S. T. Davis, *Logic and the Nature of God* (Eerdmans Publishing Co., 1983), Ch. 8.

similar in its anatomy, physiology, and the capacities for action (e.g. running, talking, etc.) which can be realized through it to those of the human bodies with which we are familiar. However, as I have argued at length elsewhere[4] and will have to assume here, what makes for the identity of a human being is not bodily continuity or continuity of apparent memory and character. For an individual could have a body formed from bits of my body and be like me in his memory claims and character without being me; I might not suffer his pains or enjoy his moments of elation. So it is necessary to postulate an immaterial core of me, which we call my soul; which is the essential part of me and whose continued existence makes for my identity over time. The soul is the subject of experience and initiator of action; and is the essential part of any human being or other person, whose possession makes any future individual that individual. It is to the soul that an individual's mental life belongs; and a body is that individual's body in virtue of being linked to his soul. An individual's mental life consists of those events in his life to which he has privileged access (that is, those events which are such that he can know better than anyone else which ones he is having—as we can know better than any outsider what thoughts we are thinking).

Now that I have introduced the word 'soul' to designate the core of every person, I can rephrase my account of God as a soul who is omnipotent, omniscient, etc. . . .

To revert to humans—there are mental events of five kinds which normal humans and many animals have. There are conscious events— sensations (e.g. patterns of colour in the visual field), thoughts (occur- rent thoughts which occur to the subject at particular moments—e.g. 'It is Monday'), purposings (tryings or endeavourings to bring about states of affairs)—conscious in the sense that the subject is necessarily to some extent aware of them while they occur. Mental states also include background states of two kinds—beliefs and desires (inclina- tions to do actions of certain kinds, to which the subject may or may not purpose to yield), which continue while the subject is unaware of them.[5] The normal soul of humans and many animals is characterized by the continued or intermittent possession of mental events of these kinds. However, as I have argued elsewhere,[6] the normal human soul, in contrast to animal souls, has four further features characterizing its mental life. The human soul is capable of logical thought (of drawing

---

[4] See my *The Evolution of the Soul* (Oxford: Clarendon Press, 1986), part 2. (Or my contribution to the S. Shoemaker and R. Swinburne, *Personal Iden- tity* (Oxford: Blackwell, 1984).

[5] On the five kinds of mental event, see *The Evolution of the Soul*, Part 1.

[6] Op. cit., Part 3.

out mentally in a sequence of thought the consequences of earlier thoughts), and of moral awareness (having beliefs about actions being obligatory or, more generally, good); it has free will (its purposings, i.e. initiations of actions, not being fully caused by earlier events), and it has to it a structure (beliefs and desires are kept in place by other beliefs and desires; we have and see ourselves as having various beliefs and desires because we have other beliefs and desires which give them support).

All of this suggests a theory of man as a being constituted by a human soul, one having the above characteristics, connected to a human body, defined as above. The 'connection' involves the subject being able to operate on the world through that body (his purposings to move the limbs of that body are efficacious and make a difference to the world), acquiring beliefs about the world through that body (stimuli impinging on the eyes and ears of that body give him beliefs about how the world is), feeling things in and desiring to act through that body.

However, this theory of human nature may be challenged on various grounds as not sufficient, or as not necessary. I consider first the challenges to its sufficiency. The first objection (which is related to a similar challenge to its necessity) is the objection that 'man', unlike, say, 'desk', is a natural kind word. What makes something a desk is a matter of observable features (e.g. shape and solidity). But, the objection goes, what makes something a man is not the features which I have listed and which are largely experienceable or observable, by which in general we rightly judge something to be a man, but the 'essence' which underlies standard examples of men and is causally responsible for the observable features.[7] The comparison is made to some more obvious

[7] This is the claim made in Thomas V. Morris, *Understanding Identity Statements* (Aberdeen University Press, 1984), Ch. 9; and developed in his *The Logic of God Incarnate* (Ithaca, N.Y.: Cornell University Press, 1986), especially Chs. 2 and 3. Morris argues (*The Logic of God Incarnate*, ch. 2) that, although humanity is a natural kind and so has an underlying 'essence', it does not follow that every individual which is human is so essentially; an individual who is human may belong simultaneously to another natural kind, and then lose its humanity while continuing to exist as a member of that kind. Morris thus understands 'essence' in a looser sense than I have understood 'essential nature'. All that follows, on Morris's understanding of 'essence', from an individual being human, is that its underlying human essence is what explains the human properties and powers which it possesses. I shall use 'essence' in Morris' sense, while using 'essential nature' in my sense in which an individual cannot lose its essential nature and yet continue to exist. Humanity, Chalcedon assumed and I believed was right to assume, is not an essential nature. A human could cease to be human and be transformed into a crocodile instead, and yet be the same individual in virtue of the fact that the former it is who suffers the crocodile's pains. On this see *The Coherence of Theism*, Ch. 13.

case of a natural kind word such as 'water'. What makes something water is not its taste, its transparency, its density, etc., but its chemical composition (H_2O), which underlies and is causally responsible for the observable properties. Something with the same observable properties but a different chemical composition would not be water. If we do not know the essence of water (as we did not before the nineteenth century), we could go badly wrong in our judgments about which samples of liquid are samples of water—even if we are the best experts available and take much trouble. Conversely, something with the chemical composition of water but which, because of external factors (change in our taste buds, odd lighting and atmospheric conditions, etc.), tasted or looked differently would still be water. Its observable features are normal but not completely reliable indicators that a substance before us is water.[8] So, the suggestion goes, 'man' is like this. The features which I have listed, and which, following Putnam, I shall call the human stereotype, are only features of a man if the underlying essence which gives rise to them is the same as in standard examples of men; and sometimes the essence might be present without the stereotype. What sort of essence are we talking about? As regards bodily features, genetic constitution is the obvious analogue to chemical constitution. Whether genetic constitution is causally sufficient to produce a human soul may be doubted,[9] and what else has to be added to it to produce a sufficient cause for the human soul is totally unclear. However, whatever the underlying cause of the stereotypic features, the issue remains whether 'man' is a natural kind term like 'water' or instead a term like 'desk'. Why should not someone with the stereotypic features which I have listed be a man, even if those features were brought about by a quite different cause from the one which operates in normal men? It seems to me that our criteria for the use of the word 'man' are simply unclear here. Some speakers might use the word one way and some might use the word another way. There is no one right answer to my question.

A similar response, in my view, must be given to the other two objections which I shall consider to the sufficiency of the stereotypic features for humanity. The next objection is what I shall call the limitation objection. It is the objection that the powers and knowledge of an individual must be limited to some extent if he is to be a man. An individual's powers over the world outside himself must be confined almost entirely to ones which he exercises through his body; his knowledge about the world must be almost entirely confined to that obtain-

[8] For this doctrine, see Hilary Putnam, 'The Meaning of "Meaning"' in his *Mind, Language and Reality. Philosophical Papers,* Vol. 2 (Cambridge University Press, 1975).

[9] See *The Evolution of the Soul*, Ch. 10 and its Appendix.

able through its effects on his body (viz. through the sense-organs). An individual's powers to move the furniture about must be confined almost entirely to the power of moving it with his arms or legs, and his knowledge of where it is must be confined almost entirely to what he sees or feels or someone tells him. A *small* amount of telekinesis and telepathy might perhaps be compatible with humanity, but too much means that we no longer have a man. A man who becomes able to move mountains on distant continents just by willing, or knows what is going on in distant galaxies without using a telescope or listening to what others tell him ceases to be man. Such is the claim of the objector. But whether his claim is correct seems to be quite unclear, because some of us might use the word 'man' in such a way that someone with such superhuman powers could not be a man, whereas others might use the word 'man' in such a way that someone with superhuman powers would be a 'man' so long as he had human powers as well. Our criteria for use of the word 'man' are just not precise enough for there to be a right answer as to whether the possession of powers far beyond those of normal men would rule out someone from being a 'man'.

The final objection to the sufficiency of the listed features is what I shall call the historical objection. Even if the stereotypic features are caused by the genetic or other essence, a being cannot be a man, the objection goes, unless his ancestry is right—unless the physical causes, viz. the genes, come from human parents or are otherwise obtained from the gene pool of the human race. If we make an ovum in a laboratory, synthesize its genes from inorganic material and fertilize it with a similar synthesized sperm cell, implant it in a tissue culture and grow the embryo in an artificial environment, the resulting being wouldn't be human—even if the genes involved are qualitatively similar in chemical make-up to human genes. To be human you have to belong to the human race. Once again, whether our criteria of humanity involve a historical criterion seems to me unclear. If they do, the further question arises how thoroughly that criterion has to be satisfied—if an individual's genes come only from his mother (parthenogenesis), can that individual still be a man? I would have thought that the use of the word 'man' by most of us is such as to yield the answer 'Yes' to the latter question.

I come now to objections to the necessity of my conditions for humanity, that to be a man an individual must have a human soul with the stereotypic features, connected with a human body, defined physiologically, anatomically and by its capacities for action. First it may be objected that an infant who has only potentially some of the stereotypic features ought to count as human. That seems right, whether or not we insist that the right causal essence ought to lie behind the infant's potentiality to develop the stereotypic features. So long as normal growth will lead to the infant possessing the stereotypic features, that infant is human. My second objection to the necessity of the stated conditions is connected with the second objection to their sufficiency—is the human body necessary? Is not a disembodied human possible; and, if so, could there be a human who was never embodied (but was human in virtue of the type of mental life he had, including sensations of a kind caused in other humans by bodily processes, and desires of a kind manifested in other humans through bodily movements)? Again, it seems to me that our criteria for being a man are just not clear enough to provide a definite answer to whether there could be a permanently non-embodied human.

Finally, why should we insist on all the stereotypic mental features? Could there not be a human who did not have sensations, but could acquire beliefs about his environment through bodily processes without their being mediated via sensations?[10] Or one without moral awareness? Or—a question of especial relevance to our main topic—could there not be a human who was not subject to desire, or at any rate to desire to do any action which he believed morally wrong? Once again, our criteria for humanity yield no clear answer.

What must now be apparent is that there are different possible understandings of 'human' (='man'). Someone clearly is human on any understanding if he satisfies all my original conditions, together with an 'underlying essence' condition, the limitation condition, and an historical condition (to meet each of the three objections to the sufficiency of the original conditions). But you get wider and wider understandings of humanity as you drop more and more conditions. There comes a point obviously where it is unreasonable to call a being human—where hardly any of the conditions apply. But there is plenty of scope for different explications of what it is to be human.

III

Given that the soul is the principle of identity of the individual man, nothing can become a man (while remaining what it is) unless it has, as its principle of identity, the soul which is subsequently the human soul. Becoming a man would involve that soul acquiring the features essential to humanity. On which understanding of what those features are, could a God who remained divine, become also man?

God could certainly acquire a human body in the sense of a body through which he acts on the world and acquires beliefs about it. Many

---

[10] On the separability of sensation and belief-acquisition as component parts of perception, see *The Evolution of the Soul*, Ch. 2.

of the effects he produces through the body will be ones he could (but need not) bring about in other ways. The beliefs which God would acquire through his body are ones he would have anyway—but now he would acquire them through a new route. He would also through his sense-organs acquire some inclinations to hold false beliefs caused by illusion or misinformation striking the ears of his human body. But these inclinations would be overborne by his strongly held true beliefs, which were his through his divine omniscience. God could also acquire sensations through a human body; and, more generally, a mental life with all the stereotypic features of a human mental life. For in acting he would have purposes; and, in so far as he was conscious of his beliefs which, traditionally,[11] he is all the time, he would have thoughts. And, with a qualification, he could even have desires. A desire is an inclination to perform an action of some kind, an inclination which causally influences the agent. It does not necessarily determine him to act, but, if there is no countervailing stronger desire, he needs to 'fight against' its influence in order not to act upon it. An agent need not desire to do actions in proportion to his beliefs about the worth of doing them. He may, for example, have no desire to do what he believes that he ought to do. For God, however, desires would have to be aligned with beliefs about worth. God could desire to do what is best to do, or desire one among many actions equally good to do, or (of two incompatible actions) desire to do the less good action so long as he had also a stronger desire to do the better action. But what he could not have is what we normal humans so often have—a strong desire, not outweighed by a contrary desire, to do the less good action, even an action believed wrong to do (i.e. obligatory not to do). For if God had such a desire, he would be less than perfectly free, subject to non-rational influence from without; and he would not in consequence be necessarily perfectly good, for he might yield to the influence of the desire.

God clearly has the four further characteristics of logical thought, moral awareness, free will, and a structured soul, possessed by humans and not animals.

What of the three suggested additional conditions? Could his body and mental life be caused by the same underlying essence as ours? Yes, an embryo which developed into God's body could have our genes, and (connected with it) whatever else was necessary to produce human mental life. The mechanism which gives rise to souls cannot dictate which soul will arise, for in general souls do not exist before birth, and so there can be no law dictating that a particular bodily process will give

---

[11] 'We know a number of things successively . . . but God sees everything at once'—St Thomas Aquinas, *Summa Theologiae* 1.14.7. See also St Augustine, *De Trinitate*, 15.14.

rise to this soul as opposed to that one. All the mechanism can do is to ensure that it gives rise to *a* soul, which will then have a certain mental life. That soul, God could ensure, without violating that mechanism, was his own soul.

Clearly God would not fulfil the limitation condition. If there is a maximum to abilities (including the ability to acquire true beliefs) if they are to be human abilities, God would exceed it. On the other hand, God could fulfil the historical condition in that the physical causes which gave rise to his body could be genes derived from the human gene pool. As I wrote earlier, he might reasonably deem the historical condition to be fulfilled sufficiently by genes being derived from one parent rather than two.

I conclude that the only qualifications on the possibility of God becoming human concern a limit to the kind of desires he can have, and that he cannot satisfy any limitation condition. Clearly the Council of Chalcedon understood 'man' in such a way that it did not involve a limitation condition. For God could not become man, if to become man a being has to have limited powers; and this is so obvious that the Fathers of Chalcedon could not have failed to notice it. We can readily suppose Councils or individuals to make claims that are internally inconsistent, but only if the inconsistency is not too obvious. If Chalcedon had understood 'man' in such a way that being man involved a limitation condition, the inconsistency in supposing that God became man (while remaining God) would have been too obvious to escape notice, and the definition would not have been adopted in the same form. If we are assessing the claim of Chalcedon we must understand their terms in their sense, in so far as that is clear. So if we don't draw the limit of the human too strictly, certainly God can become man. He would do this by acquiring a human body (joining his soul to an unowned human body), acting, acquiring beliefs, sensations and desires through it. Remaining God, he would have become man by acquiring an extension to his normal modes of operation.[12] A God who became incarnate in Christ in this way would, I suggest, have satisfied the Chalcedonian definition of being one individual with both a divine and human nature, on a not unreasonable interpretation of the latter.

[12] Chalcedon declared that Christ had a 'reasonable soul and body'; and by the 'reasonable soul' it seems to have meant an acquired 'human soul'. But the Council could not have meant by this that there were in Christ both a divine and a human soul in my sense of 'soul'. For that would have been to say that Christ was two individuals, a doctrine to which Chalcedon was greatly opposed. Rather in the affirmation that Christ had a 'reasonable soul', 'soul' is to be understood in a more Aristotelian sense of 'soul'. God in Christ acquired a human way of thinking and acting, as well as his divine way.

If God became incarnate in Christ within my limits, that incarnation would not, I think, merely satisfy formally the Chalcedonian definition, but would also satisfy the teaching of many of the Fathers and all the Scholastics about the kind of human life which Christ lived. They taught that Christ was in no way weak; he retained his divine omnipotence. And he was in no way ignorant; he retained his divine omniscience. In consequence he had before his mind the things that God alone can know, such as 'the hour' at which 'Heaven and Earth shall pass away'; the apparent denial by Christ (Mark 13.31f.) that he knew this hour was, said Augustine, to be read simply as a claim that he was not prepared to announce the hour.[13]

Despite the fact that he was incapable of sin, Christ did however, on the traditional exposition, feel pain, hunger, thirst and weariness. These feelings involve desires—hunger is the desire to eat, thirst to drink, and weariness to rest; and pain is a certain kind of sensation accompanied by a desire that it cease.[14] He could have such sensory desires, in my terminology only so long as he had as well as them a desire stronger than those always to do the good, a set of will which will inevitably not eat, rest, etc., unless it is a best action to do so.[15] If he was so placed, Christ could be tempted, for he could be subject to the desire to eat (as in Matthew 4.2ff.) when it was not overall good that he should eat, since he would also have a stronger desire to do the good. That way he would feel the pang of frustrated desire without there being any possibility that he should capitulate to it.[16] We ordinary human beings also can sometimes be in that situation. One can be subject to a sexual desire, to which there is not the remotest possibility that one will yield because of a stronger desire to do the good or to be thought well of by the object of the sexual desire. 'The impossible is still temptation', wrote Eliot.

That Christ was so placed was the common patristic and scholastic teaching, expressed sometimes in terms of Christ's two 'wills'. Christ's saying in Gethsemane, 'Not what I will, but what thou willest' was interpreted by Gregory of Nyssa as 'Not what I as man will, but what

[13] See St Augustine, *De Trinitate,* 1.23. On this see also St Thomas Aquinas, *Summa Theologiae,* 3a, 9–12.

[14] See *The Evolution of the Soul*, 23.

[15] David Brown, *The Divine Trinity* (London: Duckworth, 1985), 253f., makes sense of Christ's suffering in terms of the Chalcedonian model by his having 'such a total perspective on pain and its ultimate meaning' that it has no power over him. He thinks that in a sense this makes Christ 'impassible'.

[16] For such an account of Christ's temptations, see also C. F. D. Moule, 'The Manhood of Jesus in the New Testament', in S. W. Sykes and J. P. Clayton (eds), *Christ, Faith, and History* (Cambridge University Press, 1972), 105f.

thou and so I as God will'. Christ as man 'willed', i.e. had an inclination, to yield to various sensory desires. But he was so made that these were kept in line by the divine 'will'.[17] 'So made' is crucial. It was not that, though Christ could have yielded to temptation, in fact he always resisted it; but he could not have yielded.

In Aquinas's summary of the character of the Incarnation, Christ took upon himself death, hunger, thirst, fear, and all else that, he held, is due in us humans to the sin of Adam, except those disabilities which are 'irreconcilable with perfect knowledge and grace'; and so he did not take upon himself 'ignorance, proneness to evil, and difficulty in doing good'.[18]

IV

The trouble is that the doctrine that God became incarnate in the way just described seems, in respect of Christ's ignorance, his weakness, and the extent to which he was open to temptation, to fit badly with certain things said about Christ in the New Testament, and to fit badly with the Chalcedonian claim that in Christ God became 'like us in all respects, apart from sin', in order to effect our salvatation.

St Luke's Gospel asserts that the boy Jesus 'advanced in wisdom' (Luke 2.52), i.e. grew in knowledge, which seems to imply that he was not omniscient all the time. So too does the passage in St Mark's Gospel, to which I referred earlier, in which Jesus is reported as claiming that he, 'the Son', does not know something which the Father does know—'the hour' at which 'Heaven and Earth shall pass away' (Mark 13.31f.). And the cry of derelication, 'My God, my God, why hast thou forsaken me' (Mark 15.34) might seem to suggest that Christ at that moment ceased to believe that God was sustaining him. There is a passage in St Mark which casts similar doubt on Christ's omnipotence. It is reported that in a visit to his own country, Jesus 'could do

[17] *Antirheticus*, 32. Later writers, thinking of the 'will' not as Gregory thought of it in this discussion, as an inclination to act, but as an actual initiation of action, taught that the human 'will' of Christ, i.e. what he willed through his body in virtue of his human sources of knowledge, feeling, etc., would inevitably conform to his divine will, what he willed to do other than in this way. That was because his human ignorance would be 'topped up' by divine knowledge and human desire was kept in place by divine dedication to the good. For there was but one who willed. Such was the teaching of Maximus the Confessor enshrined in the doctrinal decrees of the Third Council of Constantinople against monothelitism. See J. Tixeront, *History of Dogmas*, Vol. III (B. Herder Book Co., 2nd edn, 1926), 180–184.

[18] *Summa Theologiae*, 3a.14 and 15.

there no mighty work' (Mark 6.5). The Epistle to the Hebrews claims of our 'High Priest', viz. Jesus, that he is not one who 'cannot be touched with the feeling of our infirmities', and that suggests (though does not entail) that Jesus is weak, and so again not omnipotent. And, finally, although perhaps not formally incompatible with any obvious biblical passage, the view that Christ's being tempted was simply a matter of his being subject to a desire to which he could never yield, does not seem the natural picture suggested by the agony of Gethsemane, nor by two remarks in the Epistle to the Hebrews. Christ is said to have 'learned obedience by the things which he suffered', and to have been 'made perfect' (i.e. over time) (Heb. 5.8f.); this might suggest that he was not immune to temptation to begin with, but by not yielding to it became immune. And if Christ was in *all* points 'tempted like as we are' (Heb. 4.15), more openness to temptation would seem to be suggested.

Some of these passsages are susceptible of other interpretations which have some plausibility; but the general feeling which many readers of the New Testament surely get is that it pictures a Jesus rather more like ourselves than the Christ of the traditional exposition of the Chalcedonian definition. Further, Christian theories of the Atonement have usually claimed that it was effected by Christ doing good when men did ill, although he was no better equipped than they for doing good; if he was as knowledgeable and predetermined to do the best as the traditional exposition affirms, that claim would be hard to justify. As St Gregory Nazianzen famously remarked, 'What Christ has not assumed, he has not healed; but what has been united with God is saved'.[19] The traditional exposition of Chalcedon might not seem adequately to affirm that he has taken on board all of us.

V

Many of the Fathers, especially the earlier ones and especially those of the Antiochene tradition, held that Christ was more like ourselves in the respects described than the traditional interpretation of Chalcedon later allowed.[20] Can we interpret the Chalcedonian definitions in a way that respects their viewpoint? I think that we can with the aid of the divided mind. It was Freud above all who helped us to see how an agent

[19] *Epistola* 101.7 (PG, 37, 181).
[20] On the ignorance of Christ, see for example Tixeront, op. cit., Vol. II, 287f.

can have two systems of belief to some extent independent of each other. In performing some actions, the agent is acting on one system of belief and not guided by beliefs of the other system; and conversely. Although all his beliefs are accessible—they would not be his beliefs unless he had privileged access to them—he refuses to admit to his consciousness beliefs relevant to his action, on which he is not acting. Thus, to take a well-worn example, a mother may refuse to acknowledge to herself a belief that her son is dead or to allow some of her actions to be guided by it. When asked if she believes that he is dead, she says 'No', and this is an honest reply, for it is guided by those beliefs of which she is conscious. Yet other actions of hers may be guided by the belief that he is dead—e.g. she may throw away some of his possessions—even though she does not admit that belief to consciousness. This refusal to admit a belief to consciousness is of course itself also something which the agent refuses to admit to himself to be happening.

Now God could not give up his knowledge, and so his beliefs; but he could, in becoming incarnate in Christ and acquiring a human belief-acquisition system, through his choice, keep the inclinations to belief resulting therefrom to some extent separate from his divine knowledge system. Different actions would be done in the light of different systems. The actions done through the human body, the thoughts consciously entertained connected with the human brain, the interpretation of perceptual data acquired through the human eyes, would all be done in the light of the human belief-system. So, too, would any public statement made through his human mouth. However, his divine knowledge-system will inevitably include the knowledge that his human system contains the beliefs that it does; and it will include those among the latter which are true. The separation of the belief-systems would be a voluntary act, knowledge of which was part of the divine knowledge-system but not of the human knowledge-system. We thus get a picture of a divine consciousness and a human consciousness of God Incarnate, the former including the latter, but not conversely.[21]

The 'beliefs' in the two parts of a divided mind may sometimes be explicitly contradictory (e.g. a belief that the son is alive and a belief that the son is dead). In such a case, it is misleading to call both 'beliefs' 'beliefs' without qualification, since at least one does not form part of a general view of the world but merely guides the subject's actions in certain circumstances. The overall constant and ever-present view of the world of a God who became incarnate in the way described would

---

[21] A model of Christ's knowledge on these lines is developed in David Brown, op. cit., 260–267. The Freudian model of the divided mind has been applied to Christology quite a bit in this century, beginning with W. Sanday, *Christologies Ancient and Modern* (Oxford University Press, 1910).

be his divine view; and so the 'beliefs' belonging to that view could be described as 'beliefs', whereas the 'beliefs' belonging to the human perspective would be mere inclinations to belief or propositions guiding a limited set of actions.

Christ's human acts are the public acts done through his human body and the private mental acts correlated with the brain-states of that body; and if it is to be a human body its capacities must not be radically different from those of our bodies. So there is a limit to Christ's power *qua* man. If God's human actions are done only in the light of his human beliefs, then he will feel the limitations that we have. God in becoming incarnate will not have limited his powers, but he will have taken on a *way* of operating which is limited and *feels* limited. So using the notion of divided mind we can coherently suppose God to become incarnate while remaining God, and yet act and feel much like ourselves.

But could he become like us in our liability to yield to temptation? For if he could, his failure to yield would seem so much more the victory over evil which the New Testament and later theories of the Atonement picture it.

Let us take a few steps backwards in order to sort out what is at stake here. Wrong is of two kinds—objective and subjective. Objective wrong is failing in your obligations (or duties) to someone whether you realize it or not: e.g. taking money which was not yours, whether or not you reasonably believe it to be yours. Subjective wrong is doing what you believe to be failing in your obligations. In both cases, a wrong is, I suggest, a wrong to someone. If you take what is not yours, you wrong the person from whom you take it. If you take, believing that you are taking what is not yours, i.e. stealing, you wrong the person from whom you believe that you are stealing. God has, I suspect, relatively few duties to men—e.g. plausibly, he could kill a man without wronging him, for as the source of his being, he may keep him in being as long or as short a time as he chooses. But, with majority Christian tradition, I suggest that God does have some duties to man—e.g. to keep promises. God Incarnate must keep his promises to men. If he failed in any of the duties he has to men, he would wrong them. He would wrong a man objectively if he failed to fulfil some duty to him, e.g. failed to keep a promise to him, whether or not he realized that he was failing to fulfil the duty. He would wrong a man subjectively if he did what he believed was failing in his duty to him.

The narrow range of duties to which God is subject does however give him vast scope for supererogatory good actions (i.e. good actions beyond the call of duty) benefitting men. We humans have a limited number of duties to our fellows, and endless scope for good action beyond the call of duty. Exactly where the line is to be drawn is disputed, but there is a line. For example, the act of saving the life of a comrade at the expense of one's own is hardly a duty owed to him, but it is evidently a good action. Doing a supererogatory act is praiseworthy, but failing to do one is not blameworthy. For by so failing you wrong no one. Plausibly, as Christian thinkers have normally maintained, God had no obligation to create a world, let alone become incarnate. If he did so, it was an act of supererogatory goodness.

A person will do intentionally what he sees reason for doing, i.e. what he believes to be good to do, in so far as he is rational. Hence he will only fail to pursue what he believes to be good in so far as he is subject to desires inclining him to act contrary to reason, and in that case if he is to do the believed good, he has to struggle against the temptation which those desires provide.[22] And if he is to do intentionally what is in fact good, he needs true beliefs about what is good.

Now it would, I suggest, have been wrong of God to allow himself to become incarnate in such a way as to open the possibility of his doing objective or subjective wrong. Hence it is incompatible with his perfect goodness that he should do so. For it is wrong of anyone to put themselves in a position where they are liable to wrong another— intentionally allow themselves to forget their duties, or to take drugs which would lead to their being strongly tempted (without having a stronger contrary desire) to do some wrong. God in becoming incarnate must ensure that in his human actions he has access to such beliefs as will allow him to be aware of his duties, and must ensure that he is not subject to a balance of desire to do believed wrong. Even though he cannot do wrong, he may however, through not allowing himself to be aware of his divine beliefs, be inclined to believe that he may succumb to temptation to do wrong and thus, in the situation of temptation, he may *feel* as we do.

Now, while it is wrong to put oneself in a position where one is liable to do wrong, there is nothing wrong in putting oneself in a position where one is liable not to do the best action. Indeed, the action of putting oneself in that position might itself occasionally be the best thing to do. A generous man might well give away so much in order to do some supererogatory good that thereby he greatly endangered the possibility of his doing even more supererogatory good in future. Compatibly with his perfect goodness, God could choose to allow himself to act on a limited set of beliefs which included inadequate beliefs about what is most worth doing; and he could allow himself to be subject to a balance of desires to do lesser goods, to a weakness of will so

---

[22] For fuller elucidation and justification of the thesis of these last two sentences, see my *Responsibility and Atonement* (Oxford: Clarendon Press, 1989), Ch. 2.

long as it did not include any proneness to wrong anyone. He would then need to discover what was most worth doing; and he would need to fight against the balance of desire to do the lesser good and it would be possible that he should yield to the temptation to do that lesser good. He might choose to put himself in this position in order to share our lot as fully as possible. God in his divine consciousness in perfect freedom would continually will (as part of the good of his incarnation) that he would do whatever (other than the wrong) he chooses to do under the influence of desire and limited belief. The former (second-order) will or choice would not be influenced by desire; only its execution would be so influenced, but it is good that it should be. Desire would have influenced God, but only to the extent to which God uninfluenced by desire allowed it to do so.

If in his human consciousness Christ were on occasion subject to a balance of desire not to do the best action, then his overcoming this balance would be a free act for which he would be praiseworthy. Almost all the actions by which he is supposed to have redeemed the world—his total sacrificial service, culminating in allowing himself to be crucified—were not obligatory but supererogatory. His doing them despite contrary temptation would be doing freely supererogatory acts, and using well the freedom which we ordinary men have abused by our sins. But if such heroic acts were inevitable, he would have had an advantage which we sinners did not, and his redeeming acts would have been taking on and rightly directing a human nature crucially unlike ours in the respect in which we had gone wrong. That he performed supererogatory good actions, while we ordinary humans did wrong, although both he and we were equally well positioned to do good or ill is crucial for many (though not all) theories of the Atonement.[23]

So, yes, God could subject himself to temptation (but only to do a lesser good, not to do wrong). The Chalcedonian definition is not merely self-consistent but consistent with the New Testament picture of Christ as acting in ignorance and weakness, and subject to temptation. God could become man in a rather fuller sense than the traditional interpretation allowed.

God being God, he must remain omniscient, but he can allow his human actions to be guided only by his humanly acquired belief substitutes. He must remain omnipotent, but there is a limit to what he can do in any human way and, when he does act in a human way, he need not be fully aware of having more power than that. Being God, he must remain perfectly good and perfectly free, but he can in perfect freedom and because of the perfect goodness of doing so, allow himself

[23] For analysis of different theories of the Atonement, see *Responsibility and Atonement*, especially Ch. 10.

to make a choice under the influence of desire to do a lesser good. But an incarnate God could not do wrong.[24]

What utilizing the modern Freudian doctrine of the divided mind involves in more traditional terminology is abandoning the full-blown interpretation of a doctrine known as the *communicatio idiomatum*[25] of the Incarnate God, the doctrine of the interpenetration of the two natures. Total interpenetration was in no way affirmed by the Council of Chalcedon but seems to have crept into much subsequent Christological thought. Full interpenetration would have the consequence that Christ as man had all the knowledge, power, and freedom which a creature could have. The full-blown interpretation of this doctrine received succinct exposition three centuries after Chalcedon from St John Damascene, when he wrote that Christ's

> holy mind also performs its natural energies, thinking and knowing that it is God's mind and that it is worshipped by all creation, and remembering the time He spent on earth and all he suffered, but has communion with the divinity of the Word in its energizing and orders and governs the universe, thinking and knowing and ordering not as the mere mind of man, but as united in subsistence with God and acting as the mind of God.[26]

It is here, I suggest, that things went wrong. Total interpenetration of natures prevents God becoming man in a way much like the way in which we are men. Some penetration on Earth, maybe, some access by Christ incarnate to divine knowledge and power in order that he should

---

[24] Not merely would Christ have been incapable of actual sin (understood as wrong-doing) on the above account, but he could not have inherited any original sin. Original sin includes minimally a proneness to sin, but has also been thought of by many as including also original guilt, guilt for the sin of Adam. Christ had on the account in the text no proneness to sin. And even if the guilt of Adam is in any way inherited by his descendants, it is a guilt in respect of an action wronging God; and so, even if Christ is in a way his descendant, it could not have been transmitted to him—given that no one can wrong himself (on original sin, see *Responsibility and Atonement*, Ch. 9).

[25] This doctrine is sometimes taken, not in the way in which I am taking it in the text, but simply as the doctrine that the human and divine attributes are predicable of the same individual, Christ. That of course I am in no way seeking to deny.

[26] St John Damascene, *De Fide Orthodoxa*, 3.19, translated by S. D. F. Salmond, *Library of Nicene and Post Nicene Fathers* (Oxford: James Parker and Co., 1889), Vol. IX. The context makes fairly clear that St John is talking about the Incarnate Christ on Earth, not the post-Ascension Christ. The *communicatio idiomatum* goes against some earlier patristic stress, especially in the Antiochene tradition, on the separateness of the two natures. On John Damascene see Tixeront, op. cit., Vol. III, 483f.

reveal it to us; and total interpenetration after the Ascension, maybe. And a subjection of the human will to the divine in the sense that Christ could not sin, and any choice of lesser goods was by the consent of the divine will. But total interpenetration on Earth is not required by the definition of Chalcedon. And without it a God, being more like ourselves and more as the New Testament pictures Christ, would be a more satisfactory means for our salvation.

Augustine's Philosophy of Being

CHRISTOPHER STEAD

Augustine's philosophy of being, the subject of my lecture, might be approached in two ways. In traditional terms, we might consider the question *quid est esse*, or alternatively the question *quaenam sunt*. This latter question is easily explained; it means, roughly speaking, what does the real universe contain or comprise, in a large and general sense. Material objects, of course, we can all accept; but what should be said about minds and spirits and the things with which they are concerned? The other question is more difficult to explain in simple terms. Suppose we translate it 'What is being?', we may seem to be asking a question about the word 'being'; what is the sense which Augustine gives to this word? But in fact we shall discover a whole spectrum of senses. 'Being', for Augustine, sometimes appears to express the purely minimal notion of mere existence; but he also uses it as a powerful symbol to formulate his deepest reflections on the spiritual life and the nature of God.

I will therefore tackle the easier question first. But before I do so, there must be a prelude. Augustine's philosophy so closely reflects his own personal hopes and concerns that we have to consider how it was influenced by the successive changes in his way of life, and not least by the new responsibilities which he assumed when he became a Christian bishop at the age of forty-one. I must therefore spend a few minutes in recalling the chief events of his career; and if some of my audience find this a familiar tale, they will be the first to admit that it needs to be told.

Augustine was born in AD 354 at Thagaste, a moderate-sized provincial town in North Africa, near the eastern boundary of modern Algeria. His mother was a devout Christian, his father a pagan, who soon recognized the potential of his gifted son and took steps to give him a good education. Augustine's interest in philosophy was aroused by his reading Cicero's exhortation to philosophy called the *Hortensius*. Like many others of its type, this book recommended the quest for wisdom as preferable to all sensual delights and worldly successes.

Augustine's next step, however, seems difficult to explain; he joined the extremist semi-Christian sect of the Manichees. No doubt he was reacting against the rather uninspiring brand of catholic Christianity which he found at Thagaste, and later at Carthage. The Manichees held out an ideal of ascetic living, which intensified Cicero's message; and they did at least profess to set their ethical teaching within a comprehensive theory of the world and its good and evil constituents. Augustine remained with them for ten years, a surprisingly long time if one considers that he still saw himself as a rising orator and statesman; not to mention the ringing tones in which he later denounced their teaching as pretentious nonsense.

He seems to have escaped from their influence by adopting a sceptical philosophy which threw doubt on the validity of *all* positive convictions; actual knowledge, it was held, is unattainable; the best we can attain is a set of probable beliefs. Sceptical views of this kind had been urged by the Platonist philosopher Carneades in the second century BC, and a sceptical tradition had persisted among Platonists down to Augustine's time. But the majority of Platonists had reverted to a positive transcendental philosophy; Augustine soon adopted their position, and later wrote a treatise *Against the Academics*, arguing that in some cases at least it is indisputable that we really know. Even if I am in doubt, I can be certain that I am doubting, and *a fortiori* that I exist. This argument, of course, resembles that later adopted by Descartes: *Je pense, donc je suis.*

Scholars have given much time and thought to enquiring what exactly was the form of Platonism which had such a powerful appeal for Augustine; in particular, they have asked whether he was influenced mainly by Plotinus or by Porphyry. This question, I believe, largely misses the point. Augustine, in his early writings at least, represents the Platonists as confirming many of the doctrines of Christianity. Their concept of three divine principles, or hypostases, seemed to him a good approximation to the Christian Trinity; their belief in intelligible realities, derived from Plato's theory of Ideas, needed scarcely any modification; the two main faults he alleges are first, their failure to envisage any divine Incarnation, and secondly, their lack of humility in relying on human reason as against divine revelation in prophecy and scripture (*Civ. Dei* 10.29; *Conf.* 7.9.14). But a modern reader of either Porphyry or Plotinus will judge that they are separated from Christian orthodoxy by a much wider gulf; Porphyry wrote as a determined opponent of Christianity; Plotinus before him shows no sign of having encountered main-stream Christianity, though he wrote against Christian Gnostics who had some resemblance to Augustine's Manichees. Plotinus usually described his three supreme hypostases as Unity, Mind and Soul; and these were in no sense coequal; on the contrary, the second and third principles reflect the first in a descending scale of purity and value. And in treating of the first hypostasis Plotinus gives great weight to the Platonic principle that pure goodness must be 'beyond mind and being'; it is an ultimate unity which has the potential to produce all ordered multiplicities, beginning with Mind or Intelligence, but remains itself undifferentiated. Thus it cannot be construed as a personal divinity who could think or be conscious, because thinking entails a distinction between a thinking subject and the object of thought; the One, for Plotinus, does not even know itself; it only generates knowledge of itself in the cosmic Mind. Nor, strictly speaking, can it be described, since description would identify it with something distinct from itself. And although it is the source of all being, Plotinus cannot envisage any creative design or intention, but only an eternal outflow of being which descends progressively through mind and soul to its humblest embodiment in matter.

All this seems foreign to Augustine, who accepted as part of his Christian faith the Nicene doctrine of a Trinity of equal Persons. Can we then find any closer approach in Porphyry? Porphyry is said to have softened the distinctions between the three hypostases—or 'telescoped' them, in Professor A. C. Lloyd's graphic phrase; but he seems to have agreed with Plotinus in detecting a principle 'beyond mind', which is also contemplated 'in a suspension of thinking that is better than thought' (*Sent.* 25). And Augustine's philosopher friend Marius Victorinus also spoke of a principle 'prior to being'.[1]

It is clear, then, that Augustine's philosophy was largely independent of these great Neoplatonists. So far as I can discover, he does not describe God as 'beyond being'; on the contrary, he tells us, *Deus est esse.*[2] And although he takes perfect unity to be an essential feature of divine being, he sees it as a unity of positive attributes; thus God's wisdom is wholly good, and his goodness is wholly wise; but we do not *misrepresent* God if we call him wise or good. Moreover Augustine is content to refer to God as Mind; he does not think that mental operations begin with the second Person, the divine Word. And he speaks of God's loving care for his creation. All these doctrines correspond with an older tradition of Platonic thought which saw no difficulty in describing God as Mind, and which could envisage the divine act of creation suggested by a more literal reading of Plato's *Timaeus*. It seems, then, that Augustine was influenced more than he admits by older Platonist writers such as Apuleius, and was therefore encouraged to read Plotinus and Porphyry attending more to their continuity with earlier Platonism than to the distinctive features identified by modern scholars. It was for this reason that Platonism appeared to offer an easy approach to Christianity.

The rest of Augustine's philosophical development can be briefly told. We soon find him at Milan, profoundly impressed by the sermons of the eloquent Bishop Ambrose, but also by the example of self-

---

[1] *Ad Candidum* 2.28, 3.7, 18.2 (Migne, P.L. 8, 1021a,c, 1028b).
[2] *Mor. Eccl.* 2.1.1, cf. *En. Psalm.* 134.4, *Trin.* 5.2.3.

sacrifice and devotion presented by much humbler Christians. He returned to the Bible, and especially St Paul. Writing later on, in the *Confessions*, he represents his conversion as an inspired resolve to fulfil the obligations which his intellect had already accepted; to submit to the authority of God's word in Scripture, and to renounce for ever all thought of sexual satisfaction. It is something of a surprise to discover that most of his writings during the next few years prove to be essays in Platonist philosophy. But the explanation has already been given. The final step towards Christian discipleship lay in acceptance of the Bible and of the ascetic life required of an uncompromising Christian. For its intellectual substructure he was still content to return to Platonism.

Augustine's philosophical activity was by no means over; indeed its most brilliant achievements were yet to come. But they were channelled into a peculiar course by the necessity of reconciling his Platonist assumptions with a Christian obedience to which his attitude was in some respects uncritical. He was hampered at times by an over-submissive acceptance of Church traditions and by a literalistic reading of the New Testament, not always proof against actual mistranslation; both these factors combined, for instance, to bring him to the abominable doctrine that unbaptized infants will inevitably suffer eternal punishment. It is hard to imagine the intellectual agony in which such a belief imposed itself on one whose belief in God's all-embracing mercy was so profound. But his philosophical enterprise and resourcefulness were irrepressible; he remains by far the most original and wide-ranging thinker of later antiquity, and only a minority of critics have ever supposed that his Christian faith in some way disqualifies him from being recognized as a philosophical colossus.

Let us then consider Augustine's picture of the universe. What sorts of things does it contain? Like the majority of ancient thinkers Augustine makes a primary division into material and immaterial reality,[3] which roughly corresponds to the biblical distinction between the visible and the invisible. Alternatively, he often speaks of the world, the soul and God.[4] This makes the useful point that the human soul acts as a bridge between the physical universe and the higher sphere; on the other hand it fails to mention the invisible part of God's creation, that is, created spirits or angels, which were firmly established in the Jewish–Christian tradition, supported by the 'created gods' of Plato's *Timaeus* 41a, as it was commonly interpreted.

But if we look more closely at the contrast of material and immaterial, we discover a very curious fact. Augustine has a clear and consistent

---

[3] *C. Acad.* 3.17.37; *Civ. Dei*, see n. 5.
[4] *Mor. Eccl.* 1.5.7–6.10, *Div. Quaest. 83*,45.

view of material beings, which appears several times in his *City of God*;[5] there is an ascending scale of value, which embraces 'stones, plants, animals and intelligent beings', as he puts it at 5:11, the latter class including both men and angels, and thus impinging on the higher sphere. But if we look for a similar brief outline of this higher world, we shall be disappointed; we discover only a multitude of elevated but conflicting suggestions. The reason for this is that for the material world Augustine can draw upon a well-established tradition of a *scala naturae* which goes back to Aristotle, and sees the natural world as arranged in a series of levels, each of which enjoys all the advantages of its inferiors but possesses some distinctive power of its own. Thus physical substances are distinguished by their consistency, *hexis*; living creatures by *phusis,* the power to nourish themselves and grow. Animals also possess *psuchē*, soul, which gives them perception and movement; and the next level is marked by reason, which belongs to man, but also to immortal spirits.

But if we look for a similar diagram of the higher world, we find no such consistent scheme. God, the universe itself, the divine Ideas, the soul of the world, star-gods, demons, angels, demi-gods and heroes, appear and disappear in a bewildering variety of combination.[6] For a brief example, we may turn to Apuleius, whose work on Plato was known to Augustine, and who presents us with three totally unrelated schemes in two chapters, 6 and 11, of Book I. In Chapter 6, the primary forms of being are the supreme God or Mind, the Forms of things, and the world-soul; this already conflicts with Chapter 5, where the initial principles are God, the Forms, and matter. Chapter 11 offers a scheme based on the four elements, which crosses the boundary between earth and heaven; there are fiery beings, the star-gods; airy beings, the demons; and those allied to water and earth, namely land-animals and plants. In the same chapter he mentions three classes of gods; the supreme God, star-gods, and local deities.

It seems, then, that in Augustine's time there was no commonly accepted map of the intelligible world; and the reason probably lies in the perplexities of Platonist philosophy. That venerable construction which we know as Plato's theory of Ideas had left behind so many discrepancies and loose ends that the later Platonists could never achieve what they so greatly desired, namely to bring together all their master's inspired pronouncements into a consistent scheme.

Let me try to indicate the position in a much over-simplified sketch. Plato was trying to solve several problems which he did not clearly

---

[5] 5.11, 8.6, 11.16.

[6] See for instance Xenocrates fr. 15 (in H. Diels, *Doxographi Graeci*, 304); cf. Eusebius, *Demonstr. Evang.* 4.5.12.

distinguish. Amongst other questions, he reflected on the nature of a term like 'justice'. This does not seem to refer to a particular thing, in the way that the name 'Socrates' indicates a particular man, or 'Crete' a particular island. 'Justice' seems to be an inclusive term which designates a whole number of possible just actions. On the other hand, it seemed likely that these just actions are so named, and form a coherent class, as approximating to an ideal standard of justice; after all, if a ring or a building are described as circular, this means that they conform to the geometrical pattern of a perfect circle. Plato thus envisages a system of classes, each one defined by its perfect exemplar; his difficulties begin when he sees that there are some classes where no perfection seems to be possible. Mud is no less real than justice; but what sense is there in imagining a perfectly muddy mud, or for that matter a perfect all-disabling disease, or a perfect standard of *injustice*?

Plato himself developed his theory along several different lines which could not be brought into agreement. First, regarding his Ideas mainly as class-concepts, he sought to arrange them in a rational hierarchy, in which the more inclusive Ideas were superior. But this is only possible if they are reduced to concepts considered *in abstracto*. Obviously the class of animals is larger than the class of horses; but what kind of creature is the animal-as-such? And what sort of qualities would the ideal animal possess? Even the ideal horse is none too easy on the mind; can we seriously picture a beast which combines the virtues of a race-horse and a cart-horse? The alternative, it seems, would be to say that their virtues are not virtues at all; one is strong and the other is speedy because they both *fail* to reproduce the qualities of an ideal horse which is neither! But despite such problems, many Platonists continued to think of the Ideas as a population of real and co-ordinate beings.

Secondly, Plato presented his Ideas as *objects* of thought; he rejected the view that they were merely thoughts, or patterns of thought; but he left it unclear whether the Ideas themselves *exercise* thought; whether they are intelligent as well as intelligible. To be sure, it is hard to believe that, say, a perfect circle can think; but there are several considerations which favour the theory of intelligent Ideas. For one thing, Plato himself declared that the soul was 'akin to the Ideas'; we can then deduce correctly that the Ideas are akin to souls. Secondly, if one accepts the old notion that like is known by like, it follows that the Ideas must resemble the mind that knows them. Thirdly, it appears that *some* Ideas at least should be intelligent; if intelligence is a virtue, then the ideal man should be intelligent. Fourthly, we are told that Plato came to think of the Ideas as definable in terms of number, or of some quasi-numerical property such as harmony or proportion; and Plato's disciple Xenocrates undoubtedly defined the soul in similar terms. Some thinkers, admittedly, treated both numbers and souls as intermediate beings, ranking below the Ideas but above material things. But if intelligence is good, there is something strange in the doctrine that the highest reality cannot be intelligent.

On the other hand, a salient fact about souls, or personalities, is that they are strongly individualized; no two souls are alike. Thus any attempt to assimilate Ideas and souls will conflict with the notion of the Idea as a class-concept, a 'one over many'. Nevertheless even Plotinus, who did not in principle set much value on diversity, came to think that there must be individual Ideas corresponding to each human individual; and less professional writers, including many Christians, made this equation without any difficulty; human souls in their unfallen state, before they enter the body, simply are Ideas; and there are similar but purer beings who are not attracted by bodily pleasures and remain in the ideal world; these are identified as 'demons' in the pagan tradition, and as 'angels' by Jews and Christians.

Finally, we should consider Plato's myth of the world's creation in the *Timaeus*. A divine craftsman makes the world of space and time according to an eternal model. It might seem, then, that he simply copies patterns of perfection which exist outside and above him. But an alternative theory was developed very early, perhaps by Xenocrates; namely that the divine craftsman himself imagined these patterns within his own mind before putting them into concrete form. This retains something of the old belief that the Ideas are simply thoughts; but it gives then objective validity, as being the archetypal thoughts of the divine creator. This view was no doubt more acceptable to religious minds; and it is worth noting that the devout but anti-Christian Porphyry came round to it under the influence of Plotinus, agreeing with his master that 'the Ideas are not outside the Intellect'.

If we now return to Augustine, we can find most of these conceptions reproduced in his writings. He gives a blanket approval to Plato's doctrine of an intelligible world, revealed by dialectics. In particular he pictures the Ideas as patterns of moral virtues, and again as archetypes for God's creations existing eternally in his mind.[7] Indeed, like many Christian Platonists, he believes that the mind is so much superior to the body that intellectual activity as such is the first step towards heavenly virtue, and that truth—any truth whatsoever—has divine authority over our minds.[8] He finds it hard to admit that any mental operation might be merely pointless or misdirected. Fortunately he is enough of a Christian realist to correct this intellectualist bias on occasion. He notes, for instance, that not all mathematicians are wise;[9]

[7] *Div. Quaest. 83*, 46.
[8] *Lib. Arb.* 2.6.14ff., esp. 2.12.33–4.
[9] Ibid. 2.11.30f.; *Gen. ad Lit.* 2.17.37.

he believes that the demons are clever, but not good; and of course he recognizes the importance of material symbols as presented in the sacraments.

But if Augustine sees the Ideas as archetypes for all God's created works, does he think there is an archetype for each individual creature? Scholars have alleged that this is so;[10] but I do not find their evidence convincing. 'Each single thing is created by its own principle', says Augustine: *singula propriis sunt creata rationibus* (*Div. quaest. 83*,46.2). But the context implies that 'each single thing' should be understood as 'each species'; Augustine has just used the standard examples of 'man' and 'horse'. In any case, the theory of individual archetypes is hardly attractive except as applied to intelligent beings; it seems absurd to suppose that God has an ideal specification for each individual flea and every grain of sand. With human individuals it may be otherwise. Plotinus thought so; and Augustine's God might reasonably have an immutable idea of what each of us should be, distinct of course from our all-too-changeable soul.

The question of intelligent Ideas is also difficult to resolve. Some of the Platonic arguments should appeal to Augustine; thus ideal faith or ideal wisdom can hardly exist without intelligence; but perhaps he did not think of these virtues as distinct intelligent beings; more probably he saw them as God's own living and creative thoughts which interpenetrate each other. Augustine does of course believe in distinct *created* intelligences, which correspond to the spirits or demons of later Platonism. But he usually describes them in biblical and Christian terms; he recognizes good angels and wicked demons, but denounces the morally intermediate demons described by Apuleius.

I have so far presented Augustine in fairly conventional terms. But a different, and rather startling perspective emerges if we try to regard him, not as a Platonizing Christian theologian, but as a renegade Christianizing Platonist. Plotinus had seen the universe as an ordered continuum in which pure spirit eternally reflects itself in lower orders of being. Augustine adopts the Christian belief in a divine act of creation inaugurating a world of time and space, and pictures intelligent spirits in transit between the eternal and the spatiotemporal realms.[11] Theologians have of course defended this concept of creation as essential for establishing the unique and personal dignity of God; and I shall not dispute this verdict. Nevertheless one has to reckon with the complications it introduces into an already complex and tangled metaphysical scheme.

[10] J. Meyendorff, *New Schol.* **16** (1942), 36; V. J. Bourke, *Augustine's View of Reality*, 5, n. 21.

[11] *Civ. Dei.* 8–9, *passim*.

First, we have noted Augustine's belief in the divine archetypes of moral virtues. These archetypes clearly function as ideals to which things ought to conform; but should we credit them with some sort of dynamic function as well? Heavenly faith, we might say, is the touchstone of earthly faith, or its formal cause; but do we see it also as an inspiration which moves us through our love for it? And if so, do we also see the heavenly right-angled triangle as thrilling us with the desire to study mathematics? However this may be, Augustine introduces another set of moving causes, the so-called seminal reasons, which originate in Stoic rather than in Platonic philosophy, and are principles of growth and development at the physical level.

Whatever be the case with the divine archetypes, it must be that these seminal reasons act on each individual thing; indeed they are pictured as present within it. And there is another link between God and his individual creatures, namely his complete and perfect knowledge of them. This knowledge relates to creatures in space and time, but it is itself eternal and unextended. It is tempting to describe it as a compound of perfect perception, perfect memory, and perfect foreknowledge; but if God is eternal, we cannot credit him with these three distinct powers.[12] In a sense, of course, God knows when things happen; he is aware that Judas betrays Jesus on a certain Thursday evening, perhaps in 33 BC; but he can never know that this is going to happen, or that it has happened. But he can, I think, know what it feels like to know these things, since he knows what goes on in the minds of his creatures. Indeed in his *Confessions* (11.13.15ff.) Augustine was prepared to define time itself in psychological terms: the past is what we remember, the future is what we foresee. On this theory, if God knows how the experience of remembering differs from that of foreseeing, he knows all that can be known about the lapse of time. But in later life Augustine did not insist on this peculiar theory.

God's knowledge, of course, raises moral problems, which can be mentioned only in passing. There is, first, God's knowledge of human sin; how can God understand sinful thoughts without in some sense admitting them? If God is a perfectly simple being, as Augustine holds, we cannot say that he understands sinful thoughts but disowns them, for that would imply a conflict between sympathy and repugnance. But perhaps the notion of absolute divine simplicity needs to be reconsidered.

Moreover, if God creates a world in which he knows that the majority of rational creatures will sin and thus be consigned to eternal punishment, how is he himself to be cleared of blame? Augustine holds that God intends to maximize the amount of goodness in the world, and

[12] *Trin.* 15.7.13.

does so by including beings of lesser value, who are therefore bound to sin. But this policy is hardly justified by its results. A second answer is to say that God acts justly towards all his creatures, but shows undeserved mercy to some. The objections to this view are obvious, but hardly belong to our subject; but we may briefly notice one subsidiary point. It might appear that if God foreknows that X will sin, then it is inevitable that X will sin; and if it is inevitable, then X is not free and cannot be blamed. Augustine replies, in his work *On Free Choice* (3.4.9–11), that God does not cause X to sin by foreknowing it; what God foreknows is that X will freely choose to sin, and his fore-knowledge depends on X's choice. In two later works he takes a different line, suggesting that God does indeed contrive that some individuals shall sin, and sin of their own free choice; he does this by omitting to supply the grace to overcome temptation (*Qu. Simp.* 2.13; *Sp. et Lit.* 34.60). I do not think this in the least acceptable as a way to vindicate God's goodness. Nor do I think Augustine gives an adequate account of human freedom. But he does maintain, consistently, that God does not cause future events *merely* by foreknowing them.

We should remind ourselves that human beings are not the only rational moral agents. There are also created spirits, which exist apart from space and time, but are in some sense capable of change. In practice Augustine divides them into two opposing classes. The better sort, the angels, choose to attach themselves to God, and so enjoy a share in his immutability; but this is properly a moral constancy, resulting not from nature but from choice. Contrasted with these are the devils, who seem to practise a kind of negative immutability in the fixity of their self-assertion and destructive intent.

A second order of intelligent beings are destined to enjoy a brief existence in space and time; namely, our human selves. Augustine does not think, with Plato, that our souls exist in time before they animate our bodies; indeed he is notably unsure about their origin. They are, he affirms, God's creatures, and destined for eternal existence; but the only eternity we can be sure that they enjoy is one qualified by their thoughts and actions in their earthly lives. It is therefore outside time, but we can only conceive it as beginning *after* their lives are completed.

How then does human life begin? It seems that God eternally pur-poses to create human souls, or at least to introduce them, in a vastly complicated temporal succession. Two points about this divine pro-cedure may be mentioned as especially strange. First, these created intelligences begin to act within the world at moments which God allows the human animals to determine in response to their own sexual passions. And secondly, although the souls proceed in purity from the creative hand of God, they are immediately thrown down into a tainted environment, so that before they have a chance to prove themselves they incur and *deserve* the indignation and righteous vengeance of God. And this apparent frustration of God's creative work results from the disobedience of Adam and Eve, that is, of only two among the myriads of human spirits. It is the measure of Augustine's greatness that he could win widespread approval for a theory which to all appearances is so improbable, inconsistent, and immoral.

So much, then, for the realities named by the term 'being' in Augustine's philosophy. We must now conclude with some remarks on the more abstruse question *quid est esse*; in other words, how does Augustine interpret the term 'being' itself.

A convenient starting-point is a passage in his Letter XI to Nebridius, which tells us that there are three aspects of being: *primo ut sit, deinde ut hoc vel illud sit, tertium ut in eo quod est maneat quantum potest*; that is to say, 'being itself, being this or that, and continuing to be'. Augustine tells us that these three aspects are distinct but inseparable, like the Persons of the Trinity.[13] There are several similar formulations, some of them using the technical term 'species' in place of 'being this or that'. Another series of passages expounds the biblical text 'Thou hast made all things by measure, number and weight' (Wisdom 11:21), which Augustine tries to interpret along the same lines.[14] This is not an easy task; in particular the term 'measure', *mensura*, does not seem an obvious equivalent for the apparently abstract notion of being itself.[15] With the second term, 'number', he is more fortunately placed, since it recalls the Platonic theory that species can be explained in mathematical terms; so he writes, *numerus omni rei speciem praebet (Gen. ad Lit. 4.3.7)*. His treatment of *pondus*, 'weight', is extraordinarily ingenious and varied, though the details hardly belong to a philosophical lecture; it stands for the ability of things to find their proper level; for the tendency of the rational will to go where it belongs; and also for a thing's internal coherence, and so for its permanence, which for Augustine is a mark of value.[16]

Let us ask Augustine a few questions about his threefold scheme, along the lines of Aristotle's *Categories*. First, how widely does it apply? For he sometimes uses the phrase 'Everything that is', but sometimes speaks of 'every nature or substance', thus referring especially to things, or what Aristotle calls substances, rather than to qualities or relations. Augustine does I think have substances chiefly in mind, which is natural enough, but sometimes misleads him; on the other hand he notes the eternal patterns of some qualities, such as virtues, and of

---

[13] *Div. Quaest. 83*,18; *Ver. Relig.* 7.13.
[14] *Gen. ad Lit.* 4.3.7ff.
[15] *C. Faust. Manich.* 20.7.
[16] *Gen. ad Lit.* 4.4.8.

quantities or numbers; and of course he uses relative terms like 'Father' and 'Son' to denote divine realities. So he recognizes the four principal Aristotelian categories. He may perhaps have adopted the Neoplatonic theory that in the intelligible world all terms are substantial; but even Aristotle noted that some things can be both substantial and relative.[17]

Next, Aristotle would like us to ask Augustine, does he think that being is capable of degrees? Can one *be* intensely, or feebly? Certainly Augustine speaks of greater and less being, and of supreme being (*magis esse, minus esse, summe esse, Civ. Dei* 12.2.9, *Ver. Relig.* 18.35); but does this apply to all aspects of being? With regard to the third of these, permanence, the answer is clear; obviously things can be more and less permanent. But to say that one can possess a specific form more and less completely sounds improbable, and is certainly a direct contradiction of Aristotle; while common sense insists that either a creature is a horse, or it is not. But Augustine clearly did believe that a specific form, for instance humanity, can be more and less perfectly realized; and this belief is linked with his theory of evil as a defect of being. We cannot stay to examine this theory, though I myself distrust it. At the very best, it needs a good deal of elaboration to make it even plausible. Physical deformity, mental deficiency, and moral obliquity can all stand under the broad umbrella of defective humanity. No doubt all are bad; but they are bad in very different ways.

What about the first term of the triad, namely being as such? Here I think Augustine is imprecise. Sometimes his words imply something very like our notion of bare existence; he uses the phrases *utrum omnino sit* and *quo constat (Div. quaest. 83,*18), which recall the language of the law-courts, where one has to establish that a piece of property does actually exist before disputing its ownership.[18] Here there is a straight contrast of the real with the fictitious. In another passage (*Civ. Dei* 11.27) Augustine uses the phrase *ipsum esse* to mean the mere existence, or life, which all creatures try to preserve; this makes a rather different point, for real creatures obviously do not struggle to prevent themselves from becoming fictitious! But yet again, this same phrase *ipsum esse* is used to indicate divine being. This has some analogy with mere existence, as it is in some sense unqualified; God clearly does not belong to any created species. But what exactly is meant by referring to God as pure being?

In fact Augustine declares that God is the source of measure, number and weight—or their various equivalents—but is superior to all of them. On the other hand, as we noted, he can say, *Deus est esse*; he does not appear to have pronounced that God is beyond being. But I am

[17] Plotinus, *Enn.* 6.1.3; Aristotle, *Categ.* 7, 8 a 13ff.
[18] Cf. Quintilian, *Inst.* 7.6.36.

inclined to think that he has two different conceptions in view. He reproduces the traditional Platonic-Christian concept of a creative intelligence which foreordains what variety of things are to exist in the world, because it is best that it should be so. But beside this appears the more difficult, and more characteristic idea of the One as a source of being, pure being, from which the distinct varieties of being descend by a process of diminution, rather like the refraction of white light to produce the various colours.[19] Pure being, in this sense, is an intensely powerful reality; Augustine describes it as the source of life, sensation and purposive motion (*c. Faust. Man.* 20.7); elsewhere he associates it with unity, goodness, and truth. But he offers us the paradox that the highest form of life is found in a Being which lacks all the characteristics which we associate with life, unless unity, goodness and permanence can provide some sort of bridge; and the approach to such a being should be to lay aside not only action but thought, indeed everything that is regulated by number and proportion, and to lose oneself in the contemplation of the absolute One.

I think, then, that the alternative conception better expresses the Christian doctrine of creation, indeed of divine being; and it should also be more acceptable to us moderns, impressed as we are by Darwinian theories of evolution; for we normally think that new species have evolved by developing new positive capacities which enable them to compete and survive, rather than by the self-restriction of an undifferentiated source of being.

Both these theories, however, presuppose an optimistic view of the universe, as expounded by many Stoics and Platonists; and both are difficult to reconcile with Augustine's vision of a universe which God knows from all eternity will be darkened and corrupted by sin. The problem would be eased if we could believe, with John Lucas, that God's foreknowledge is not absolute, so that there was at least a chance that Adam would not sin; or better still, if we could persuade Augustine that man's absolute need of God's grace need not imply an absolute entanglement in corruption. As it is, I suspect that he has involved himself in a contradiction from which even his own masterful ingenuity could find no way of escape.

I will conclude with some further remarks on the subject of permanence; for permanence is a characteristic which Augustine values highly; he thinks it an essential mark of true goodness and of God's being. But the connection between permanence and value is not immediately obvious. Aristotle indeed challenged Plato on this point, observing—perhaps not very seriously—that a white post that lasts a long time is no *whiter* than one which lasts for a day (*NE* 1096b, 4). We might of course

---

[19] *Civ. Dei* 8.6, 12.2; cf. *Nat. Bon.* 3.

object that this is not a good analogy for moral qualities. If we call a man generous, we mean that he has a permanent disposition towards unselfish giving. Thus an isolated impulsive action cannot count as generosity; to quote Aristotle again, it is virtuous only if it proceeds from a fixed intention (ibid. 1105a, 34). But unfortunately for this argument, it applies to vices as well as to virtues; and just as a throw-away largesse doesn't prove a man generous, so a momentary panic doesn't brand him a coward. Augustine is obviously captivated by the old Platonic doctrine that instability is a mark of vice, and *per contra,* that stability is necessary for virtue; but once again, he is not consistent; he can insist that some men acquire a habit of self-assertion and wrong-doing which determines all their actions (*Gr. Xti.* 18f.). It seems to follow that stability or permanence is a necessary condition of moral goodness; but it cannot possibly be a sufficient condition.

In dealing with God himself, Augustine introduces the much stronger notion of immutability, which we cannot discuss at this stage. But even the requirement of stability poses problems for the moralist; how can one acquire it without becoming inflexible and insensitive? And *per contra*, what can a philosopher make of those delightful acts of spontaneous generosity which we associate with the alabaster cruse of ointment and with St Francis of Assisi? No doubt the answers to such questions are implicit in Augustine's writings; but he does not present them in worked-out form. And the happy tribe of Augustinian scholars who quote the master's words with placid approval have seldom explored these problems, and give us little help towards their solution.

The moral, I think, is that it is more important to be stimulated and inspired by Augustine than to put together an Augustinian system. Augustine is a fascinating character; devout, yet ingenious; authoritarian, yet sympathetic. As a philosopher he has one outstanding weakness, namely his uncritical acceptance of a Church tradition that had been fixed through the labours of lesser men; and this of course includes an approach to the Bible which we moderns have been forced to discard. But no one can wholly free himself from the influence of his predecessors. Augustine is not only a saint, but an innovative genius whose work will hold a permanent appeal.

Predestination and Freedom in Augustine's Ethics

GERARD O'DALY

In his great poem *The Wreck of the Deutschland* Gerard Manley Hopkins evokes the conversions of Paul and Augustine as two contrasting examples of the way in which God may intervene in human affairs:

> With an anvil-ding
> And with fire in him forge thy will
> Or rather, rather then, stealing as Spring
> Through him, melt him but master him still:
> Whether at once, as once at a crash Paul,
> Or as Austin, a lingering-out swéet skíll . . .[1]

For Hopkins, the sudden conversion of Paul on the road to Damascus, and the gradual conversion which Augustine describes in the *Confessions*, and which culminates in the garden at Milan, are both manifestations of the one God who is, paradoxically, 'lightning and love . . . a winter and warm', who is the God of mercy, but also of mastery.

In the *Confessions* the conversion of Paul does not figure among the examples presented by Augustine as parallel to his experience, despite the Pauline colouring of the conversion account itself. The reason must lie in the contrast expressed in Hopkins' poem. Augustine's long process of conversion, and the part which human intermediaries, wittingly or unwittingly, play in it, have no parallels in the accounts of Paul's conversion in Acts.[2] Yet in two works written towards the end of his life, works composed in the aftermath of the Pelagian controversy but still dominated by the issues of that controversy,[3] Augustine turns to

---

[1] *The Poems of Gerard Manley Hopkins*, 4th edn, W. H. Gardner and N. H. MacKenzie (eds) (Oxford University Press, 1967), 54.

[2] Cf. Acts 9, 22, and 26. For a perceptive discussion of these accounts, Pauline references to his conversion, and Augustine's exploitation of Paul see P. Fredriksen, 'Paul and Augustine: Conversion Narratives, Orthodox Traditions, and the Retrospecitve Self', *Journal of Theological Studies* NS **37** (1986), 3–34.

[3] On the issues see the lucid account of G. Bonner, *St Augustine of Hippo: Life and Controversies*, 2nd edn (Norwich: Canterbury Press, 1986), 352–393. The progress of the controversy is described by P. Brown, *Augustine of*

Gerard O'Daly

consider both Paul's conversion and his own, and finds the same underlying factors at work in both. In Paul's conversion there is no apparent trace of free choice: 'For the call to come from heaven, and for him to be converted by so great and effective a call, there was the grace of God alone; for he merited much, but much evil' (*De gratia et libero arbitrio* 5.12). In the same passage Augustine quotes a number of Pauline texts which assert the co-existence of divine grace and free will, particularly 'not I, but the grace of God with me' (1 Cor. 15:10). It is not the aspect of human will, but the manner in which divine grace implants faith in the human being without any antecedent merit on his or her part, that Paul's case exemplifies. When he turns to his own conversion account in the *Confessions* and reconsiders it, Augustine likewise emphasizes the divine gift of faith which, in his case, makes an active enemy of Christianity into a willing believer (*De dono perseverantiae* 20.53). In this late reassessment of his conversion, Augustine has subtly modified the *Confessions* account to make it sound more like that of a Pauline conversion: 'I was ravaging [the faith] with most pitiable and raging talkativeness'. The gradual aspect of his conversion is not denied, but it becomes external to him (his mother's persistent faith, and its intermediary role, is stressed), and it is the unmerited gift of grace that is dominant. The conversion of Augustine's will is not omitted, but as with Paul, it is God's gratuitous initiative that is now the most striking fact about Augustine's conversion. In the late Augustine, the road to Damascus and the garden in Milan have become settings for the same divine drama, in which God's enemy becomes God's servant.

Yet this alignment of two apparently different conversion experiences does not mark any late, radical change in Augustine's theory of grace and election. It is, rather, a reflection of the fact that, at the end of his career, as Gillian Evans has observed, 'Augustine finds the internal coherence of his account of the matter growing tighter at every point, each principle supporting the rest'.[4] Only a slight shift of emphasis is needed, and the inherent similarities of the two conversions are revealed. In fact, the principles of Augustine's account of grace, election, and freedom were, as is well known, established as early as 396 or 397, when he wrote in reply to questions sent him by Simplicianus of Milan (*Ad Simplicianum*). There, in a work completed before he begins the *Confessions*, and which antedates the Pelagian controversy

[4] G. R. Evans, *Augustine on Evil* (Cambridge University Press, 1982), 168.

Hippo: A Biography (London: Faber & Faber, 1967), 340–407, and (with full documentation) by O. Wermelinger, *Rom und Pelagius* (Stuttgart: Hiersemann, 1975). See also J. P. Burns, *The Development of Augustine's Doctrine of Operative Grace* (Paris: Etudes Augustiniennes, 1980).

by many years, he argues that God determines our wills when we will what is good, and also that such willing is none the less free choice, for which we are responsible.[5] Augustine's subsequent writing on the subject is exploration of these two assertions and of their ramifications. They are the corner-stone of his doctrine of predestination, and concomitant defence of human freedom. To the details of that doctrine we must now turn.

Much of the detail of Augustine's account of free will and predestination is concerned with humanity after the Fall. But it is none the less important to understand what Augustine believes to have been the nature of Adam's freedom before the Fall. Adam in Paradise enjoyed divine grace as a 'help without which' (*adiutorium sine quo non*) he could not choose the good, or even avoid evil. Divine grace for Adam in Paradise was a necessary, but not sufficient condition of his free choice of the good. It did not render him incapable of sin, but it ensured that he had the means of choosing good. But even in Adam's prelapsarian state, freedom of choice on its own was not a sufficient condition of doing good. Only free choice and divine grace together suffice for good.[6]

Adam (and the fallen angels) had the power to avoid sin. We need not, in the present paper, consider the reasons for the Fall, but we should note one reason which Augustine gives for its possibility in a being of Adam's intellectual and moral integrity. Adam, and all created beings, according to Augustine, are liable to sin because they are created out of nothing.[7] This 'ontological weakness' does not entail their sinning, but it makes it possible that they will choose evil. Augustine does not elaborate on this endemic weakness in all created rational beings, but his assumption that it is present influences what he has to say about the nature of the elect, as will be seen later in the paper.

In his early work *De libero arbitrio (On Free Choice)* Augustine distinguishes between three kinds of goods. The 'great goods', the highest kind, include the virtues, and can be used only for good, whereas the lowest or minimal goods, to which all kinds of physical beauty belong, and the intermediate or middle goods may be used for both good and evil ends. Will is a middle good, and what distinguishes it from the lowest kind of goods is that its activity is necessary to 'living rightly', whereas the possession of the lowest goods is not necessary to

---

[5] *Ad Simplicianum* 1.2.

[6] Cf. *De civitate Dei* 14.26; *De correptione et gratia* 10.28–12.34. See G. Bonner, 'Adam', *Augustinus-Lexikon* 1, fasc. 1/2 (1986), 63–87, especially 78–80.

[7] Cf. *De civ. Dei* 12.6; 14.13; *Contra Iulianum opus imperfectum* 5.39. See Bonner, op. cit. (above n. 3), 369.

virtue (*lib. arb.* 2.19.50–53). Augustine here advocates a concept of will that could be described as morally indifferent: the neutral will can be used either rightly or wrongly. The work *On Free Choice* was completed by 395. In the *Confessions*, begun some two years later, Augustine has already moved away from the notion of the will as an indifferent instrument, used for good or ill, to the concept of will as good or evil, depending upon the value of what is willed.[8] This latter concept of a will that is morally determined represents Augustine's mature thought on the subject. The Pelagian controversy, however, focused attention on Augustine's views in the work *On Free Choice*, in which Pelagius and others found evidence that appeared to make Augustine hold views akin to theirs.[9] It is surely no accident that, as Robert Evans has pointed out, Augustine implicitly disclaims his theory of the indifferent will in his first anti-Pelagian treatise *On the Merits and Forgiveness of Sins (De peccatorum meritis et remissione)*.[10] Here he repudiates the idea that the will can somehow be 'in the middle' (*in medio*), and neither good nor evil. Will is either good or evil, and a good will is 'from God'. Moreover, a good will cannot be misused for evil (*De pecc. mer.* 2.18.30). This was Augustine's view in 411 or 412. In the course of the discussion he refers to his earlier concept of will as a natural good that can be misused, and which is 'freely directed in this direction and in that', thereby acknowledging the phenomena of choice, moral conflict, and apparent abuse of freedom. But the progress of the discussion leaves the reader in no doubt that, although Augustine wishes to maintain that the will, like all created things, is a good, even when it is corrupted, he repudiates any view which makes the will a morally neutral power. Augustine's terminological imprecision can sometimes puzzle and dismay his readers. In his work *On the Spirit and the Letter (De spiritu et littera)*, written shortly after *On the Merits and Forgiveness of Sins* in 412, he resurrects the description of the will as a 'middle power' (*media vis*), capable of being turned to faith or unbelief (*spir. et litt.* 33.58), even if he reaffirms in the same context the view that the will to believe is received from God. But, once again, the larger context of the work makes it clear that the middle power of the will is not a description of its neutral or indifferent nature, but rather of its capacity for change. 'The human will is not removed, but is changed from an evil into a good will by grace', a view expressed by Augustine in a later work (*De gratia et libero arbitrio* 20.41), might also be the motto of *On the Spirit and the Letter*.

[8] Cf. especially *Confessions* 8.8.19–9.21, discussed later in this paper.

[9] See Augustine's reaction to Pelagian views of *De libero arbitrio* in *Retractationes* 1.9. Cf. *De natura et gratia* 67.80–1.

[10] R. F. Evans, *Pelagius: Inquiries and Reappraisals* (London: A. & C. Black, 1968), 87–88.

Pelagius's description of human freedom of choice as a *possibilitas utriusque partis*, a 'power to take either side',[11] and his comparison of this power with a fruitful and fecund root that can produce either the blossom of virtue or the brambles of vice, leads Augustine to deny explicitly that the same will can choose good and evil. Augustine counters Pelagius's metaphor with a related one from Scripture: 'A good tree cannot bring forth evil fruit, neither can a corrupt tree bring forth good fruit' (Matthew 7:18). The causes of good and evil actions are twofold good and evil wills, determined in turn by grace or sin (*De gratia Christi* 18.19–20.21). Augustine wrote these words in 418. Controversy with Pelagius had elicited an unequivocal expression of his views on the will from him.

Will, for Augustine, is never a mental faculty, never, in the Platonic sense, a 'part of the soul'. Even in the early *On Free Choice* it is no more and no less than a kind of mental power or capacity, like memory, with which it is compared in that work (*lib. arb.* 2.19.51). In Augustine's later theory will is evidently, in John Rist's words, 'the human *psyche* in its role as a moral agent'.[12] The will reflects a person's moral standing. That is certainly the way in which Augustine understands the 'men of good will' of Scripture (Luke 2:14): they are, simply, the good (*De gratia et libero arbitrio* 1.4). But as well as referring to our will in the singular, and calling it good or bad, Augustine also speaks of two or more wills in us, as when, for example, he wishes to suggest moral conflict. In such contexts, our wills are the range of possible courses of action upon which we are inclined or deliberating. I shall return to this second sense of the term 'will' in Augustine later in the paper.

It is now time to go on to further details of Augustine's views on grace and election, views which can only be understood against the background of his concept of the will which we have been examining. I shall remind you briefly of the main points of Augustine's doctrine, and dwell only on some of its obscurer or more controversial aspects.[13]

Humanity after the Fall retains the power of free choice (*liberum arbitrium*), but fallen man's freedom is merely the freedom or power to sin. Even faith in God is impossible without grace: *initium fidei donum dei* ('the beginning of faith is the gift of God', *De dono perseverantiae* 20.52). Augustine criticizes his early view that such faith is naturally

---

[11] Or 'a power to X or not-X'.

[12] J. M. Rist, 'Augustine on Free Will and Predestination', *Journal of Theological Studies* NS **20** (1969), 421.

[13] For the following see, apart from Bonner, op. cit. (above n. 3), 358–393, and Rist, art. cit. (above n. 12), 420–442, the classic account of O. Rottmanner, *Der Augustinismus* (Munich: Lentner, 1892), reprinted in *Geistesfrüchte aus der Klosterzelle* (Munich: Lentner, 1908), 11–32.

possible in the late work *On the Predestination of the Saints (praed. sanct.* 3.7). He never tires of quoting Proverbs 8:35: *praeparatur voluntas a domino*, 'the will is prepared by the Lord', in references to the genesis of the good will in us.[14] The good will is not merely prepared by God, but God eternally and timelessly foreknows that it will be. Therefore God foreknows both the salvation of the saved and the damnation of the damned. Now, when Augustine speaks of divine foreknowledge (which, since it is timeless, he prefers to call 'divine knowledge'), he understands it to be a knowledge that does not necessarily determine the foreknown event.[15] He distinguishes clearly between divine foreknowledge and predestination: predestination, the determining of certain events by God, entails God's knowledge, for God is omniscient, but the converse does not follow (*praed. sanct.* 10.19). At the same time, there is an inevitable parallelism in Augustine's accounts of divine foreknowledge and predestination. Thus God's predestination of the saved as well as of the damned—and, contrary to the view sometimes expressed, Augustine does speak of the predestination of the damned[16]—is eternal and timeless: it 'precedes' the creation, in the sense that his foreknowledge does.[17] Predestination to damnation is simply the withholding by God of grace from those he does not will to save. That is to say, whereas predestination to salvation is actively caused by God, God merely permits the damned to suffer the consequences of Adam's sin. Augustine suggests that nothing (not even the sins of Satan and Adam) happens 'apart from God's will' (*praeter voluntatem dei*), even if some things do happen 'against his will' (*contra voluntatem eius*). God lets Adam sin, but does not cause him to do so (*Enchiridion* 100). We might say that the predestination of the damned is a negative condition of their damnation. Condemned through the solidarity of all humans with Adam, they are predestined because God foreknows that he will not give them the grace to be saved.

But it is with the predestination of the elect that Augustine, and we, are chiefly concerned. Their predestination is *gratiae praeparatio*, 'the preparation of grace', and grace is its effect (*praed. sanct.* 10.19). Augustine suggests that God's promises to Abraham in Genesis 17:4–5 are a pre-eminent instance of predestination. The implementation of the divine promises does not depend on human wills, though they are

---

[14] Cf. A. Sage, 'Praeparatur voluntas a Deo', *Revue des Etudes Augustiniennes* **10** (1964), 1–20.

[15] See R. Sorabji, *Time, Creation and the Continuum* (London: Duckworth, 1983), 253–267.

[16] Cf. *In Iohannis evangelium tractatus CXXIV* 48.4,6; 107.7; 111.5.

[17] Cf. *In Io. ev. tract* 68.1; *De Genesi ad litteram* 6.11.19; *De praedestinatione sanctorum* 9.18.

implemented through human actions. The notion that God's promises should depend for their fulfilment on humans alone is untenable (ibid.). Fallen humanity cannot achieve goodness on its own.

It follows that God's determination of our wills through grace precedes any merits of ours. But Augustine is no less insistent that divine determination of our wills does not make us mere passive recipients of grace. He repudiates the view of Julian of Eclanum that his (Augustine's) doctrine of grace is a doctrine of absolute determinism or *fatum*.[18] For Augustine, the notion of 'compulsion of the will' (*cogi velle*) is nonsensical (*Contra Iulianum opus imperfectum* 1.101). Augustine takes this view because he is convinced of the self-evident nature of the fact that we will, that we have the power to do X through, and only through, the means of willing X. He believes that this fact about us is ascertained by infallible introspective analysis of the mechanism of our behaviour, and by deductions from the observed behaviour of others.[19] It is corroborated by the authority of Scripture, where divine commands, promises, and threats, and the whole apparatus of divine rewards and punishments, entail the concept of human freedom and responsibility.[20] Even the elect cannot be rewarded for something for which they are not responsible.

The importance of Augustine's theory of action cannot be underestimated in an account of his views on grace and free will. The activity of *intentio*, of mental concentration or attention, is an essential ingredient of the processes of sense-perception, imagination, and memory. *Intentio* is the necessary mental prelude to all action. And *intentio* is none other than the activity of willing in its basic form.[21] Neither at the level of sense-perception, nor in the activities of imagination or memory are we passively determined beings. The notion of passive determination is contradicted by the evident facts of human psychology. The mind's movement, says Augustine, is activated by the will, and it is not like the movement of a stone which falls to the ground by a law of natural necessity (*lib. arb.* 3.1.2).

When Augustine applies his psychological theory to problems of grace and free will, he argues that the only way in which grace may become operative in humans is by the attraction of the will to what is good and true. The will is always goal-directed, it is active, but only to

[18] Cf. *Contra duas epistulas Pelagianorum* 2.5.9–6.12.

[19] See A. Dihle, *The Theory of Will in Classical Antiquity* (Berkeley, Los Angeles and London: California University Press, 1982), 123–132, 231–238.

[20] See e.g. *De lib. arb.* 2.1.

[21] Cf. G. O'Daly, *Augustine's Philosophy of Mind* (London: Duckworth, 1987), 43–45, 84–87, 108–111, 132–133, for the role of *intentio* in perception and other mental activities.

some purpose. Augustine speaks of the 'delight' (*delectatio*) of the will in its objects. This delight is said to be 'conquering' or 'victorious' (*delectatio vincens/victrix*) when a particular choice is made or course of action adopted. *Delectatio* is a feature of the good, but also of the evil will: it can be *delectatio iustitiae*, but also *delectatio peccandi*.[22] When John Burnaby situates this concept in its larger context of Augustine's idea of love (*amor*), he rightly points out that Augustine 'is simply isolating for the moment the affective aspect of *amor*'.[23] That is to say, Augustine's reader should not forget that the affective element in Augustine's concept of *amor* is balanced and complemented by its conative counterpart. Delight and willing are aspects of the same process. If I will X, then my willing is necessarily accompanied by delight in X. But Augustine argues that this is none the less not a total determination of my will by something external to it. I will actively, deliberately, and freely. *Delectatio* is not an instinctive reaction to external stimuli, not a reflex action: when Augustine wishes to distinguish such phenomena from the rational assent that is present in *delectatio*, he sometimes uses the verbs *placet* and *libet* in binary opposition, *placet* to connote *delectatio, libet* to suggest instinctive reactions (*Contra duas epistulas Pelagianorum* 1.2.5, 1.13.27).[24] Augustine insists upon the active nature of human responses to divine grace: 'God makes man act' (*ut . . . faciat homo deus facit, contra Iul. imp.* 1.134). It is both the case that we will and act, and that God makes us will and act (*De gratia et lib. arb.* 16.32).

The conclusion is unavoidable that, for Augustine, divine grace is irresistible, in the sense that it is not within our power, if we are predestined, to reject it. This does not make of Augustine a Jansenist determinist, for he is not arguing that grace compels us. What Augustine is emphasizing is, as Burnaby says, 'the Almighty providence which rules the issues of all human willing'.[25] Grace transforms and activates the human will: men 'are acted upon that they may act, not that they may be themselves inactive' (*aguntur . . . ut agant, non ut ipsi nihil agant, De correptione et gratia* 2.4). When, in the work *On the Spirit and the Letter*, Augustine asserts that 'to consent to God's call . . . is the act of one's own will' (*spir. et litt.* 34.60), he is proclaiming

[22] Cf. *De peccatorum meritis* 2.19.32; *Contra duas epist. Pelag.* 1.2.5; 1.10.22; 1.13.27; 2.9.21.

[23] J. Burnaby, *Amor Dei: A Study of the Religion of St Augustine* (London: Hodder & Stoughton, 1938), 222. Burnaby's discussion of grace and reward in Augustine (op. cit., 219–252) is brilliantly perceptive.

[24] Cf. G. Bonner, '*Libido* and *Concupiscentia* in St Augustine', *Studia Patristica* 6 (=*Texte und Untersuchungen* 81) (1963), 303–314.

[25] Burnaby, op. cit. (above n. 23), 231. Rist, art. cit. (above n. 12), 434–440, argues for the irresistible function of grace in Augustine's theory.

his own particular brand of determinism, a determinism which he believes to be compatible with human freedom. Here, and elsewhere in his writings, he is putting forward the view which J. B. Mozley succinctly summarizes: 'consent is . . . the necessary mode in which the will receives a gift'. But Mozley's conclusion is unavoidable: 'to say that the will must consent in order to receive, is nothing more than to say that the will must receive when it receives'.[26] Augustine is aware of the paradoxical nature of his claim, and expresses it in the paradox that grace enables us to escape from the freedom to sin, which is, in fact, a form of slavery, so that we may enjoy true freedom, which is willing and obedient slavery to the will of God (*Enchiridion* 30).

* * *

I should now like to turn from consideration of Augustine's views to an examination of their cogency. What are the underlying philosophical principles and assumptions of Augustine's doctrine? Is it a philosophically tenable doctrine? I shall begin by returning to a text which I referred to earlier, the passage in the work *On the Grace of Christ* in which Augustine counters Pelagius' description of freedom of choice as 'a power to take either side'. Augustine is, in effect, arguing there against the conception of freedom later known as liberty of indifference, the ability to do otherwise, to do or not to do X, or to do X while being able to do its opposite. The ground of Augustine's objection to liberty of indifference is that 'it has established one and the same root of good and evil', that is to say, that it posits the same cause of opposite effects. I do not think that Mozley is right to suggest that Augustine is here using substantially the same argument as that of the eighteenth-century Calvinist theologian Jonathan Edwards in his book *Freedom of the Will*.[27] Edwards is arguing, against the theory of liberty of indifference, that an act of choice cannot be simultaneous with a state of indifference.[28] Augustine is arguing that the same cause cannot produce opposite effects. But it may be that Augustine and Edwards share substantially the same theory of mental causation. Does Augustine, like Edwards, believe in causally effective volitions, which are the necessary antecedent mental events that make actions voluntary? That would appear to be the implication of his argument against Pelagius in *On the Grace of Christ*. But such a possible interpretation of Augustine's argument in that one passage is not an adequate demon-

---

[26] J. B. Mozley, *A Treatise on the Augustinian Doctrine of Predestination* (London: John Murray, 1855), 241.

[27] Mozley, op. cit., 228.

[28] J. Edwards, *Freedom of the Will*, P. Ramsey (ed.) (New Haven: Yale University Press, 1957), 190–212.

stration of Augustine's dependence upon a theory of causally effective volitions. Further evidence must be adduced.

One of the most extended discussions of willing in practice in the writings of Augustine is his account of his state of mind in the time immediately prior to his conversion in Book Eight of the *Confessions*. There Augustine distinguishes between the will to perform bodily actions, such as walking or beating his forehead, and the power or ability to perform them: I might will to walk but be unable to do so because I am ill or tied up (*conf*. 8.8.20). The bodily action, if accomplished, is an effect of willing it: 'I did it because I willed to' (ibid.).[29] Augustine makes a further distinction between actions of this kind and mental activities where will and power coincide, where to will is to perform. In acts of this latter kind (of which Augustine's will to devote himself to God is the pre-eminent relevant example) the willing appears to be both cause and effect, for it is through and in the act of choice that the voluntary action is realized. The act is one and the same thing or event as the choice of the act (*conf*. 8.9.21). Yet in his discussion of this second kind of act Augustine none the less uses the same language as is used in the account of the first kind. He speaks of distinguishable causes and effects: 'The mind commands the mind to will, the mind is itself, but it does not do it . . . it does not totally will' (ibid.). Now clearly the willing agent here is not external to the mind, for it is the mind itself. It is not separable in the way that the mind is separable from the body in Augustine's account of the first kind of actions. But Augustine is none the less suggesting that there is a 'commanding' power whose commands can be inefficacious, that is, not have the desired effect. The implication of this language is that willing is analogous to doing. This second type of behaviour is frustrated action, if it is unsuccessful, and completed action, if it succeeds. Now Augustine, as we have seen, does not regard the will as a faculty that makes decisions. Moreover, he can speak of two or more wills in conflict in one person: these conflicting wills may be all good, or all bad, or a mixture of both good and bad. One mind may be 'torn' by such diverse wills (*conf*. 8.10.24). But even if he does not consider the will to be a decision-making faculty, and postulates a plurality of possible wills active in one person in any situation, he none the less identifies the kind of mental process or activity called willing as a process with a causal function. And, as has been seen, he distinguishes, in the case of mental processes such as the willing of his own conversion, between willing and execution, cause and effect.

[29] This and the following citations from the *Confessions* are in F. J. Sheed's translation (London: Sheed & Ward, 1944), 135–139.

Now it might be argued that Augustine appears to say that frustrated acts of the will of the second kind are not acts of the will at all, and that that is the reason why nothing is achieved. He does say that the mind 'does not totally will', and that the will, therefore, 'does not in its fullness give the command' (*conf*. 8.9.21). But his language also suggests an activity of willing: 'It commands in so far as it wills . . . what it commands is not done' (ibid.). His use of such terms as 'command', 'do', 'disobey' indicates that he considers this activity to be one of frustrated intention, rather than absence of intention. His willing may be inadequate, but it is willing none the less. What he appears to be describing is weakness of will, as that concept is understood by Aristotle or Ryle: 'I was frantic in mind, in a frenzy of indignation at myself for not going over to your Law and your Covenant, O my God, when all my bones cried out that I should be, extolling it to the skies' (*conf*. 8.8.19).[30]

The implication of this account of Augustine's discussion of willing in the *Confessions* is that, even if he does not subscribe to the same theory of action as that found in Locke or Edwards, he none the less subscribes to the same assumptions about the causation of voluntary actions. Willing is an event which may give rise to a free action, and free actions are caused by the will.

A consequence of these assumptions is that Augustine, like Edwards, needs to identify a cause of acts of the will, for willing is not self-determining. But Augustine, unlike Edwards, does not appear to be aware of the infinite regress inherent in the theory of liberty of indifference, if that theory is assumed to entail a concept of causally effective volitions.[31] In fact, he is not totally opposed to the liberty of indifference notion. He may reject his version of it in his early work *On Free Choice*, but it presumably applies to Adam in Paradise before the Fall. He cannot, therefore, have cogent grounds for rejecting its tenability *per se*. But it does not square with the facts of the psychology of fallen humanity. Our wills can never in this earthly existence have the neutrality which the theory of indifference seems to entail for Augustine. Our wills are always either good or bad, and even the good wills of the elect can only remain so through the gift of perseverance. Augustine's analysis of human psychology more than halfway meets his interpretation of the Christian doctrines of grace and election.

---

[30] Cf. *conf*. 8.9.21: '. . . partly to will, partly not to will . . . a sickness of the soul to be so weighted down by custom that it cannot wholly rise even with the support of truth'. Weakness of will: Aristotle, *Nicomachean Ethics* 7.1–10; G. Ryle, *The Concept of Mind* (Harmondsworth: Penguin, 1963), 67–72.

[31] See A. Kenny, *The God of the Philosophers* (Oxford: Clarendon Press, 1979), 83–85, for a brief discussion of Edwards's arguments.

We have seen that Augustine attempts to preserve freedom of the will, even if fallen man cannot reject divine grace. Mozley considers Augustine's talk of free will to be a description of a mode, rather than a source, of action, and he suggests that, for Augustine, the will is a mediate, and not a first cause, of action.[32] In fact, Augustine's view of free will amounts to liberty of spontaneity. It is not so much the ability to do otherwise, as the ability to act free of compulsion or constraint. Augustine, like Luther, allows such spontaneity to human action, even if, unlike Luther, he argues that such a will is free.

Are Augustine's assertions of this freedom mere words, a metaphorical form of expressing the vision of the elect as slaves of God? Is Rist right to conclude that Augustine's man is 'a puppet', who enjoys no freedom in any acceptable sense of the term?[33] I should like to suggest, at the conclusion of this paper, that this is not the only philosophically legitimate reading of Augustine's ideas. Anthony Kenny has argued for the compatibility of freedom with determinism.[34] The power of alternative action, which constitutes genuine freedom, can, he suggests, be present even when it may be predetermined, for example physiologically, that it will not, in fact, be exercised. This power involves both the ability and the opportunity to act. Let us apply Kenny's argument to the case of a recipient of divine grace, one of the elect. Even with grace, he will have the ability, in Kenny's sense of the term, to act otherwise. For if he wanted to sin, and there was an opportunity to do so, he would sin, even if, in fact, he is not now sinning. Furthermore, Augustine's predestined man may possess the opportunity to sin, provided that nothing independent of his own wants prevents him from sinning, even if he does not make use of that opportunity by sinning. So Augustine's *praedestinatus* has the power to commit sin, as an alternative to being good, even when it is predetermined that this power will not be exercised.

This argument may, if it is tenable, save freedom in a deterministic system. Augustine's position is, perhaps, not so philosophically unrespectable after all. But, as Kenny points out, to accept the compatibility of freedom with determinism in this manner is to make it difficult to avoid the consequence that God is responsible for sin. Even if we maintain that not all that happens in the world is determined by God, God cannot escape responsibility for states of affairs brought about voluntarily, if not intentionally, by him. The distinction between causing and permitting would not, then, be possible to maintain with

[32] Mozley, op. cit. (above n. 26), 242, 244–245.
[33] Rist, art. cit. (above n. 12), 440.
[34] A. Kenny, *Will, Freedom and Power* (Oxford: Blackwell, 1975), 145–61; Kenny, op. cit. (above n. 31), 85–86, summarizes his argument.

application to God.[35] Augustine, as we have seen, regards Adam's choice as permitted rather than caused by God, and so sin as occurring against, but not apart from, God's will. But that indeterminist position fits ill with his deterministic account of the operation of grace. A philosophical defence of Augustine's notion of freedom of the will seems impossible: it remains a glorious and influential failure. His graphic late accounts of the conversion of Paul and his own conversion, which minimize the role of the human will, may reflect a position that he would not have cared to admit.

[35] Kenny, op. cit. (above n. 31), 86–87.

God as Creator

KEITH WARD

'In the beginning God created the heaven and the earth' (Genesis 1.1). For millions of Jews, Christians and Muslims this has been a fundamental article of belief. Nor is it unknown in the classical Indian traditions. The Upanishads, taken by the orthodox to be 'heard', not invented, and to be verbally inerrant, state: 'He desired: "May I become many, may I procreate" . . . He created (or emanated) this whole universe' (Taittiriya Upanishad, 6). The belief that everything in the universe is brought into being by an act of will or desire on the part of one uniquely uncreated being is widespread and fundamental in religion. Historians of religion generally suppose that it is a rather late belief in the Biblical tradition, having developed from an earlier stage at which Jahweh was one tribal deity among others. By the time of the major prophets, however, the notion was firmly established that there is only one God, creator of everything other than himself. Christian theologians always seem to have had a great interest in conceptual problems, and the idea of creation has proved a very fruitful one for generating philosophical puzzles. Those puzzles are still of great theoretical interest, and I shall consider some of them with reference to the work of Augustine and, to a lesser extent Thomas Aquinas. Their views have been so influential that they may fairly be called 'classical', in Christian theology.

The problem which appeared to strike Augustine with most force arose from consideration of the phrase, 'In the beginning'. Augustine asks, 'What made God create heaven and earth then, and not sooner?' (*City of God* 11.4). What was God doing before he created the universe? And what made him decide to make it at just the moment he chose, rather than at some other moment? The picture is of God existing for a time so long that it has no beginning or end; and, at a particular moment, deciding to create this universe. If one has this picture, it is not an idle question to ask if God had a good reason for creating the universe at just the precise moment he decided upon.

Augustine, however, rejects this picture entirely. God, he holds, does not exist in time at all. In his *Confessions,* Book 11, he writes that 'in the Eternal nothing passes, but the whole is present'. So, in the *City of God* 12.17, he says, 'He is never affected, nor does His nature admit anything that has not been ever in Him'. There is no past, which has ceased to be and may only be remembered, in God. There is no future, which does not yet exist, and may only be foreseen, in God. There is no present, which continually passes from moment to moment, and is constantly changing, in God. There is one unchanging reality, subject to no temporal relations whatsoever.

Augustine accepts from Aristotle the idea that time is 'a measure of motion' (*Physics* 221a1). As he puts it, 'Where no creature is, whose motion may bring forth time, there can be no time' (*City of God* 12.15). Time only exists as a certain relation between objects, such that one exists before or after the other. Time *is* that relation, and without objects which change, which have that relation to one another, the relation does not exist. Since time depends upon change, and there is no change in God, there is no time in God either.

Two major puzzles arise immediately. First, can one really conceive of a timeless being? It is clear that Augustine, and others who follow him, constantly use temporal terms in speaking of God. In Chapter 12, he writes, 'God's pause before man's creation being from all eternity was so great that compare a definite number with it of ever so unspeakable a quantity and it is not so much as one half drop of water compared with the whole ocean'. The analogy is unfortunate; for the ocean is of the same kind as the drops of water, though much greater in degree. Augustine sees this, of course, and is at pains to point out the inadequacy. Yet he still declares that anything which has a beginning is tiny when compared to that which has no beginning at all. The implication is that God endures through and beyond all times at which the universe exists; that he is temporal, but without beginning or end. But that is not an implication Augustine wants; the wholly timeless can be neither temporally greater nor temporally smaller than anything temporal.

In addition to speaking as though God is temporally greater than anything with a beginning, Augustine uses phrases which impute existence in the present to God. Having said that nothing passes in the Eternal, he asserts that 'the whole is present' to it. In some sense, 'presentness' must be applicable to God, who is 'from eternity' and has knowledge of all things. Must God, as knower, not be present *at the same time as* the objects of his knowledge, at least as they are known to him? I suppose Augustine's argument would be that, if time is a relation between changing objects, a wholly unchanging object, though in some sense co-present with its knowledge, its intentions and its actions, would yet be timeless. If God is simple, then co-presence may be denied, since there are no parts in God, even conceptually, to be co-present. But this confirms the suspicion that an eternal God is wholly beyond our conceptual comprehension. One might expect that much of God would be incomprehensible to us; but holding that he is completely incomprehensible is in marked tension with our claims to speak comprehensibly of him at all.

Suppose, however, that we grant Augustine his slightly contentious definition of time. What he wants to say of God is that he is wholly changeless and yet that he knows, intends and creates all things other than himself. The second puzzle now comes to the fore—how can a being create a changing world without himself changing? Normal cases of creation, of bringing into being something that did not previously exist, imply a change in the agent as well as in some object. If I compose a tune that has never existed before, I change the world by constructing a sequence of sounds which has not, so far as anyone knows, previously existed. In doing so, I also change myself in at least two ways. I exert mental effort in a way I have not previously exerted it, so that my mental state changes by activity. And I come to apprehend a tune as existing in reality I had not previously apprehended in that way, so that my mental state changes by the addition of new experienced data.

If God creates the universe, he brings into existence something which has not previously existed. Since he creates everything other than himself, he creates *ex nihilo*: there is nothing other than himself out of which he creates the universe. Nor does he make it out of his own substance, which is non-material and non-temporal. He simply causes it to be, when previously it was not. This word 'previously' threatens trouble. But it can be construed satisfactorily by saying that God causes a sequence of changes to be. Time is the relation, T, which obtains between the members of this sequence, which has a first member. That first member is related by T to events after it; but is not related by T to anything before it, since there are no events before it. Saying that the sequence has not previously existed amounts to saying that there is a first member of the sequence; and that the sequence has never been repeated. It is not saying that there was a time before time began. As Augustine puts it succinctly, 'No time passed before the world, because no creature was made by whose course it might pass' (Ch. 6).

God does not create the world in time; he creates time, and with it, all the events which are related by it. So Augustine's main problem disappears, of why God made the world when he did. He did not create it at any time. He created time; and it is senseless to ask when time was created, or what happened before it. Time is a finite created sequence of changes; and it is created by a being who is wholly changeless, and therefore beyond time, in the sense defined.

But must God not change by the mental activity of creating and by the new mental state of now apprehending what previously did not exist? Augustine accepts that we think about things, plan them and then bring them about, in a temporal sequence. But he proposes that for God, 'all that ever He created was in His unchanged fixed will eternally one and the same' (Ch. 17). God does not run over new plans in his mind, or make new and surprising decisions. As God is changeless, so 'the will of God belongs to his very substance' (*Confessions* 11), and is incapable of change. I may create things one after another, by great effort and after much hesitation and many false starts. But 'eternity, ever standing still, neither past nor to come, utters the times past and to come' (*Confessions* 11). The changing world flows from an unchanging God, and causes no change in him. Nor does his knowledge change as a result of its existence; for he always knew exactly and in every detail what it was to be. Its real existence never lies in God's future; but lies before him perfectly in his changeless present.

We are not to think of God as becoming lonely and deciding to create a universe. God never becomes what he is not already; so the creation is eternally and changelessly fixed in the Divine will. It follows that creation, in Augustine's sense, is wholly misunderstood if it is taken to be an act of God at the beginning of the universe, as though it was itself a sort of first event or act. 'Creation' signifies that a finite sequence of changes, taken both as a whole and in every part, is entirely dependent upon the fixed intention of a changeless and causally independent being. Aquinas points out that the word 'creation' is often taken to refer to the beginning of time; but in fact God's continually conserving activity is needed for the existence of all things; and the distinction between creation, in this sense, and conservation, is a conceptual, not a real one. (*Summa Theologiae* 1a, 45, 3).

How are we to understand this relation of causal dependence between the world and God? Kant argued that causality is a category which loses any content if the cause has no temporal relation to its effect. He did not argue that causes must precede their effects in time; they may be simultaneous; but at least there must be some temporal relation between them.(*Critik der Reinen Vernunft, Zweite Analogie*). For Augustine, God as cause does not exist before, after or at the same time as the universe or anything in it. In what sense, then, can the universe *depend* on God? Perhaps one can distinguish the idea of (a) 'that which exists, and would exist whatever else were the case, without dependence upon any other thing', from the idea of (b) 'that which exists, but would not exist without some other thing, which exists only if that other thing exists'. If one allows the former idea its full force, it provides the idea of a 'necessary being', in a stronger sense than that commonly used by Aquinas, of a being not liable to corruption. A being which would exist whatever else is the case is a being which exists in every possible world. There is thus no alternative to its existence. It could not have been different in nature; nor could it have failed to exist.

It has been commonly said, since David Hume made the point, that anything whatsoever may or may not exist. A thing may be wholly independent of any other thing; and yet it might have been non-existent. This is the world of Hume's supposed atomism, in which everything is discrete and independent of everything else; but in which absolutely anything may happen or not happen. In this world, each thing may exist whatever else is the case; but it may itself have been different or non-existent. No members of type (a) exist, since nothing *would* exist whatever else is the case; each thing may or may not exist. But there are no members of type (b) either, since nothing depends for its existence on anything else.

Augustine's world is different. It is a world in which some things cannot exist without others; in fact, in which all things but God cannot exist without God. What is the nature of this 'cannot'? It is not formal logical entailment—what is sometimes these days called 'necessity *de dicto*'—since I can say that things exist without God without apparent formal contradiction. It must be a real necessity—necessity *de re*—which obtains between elements of the world, not primarily of language. In Hume's world, there are no real necessary connections. In Kant's world, there are necessary connections, but only within the space–time world of humanly perceptible phenomena. In Augustine's world, as in that of most classical theologians, there are necessary connections between things as they are.

Are these all possible worlds? And if so, which one is ours? The oddity is that within each of them the others are declared to be impossible, not just non-actual. Hume will say that there *cannot* be necessary connections. Augustine will say that things *cannot* just happen to exist for no reason. Kant will say that we *cannot* speak of things in themselves. Hume's argument is that it is unintelligible to speak of necessary connections. One cannot see how one thing could be necessarily connected to another; and one can always think one thing without the other. What I can think can exist; therefore no connection can be truly necessary. Augustine's argument would be that it is unintelligible to deny necessary connections; for then there would be no reason why anything should be as it is. Anything could happen; and we could never be sure of understanding the world at all. But the world is rationally ordered.

The basic premises underlying both these views are disputable. It is not necessarily true that 'what I think can exist' (I can say that 'some things I can think cannot exist' without contradiction). From Augustine's point of view, I may think of, say, a carrot existing entirely on its own, with nothing else in the universe. But if I do so, I am thinking of the carrot confusedly and imperfectly. As Aquinas would argue, we can define a carrot without reference to its cause (admittedly he does not speak specifically of carrots); but in fact carrots 'share in' existence (*participant esse*). They only exist by participating in sheer existence subsisting of its very nature (*ipsum esse per se subsistens*) (*Summa Theologiae* 1a, 44, 1). Carrots have no power of existing by themselves; they essentially receive existence from that which is existent of itself alone. If I comprehend this, which it may be beyond human capacity to do fully, then even a properly conceived carrot does entail the concept of that which exists of itself alone, in the fullest sense (*perfectissime*). Thus I may think of a solitary cosmic carrot (my thought being imperfect, unknown to me) and yet such a carrot really could not exist.

But from Hume's point of view, it is not necessarily true that all existent things must receive existence from *esse per se subsistens*. Indeed, such a notion may itself be incoherent. It is easy to deny that such a difficult idea has content. To say a carrot exists is just to say that it is located in space and time. There is no receiving or participating in a mysterious quasi-property of '*esse*'.

John Findlay made the claim, in a much-quoted article, that all existential propositions are contingently true. It is not so often mentioned that he later renounced this view. The reason for his former claim was the Humean point that we just cannot see what sort of connection could be necessarily true, except the strictly deductive one where the alternative is a self-contradiction. As Kant remarked, the concept of real necessity is a veritable abyss of thought. But the logical nemesis of the Humean view is that it is not necessarily false (it is not self-contradictory to say) that some propositions are such that they are true in every possible world, even though they can be denied without contradiction. So it may be the case that some existential propositions are necessarily true. But what, we might ask, could *make* them true? The defender of real necessary truths does not have to be able to answer this question, any more than anyone can say what makes any contingent proposition true. Still, a contingent proposition just happens to be true; there is no reason why it is true; so nothing has to make it true. It may be thought that a necessary proposition cannot just happen to be true; there must be a reason which determines its truth. Most Rationalist philosophers have accepted this point, and have embraced the principle of sufficient reason in some form (even Kant embraced it, only restricting it to the phenomenal world. For him, what determines necessity is the transcendental self; though he leaves teasingly unanswered the question of what determines the necessity of its constitution). All facts are determined by good reasons; and the process terminates in a supreme all-determining fact to which there is no alternative, the exhaustive substratum of all possibilities, the *Ens Realissimum*.

It is clear that the Fathers accepted such a Rationalist scheme, in general, for they held that all things necessarily depend upon God as creator. They do not just happen to depend on God, though they need not have done. Dependence is part of creaturely nature. Solitary cosmic carrots are precluded from existing because the all-inclusive principle of sufficient reason excludes the radically arbitrary. Real necessary connections and God go together; for the whole point of asserting necessary connections is lost if those connections are themselves rooted in something contingent. There would then be a reason for all events in the temporal sequence, but no reason why the sequence as such is as it is.

It is misleading to suggest that Thomas interpreted 'Divine necessity' to mean just independent and non-temporal existence, as Kenny and Swinburne claim. Certainly, Thomas speaks of necessary substances like angels and the supra-lunar spheres as ones which are not liable to corruption. But they still depend upon God, and thus are not absolutely necessary. Divine necessity is not like that. If it were, God could have been non-existent or different in nature. Thomas's idea of God, however, is of a simple, unlimited fully actual being, whose essence is his existence. His being exhausts actuality and excludes only what is not. There is thus no alternative to his existing and being what he is. Only such a God can exclude irrational carrots from appearing all over creation.

We cannot say that a Humean world and an Augustinian world are equally possible, except in the sense that we can present them as alternative conceptual frameworks for understanding the world. If Hume is right, the Augustinian world is an empty and impossible fantasy. If Augustine is right, the Humean world arises from a failure to understand how things are and necessarily have to be. This does not establish that Augustine's understanding of creation is non-vacuous. But it helps to fill out the underlying conceptual framework upon which it depends. In particular, it brings out the fact that God is not conceived as a being who as a matter of fact depends upon nothing else, but who might have been different or non-existent; who might have created no world or a different world instead of this. On the contrary, God is the fullest actuality, in which all finite things participate in some manner. 'Esse per se subsistens' could not have a different character, since it is the fullness of all possible actuality. And it could not be non-existent, without there being no such possible concept as that of such a God. It is in this sense that the so-called 'ontological argument' is in one way accepted by all those in the classical Christian tradition of theism. That is, if the concept of 'being existent of itself' is possible, then that concept is, uniquely among all concepts, instantiated in all possible worlds. What Aquinas adds, quite correctly, is that this is not actually a demonstration that God exists. For we cannot demonstrate that the concept is non-vacuous.

Creation can now be construed as the relation which holds between a necessarily existent being whose existence is the fullest actuality, not arising either from another or from nothing, but being wholly of itself; and a realm of changing, limited beings which derive their existence by ordered participation in that unoriginated One. This is not a relation between a cause and its successive or co-temporal effects. It is a relation between the Unoriginated Unchanging One and the beginning, changing many which are bounded and defined by the temporal series itself. Thus Augustine, pressing thought beyond the point at which he dares to affirm, supposes that there may be a beginningless series of created things, universe succeeding universe (Ch. 19), *saecula saeculorum*.

He denies the neo-Platonic and Vedantic speculation that the universe repeats itself infinitely, on the ground that liberated souls are freed for endless life in God, without any return to worldly misery. But, accepting what he takes to be the Biblical view that this universe has a beginning, he has no philosophical difficulty in thinking that there may be an endless number of others before and after it. Even so, he declares, 'Time, being transitory and mutable, cannot be co-eternal with unchanging eternity' (Ch. 15). God might have always had creatures to be Lord over; yet all would be created out of nothing, not co-eternal with Him. Time and eternity are entirely diverse in nature; the former depends wholly upon the latter, which remains unchanged by even an infinite sequence of temporal universes. Aquinas, too, had no theoretical difficulty with the idea that time might always have existed. He held that Christians believe that time began simply on the basis of Biblical revelation (*Summa Theologiae* 1a.46.2).

Why would such a God, to whom the universe makes no difference, create? One answer would be that, since God is immutable, he never had the opportunity to do anything else. It is in his nature to create the universe; and that nature cannot be changed (cannot logically be changed, if time is necessary for change, and God is not in time). But what Augustine actually says is rather more positive. 'He needed none of these creatures, but created them of His pure goodness, having continued no less blessed without them, from all unbegun eternity' (Ch. 17). God does not create because it will change him in any way, for better or worse. It will not; what happens in the world will change God not at all. Because he is good, he creates a world that is good. It is an overflowing of his essential goodness; a series of partial manifestations or reflections of his own unlimited perfection.

What is the difference between a necessary emanation, such as the neo-Platonist Porphyry postulated, and a free creative act, such as Christians accept? The difference, for Augustine, is not that God might or might not have created the world; or that he might have created it very differently; or that he may respond to what happens in it in a personal way. God, being wholly immutable, had to create precisely this world, and he cannot respond to what happens in it in any way not already determined in his eternal being. The difference is twofold—that the world is positively good (not, as neo-Platonists tended to think, some sort of punishment for ignorance or past evil); and that it is in accordance with the desire and will of an all-knowing being. The world does not overflow by mistake, with the ultimately real not knowing about it or even regretting it. The world originates by desire and with conscious purpose—the purpose that some creatures at least should possess endless joy.

Augustine has constructed a remarkable intellectual vision which seems coherent and profound. But few Christian philosophers today are happy with it. One reason can be found by further analysis of the proposed relations between the eternal and temporal, the necessary and the contingent, the immutable and the mutable which are entailed by Augustine's account.

In one way, Augustine has resolved the problem of evil completely. For if the world is necessarily entailed by the changeless existence of God, he cannot be held blameworthy for anything. One will just have to accept that things are necessarily what they are. But in another way, he forces himself into an insoluble dilemma. He holds that God creates the world because it is good. Yet he not only sees how much suffering there is in the world; he compounds it by believing that most people are destined for eternal torment. This is where most contemporary theologians draw back. If things are necessarily as they are, how can such torment be just and such a world good? Augustine replies: 'Punishment falls justly upon those acts which are wills and not necessities' (8).

Distinguishing between the natures of angels and men, which are created and remain good, and their wills, he holds that the will can perversely prefer a lesser to a greater good. There is no cause for this outside the will itself: 'Seek the cause of this evil will, and you shall find just none' (6). He does not mean that the wills are arbitrary or wholly random causeless phenomena. He means that there is no cause in the universe outside the will which determines it to decide as it does. It is itself the only cause of its decision for good or evil. So it bears sole responsibility for the consequences of its choice. Such irrationally evil wills deserve punishment, for turning away from God to their own selfish good. God knows their turning and their end; but knows also that he will bring good out of their choice, for the universe as a whole. The world is good, then, because in it many will be brought to supreme joy; because even out of evil much good will be brought; and because evil wills are justly punished. All this, besides the moral questionableness of the doctrine of endless torment, focusses attention on the idea of *a will, not a necessity*, which may be justly punished for its choice. Can

Augustine legitimately make such a distinction, given his belief that the whole world flows from the immutable and necessary being of God? The argument can be set out as follows:

(a) God is immutable; so he cannot do other than he does. Moreover, as perfect actuality, God could not have been other than he is. So God could not have done other than he does.
(b) All temporal events are caused by God.
(c) Therefore no temporal event could have been other than it is.
(d) Acts of willing are temporal events, even though not causally determined by any other temporal event.
(e) Therefore all acts of will are necessarily what they are.

Of course one can distinguish between events which are causally determined by other events, and events not so determined, or which are determined by desires of the agents, and call the latter 'free'. It is clear, however, that free events are causally determined by God, even if they are in accordance with the desires of the agent. Why should an act of will be justly punished, if it is determined by God and not, secondarily, by any other event? The point of Augustine's argument is surely that one should only be punished for what one is solely responsible for. That is why acts of will can have no external physical cause, which would pass on at least part of the responsibility. But it turns out that they all have a cause external to the will itself; namely, the eternal decision of God.

It is no use saying that God can create a will so that it is free to choose either x or y. For if choice is made of x, many events will follow which will be quite different from those which would follow from the choice of y. God has to bring all those subsequent events into being. So if he left the choice truly undetermined, he would have to let his subsequent creation depend upon some creaturely act. That he cannot do, since he is unaffected by creatures in any way, being wholly immutable.

It is no use saying that God can leave the will indeterminate, and yet foreknow how it will choose, and act accordingly. Such foreknowledge would still be a knowledge caused by some creaturely act. Augustine says, 'The creatures also do they (the angels) know better in the wisdom of God, the workman's draft, than in the things produced' (11.29). God does not wait until things actually exist in order to know them; but he causes them to exist as a result of his changeless knowledge: 'He saw that what He had made was good, because He foresaw that He should make it good' (11.21). There is no escaping the conclusion that God wills to bring into existence finite wills, angelic and human, which he necessitates to choose evil, by their non-finitely caused acts. Contemporary theologians tend to recoil from this double outrage, as it seems to them, of determining a will to make a choice which is then punished eternally. God cannot help it, being necessarily what he is. But few will call such a God 'just' as readily as Augustine did.

The simplest way to mitigate the outrage is to take the course that Origen and Gregory of Nyssa took, and guarantee final salvation and unending bliss to all. The combination of Divine necessity; the possession of full, perfect and supremely desirable reality by God; and a guarantee of final universal bliss may indeed convince even Ivan Karamazov that his ticket is non-returnable, that moral outrage is misdirected, and that life's journey will lead out of despair. And there we might happily leave the matter, if it were not for the nagging suspicion that Augustine has touched on something of fundamental importance in his distinction between 'will' and 'nature', between 'choice' and 'necessity', however unsatisfactory his treatment of it may be. Is there not, after all, more to be said about human malice and evil than that it is inevitable? Is there not more to be said about Divine judgment and mercy than that they are necessary attributes of a being who cannot be other than he is? Are there no deeper senses of divine and human freedom than this?

Contemporary Christian philosophers tend to place a much greater emphasis on Divine and human freedom than Augustine and Aquinas did. And it seems that the concept of the wholly immutable God which the classical tradition developed does not find much support in the Bible. One of the central strands of Hebrew theism is the prophetic declaration of the judgment of God on human sin. We might like the idea of a purely non-judgmental and reformative attitude to evil-doing, which arises from the acceptance that sin is a necessary part of how things are. But the Biblical God does not have such an attitude. He declares that sin will be punished to the third and fourth generation. The notion of moral retribution—and of reward for good works—is a marked feature of the Biblical writings. It eventually gave rise to belief in resurrection, when the due consequences of one's earthly actions can be properly worked out. The prophetic call is for repentance and trust in God. That implies a stress on choice, on acceptance of responsibility for one's actions, and on a belief that one should, and therefore could, have done otherwise, with which necessitarian views find it hard to cope.

God himself is spoken of as responding to human choices. He promises judgment on Nineveh; but changes his mind when the people repent. He vows to destroy the Israelites; but changes his mind in response to Moses' prayer. Again and again he gives conditional promises to his people—'If you repent, I will be merciful'. The natural way to take all this is to say that some of God's actions, in judgment and mercy, are dependent upon human choices. The church Fathers offer a very sophisticated account of it, requiring almost all such talk of God to be metaphorical and in need of drastic philosophical re-interpretation. It is ironic that they placed such a high reliance on the authority of scripture, while feeling free to re-interpret it so radically with regard to God, if not in regard to history. Nor is it only Christians who have done this. Maimonides is, if anything, even more ready to take all Biblical language about God as literally false, explicitly holding that every positive statement about God must be denied.

Suppose, however, that we posit finite choices which are not determined by God, which he leaves truly indeterminate, what might follow for an account of creation? Most obviously, each choice will open a set of alternative futures; and the set of alternatives will multiply exponentially, as further choices of many different creatures arise. These alternatives are 'open', in that God, at the moment of creating the first choice, cannot have determined which of them will exist. God may know what all the alternative possibilities are; but he cannot know, in advance of finite choices being made, which alternatives will be actual. It may be said that he can *foreknow* which will be actual. But, if the choices are truly undetermined by him, that foreknowledge will depend upon what the creatures decide. God will be passible, in that his knowledge will be partly determined—as to which possibles are actual in this universe—by the acts of creatures.

Further, since God cannot decide what further events to create until he knows which world-line has been actualized, he cannot be said to create the whole universe in a single non-temporal act. He will first have to create a choosing will; then see what it chooses; and only then can he create the next segment of the actualizing world. God's creative action will be continually responsive to creatures; it must therefore have an internal successiveness, in which he does one thing after another.

God can only foreknow x if x will actually be the case; and this is determined by the choice of P, where P is some finite will. God can predetermine his response to x, as foreknown by him; so one might suppose that God could still foreknow and decide upon the whole state of the universe before he brings it into being. But what God cannot do is to envisage a possible, but non-actual, universe in which P chooses x, and decide to create *that* universe in view of the choices which he foresees being made in it.

One may argue thus: God can create any possible universe. There is a possible universe in which P chooses x. Therefore God can create that universe. This argument is used by J. L. Mackie to support his view that God could, and should, create the universe in which all free agents always make good choices. But it does not work. For the fuller description of the universe in question is that, in it, P *freely* (i.e. not determined by God) chooses x. That is a possible universe; but it is not a possible universe that God can wholly determine of himself. Then we would have the contradiction that God determines wholly a universe in which some things are not determined by God; i.e. there is some event which God both does and does not determine.

So there are many apparently possible universes that God cannot create, since creating them would be self-contradictory. He cannot wholly determine any universe in which some events are free (i.e. not wholly determined). He can, of course, create any universe in which there are free agents; but he cannot know, before they choose, which of the alternatives he places before them they will choose. He can thus only foreknow such a universe as about to be actual if it will actually exist. And that cannot be wholly within his power of choice.

One may wonder now if the concept of foreknowledge has any point, apart from a desire to cling to a specific philosophical interpretation of the term 'omniscience'. In Augustine's scheme God's foreknowledge did not depend on any creaturely act, and could not be changed by any such act. But on this scheme, his foreknowledge depends logically upon free creaturely choices having occurred. Further, his creation of succeeding states of that universe depends upon his dependent knowledge; so his foreknowledge of what he himself is going to do is dependent upon creaturely acts. God must now logically be conceived as having successive states of knowledge and action in his own being; a primal state of causally independent knowledge and a successive series of states, each of which causally depends upon the others. To speak of God foreknowing will involve the idea of backward causation, from a future event to a past knowing of it. But it will also entail that there is some state of God in which he cannot know as actual something that will be actual—namely, the primal state which is wholly independent, and therefore cannot include any causally dependent knowledge, resulting from creaturely acts and his responses to them. When one has to attribute successive states of increasing knowledge to God, there may well seem to be no merit in placing all these states before the beginning of time (with all the difficulties of backward causation that involves) as opposed to accepting that Divine knowledge increases co-temporally with the sequence of created temporal states.

Does this limit God by making him at some time ignorant of future facts and by making him increase in knowledge, and thus presumably evolve from worse to better? It is no limitation if one accepts the premise that future contingents are not actual. One can then say that God knows as possible everything that is possible and as actual everything that is actual. Clearly, then, he knows all possible futures; but at many times he does not know as actual what is not actual. That is no defect. The increase of knowledge which consists in knowing more facts as actual when more of them are actual is not an increase in the perfection of knowledge, which consists in knowing everything actual at every time. Nor does it attribute imperfection to earlier states of God, when he knew fewer facts as actual, because fewer were actual.

This beginning from free creaturely acts thus results in making God possess temporal attributes, in making him passible and successive in many respects. There is no reason, however, why this should be thought to deprive him of power, as though the future might get out of his control. It is true that many free creaturely acts will create many openly possible futures. But the nature of those possible states can remain wholly under Divine control. God always lays down the alternatives between which free creatures can choose. It is even true that a large aggregate of unpredictable choices may result in a perfectly predictable outcome, as any competent statistician could show. So there need be no fear that such a God will be unacceptably limited by the world; that he may be at its mercy or restricted by it in creative power. Indeed, it may plausibly be argued that God's creative power is enhanced by giving him the capacity to create autonomous agents and to bring about an infinite number of genuinely new states of being. Augustine's God, after all, has no alternatives; he does what he has to do. Is this a greater power than the possession of a capacity to act in ways which are not determined by necessity, to be radically and creatively free?

A temporal view of God adds a powerful argument to theodicy; in the form of the 'free-will defence' it suggests some reasons for the presence of much suffering in the world. However, it also seems to deprive Augustine's theodicy of its main advantage—namely, that God cannot help creating this world. If we now have a temporal God, who is presumably free to choose between many possible worlds, why should he choose this one, wherein the possession of freedom, while making some suffering comprehensible, may not be considered to be worth the degree and amount of suffering it seems to involve? Give God truly radical freedom, and the existence of any world with great suffering in it, if there are alternatives, becomes so much harder to justify. It is natural to see if one can get the best of both worlds, and find a way of holding both necessity and freedom together in God. It is imperative to do so, if one wishes to hold, with the classical tradition, that God is necessarily wise, powerful and good, the creator of all things; while considerations of moral freedom lead one to ascribe contingency and temporality to him.

The admission of contingency in God complicates the account of necessary connections in nature already given. For that account employed a version of the principle of sufficient reason, which is a principle of complete determinism. Given the cause, no other effect can exist. The complication is, however, quite a small and simple one. One says that there is a being which necessarily exists as a plenitude of infinite reality. But, since contingent worlds are logically possible, that being also possesses the capacity contingently to create them. God will be the necessary cause of any universe, but not the sufficient cause of any. He will determine, of necessity, many features of any universe he creates, in accordance with the exemplars existing in his own necessary being. But he will not so determine all features, thus allowing creaturely freedom to exist. We can now say that there are necessary connections in the world (and in any possible world), determined to be what they are by the exhaustive reality of the Divine being. But not all connections are necessary; many of them will take the form of processes conditional upon contingent acts, and will terminate in subsequent occasions of finite or Divine creativity. So there can be a place for freedom in a largely determined universe. And if for freedom, there can also be a place for chance, for the indeterminacy which allows the possiblity of subsequent freedom, in the course of evolution. That chance will operate within clearly limited parameters, and thus it is possible for necessity and contingency to live together both in God and in any world he creates.

So in response to the problem of evil, which threatens the doctrine of the goodness of creation, it is possible to combine the defence of necessity and defence of free-will in one coherent account, by supposing that God may choose to create a particular world freely; but will be limited in any creation by necessities internal to and rooted in his own immutable being. This also provides a powerful reason for creation, which is not available to anyone who thinks that the world makes no difference to God. This account can say, not only that God expresses his own being in creation; not only that he creates other subjects who can share in his goodness; but that he himself will realize new and emergent sorts of good, by relation to finite and free creatures, which would not otherwise exist. The Christian revelation might further suggest that not only does God respond to the acts of his rational creatures; but he brings them into the unity of his own being, as finally liberated souls whose destiny is to become one in Christ. That would make God passible in the sense that he can even include creatures within his own temporal being.

Moreover, creation can be viewed, not just as a sort of necessary overflow from the Divine plenitude, which leaves God quite unchanged, but a continual creative and dynamic exercise of the divine imagination. More truly like a creative artist than the classical tradition allows, God can be seen as continually seeking to realize new forms of beauty and order; so creation becomes the exercise of unlimited potency. Ironically, we can call in support of this view precisely the same text that Aquinas appeals to in support of his—'I am that I am'. For now we know that a better translation of this obscure Hebrew phrase *Ayeh asher ayeh* would be, 'I will become whatever I will become'. Theodicy becomes even stronger if we add that God, as essentially a supremely imaginative creator and a source of dynamic love which seeks to relate to others, necessarily creates some universe or other; that none is without the possibility of evil similar in general respects to what we find in this universe; and that the goods of each possible universe are distinctive and unique. But it may be enough to say that God necessarily *can* create a universe, though he need not create any, since he will choose one on the ground of its unique sorts of goodness anyway. Either way, once we concede necessity *de re* at all, we have the makings of a coherent account of how a necessarily perfect God, possessing the maximal power that a perfect being can possess, can create a world like this.

The key question for the classical view is whether contingent states are factually possible (possible *de re*). We might hazard the supposition that it is a richer reality which includes contingent as well as necessary states. Thomas himself appeals to such a principle of plenitude in 1a.19. But although Aquinas wishes to distinguish between necessary states and contingent states, his doctrine that God is necessary, simple and immutable, the creator of all things, entails that everything that is created must be as it is. Whatever a wholly necessary being causes must itself be necessary. Aquinas tries to resist this conclusion; and he deploys a bewildering number of senses of 'necessity'. At 1a.19.3 he raises the question of whether God is bound to will whatever he does will. In replying, he makes a distinction between absolute necessity and necessity '*ex suppositione*'. The former he defines as expressed in propositions in which the predicate is entailed in the definition of the subject. A proposition is absolutely necessary if the meaning of one term is part of the meaning of the other. In this sense, God does not will the world by absolute necessity, since the meaning of the term 'God' does not entail the meaning of the term 'world'. God wills his own goodness necessarily, since 'the will' is defined as a tendency to seek the good, and God's will is identical with his nature. But he wills the world with only hypothetical necessity—if he wills it, it cannot be unwilled.

The idea is that God's complete goodness can exist without the world. The concept of the former does not entail the concept of the latter. However, Thomas gets into deep trouble when he says, 'As the divine existing is essentially necessary, so also is the divine knowing and the divine willing'. The divine knowing is of things as they exist in God—he knows all things in his own being. But this must include, of the things he actually wills to exist, that they do actually exist. He must therefore know changelessly what he wills to exist. So if it is true that, 'whatever God knows he knows of necessity', he must know of necessity what he wills to exist. Can it be true that it is not the case that he wills of necessity whatever he wills? We would then have: necessarily, God knows that he wills p; but not necessarily he wills p. Can God know of necessity what he wills contingently? It may be necessarily true that he knows whatever he wills. That is, he will necessarily know whatever he wills, when he has willed it. But it cannot be necessarily true that he knows he wills p, when he does not necessarily will p. For that necessity will be conditional upon his willing p, which is not necessary. It will be necessary *ex suppositione*. But God's willing and his knowing are identical; so one cannot be conditional upon the other. It looks as though the doctrine of Divine simplicity compels us to ascribe the same sort of necessity to God's willing as to his knowing, and so to say, against Thomas, that it could not have been other than it is.

God, being necessarily what he is, and containing no distinctions, must necessarily do whatever he does. This is necessity *de re*, necessity determined by the immutable Divine will, which is identical with the Divine nature. Thomas nevertheless wishes to say that the creation of the universe is contingent, in the sense that it is not *logically* necessary. There are logically possible alternative universes (including the possibility of no created universe at all).

If by 'logical possibility', one means: what can be stated without apparent self-contradiction, then indeed it seems that many states are logically but not really possible—for instance, the existence of an uncreated universe, or the non-existence of God. But, for Thomas, is this not just because we are unable to conceive the nature of things correctly? Does it not belong to the nature of creatures, fully understood, that their existence is derived from another? Does it not belong to the nature of God, if we could understand it, that his essence is identical with his existence, so that if he is possible he must exist, and be in all respects exactly what he is? Our logical possibilities, then, depend upon our imperfect apprehension. To a perfectly intelligent being they would dissolve. For instance, every truth about an apparently alternative universe would in fact contradict the truth that it belongs to the nature of any universe to be created by a God whose nature, being essentially unalterable, could not have done other than it does.

Logical possibilities, as we understand them, are formulations due to the imperfection of our intellects. The *de re* and the *logical* coalesce for any perfect understanding. So, in what we may term a Divine or fully understood sense of logical possibility (one understood by God), nothing other than what actually exists is logically possible. Though God creates a world that seems to us to be one logical possibility among others, there is nothing that God could do other than what he does. This is a rigorous and subtle doctrine; but it may be doubted whether it captures the sense of Divine freedom that is so strong in the Bible, or whether it can adequately cope with the Christian belief that God was free to create or not to create any world he chose.

Suppose, however, that we admit the real possibility of alternative and mutually exclusive contingent worlds. Then God may still be, as the classical tradition supposes, a uniquely perfect actualization of value. What is necessarily true of him is immutable (true in every possible world and state). Many things are necessarily true of him—his existence, his possession of unrestricted intelligence and bliss, and his conception of all possible worlds, which, as possible, exist immutably and necessarily in him. Nothing can exist which is incompatible with his being and nature. But a number (perhaps an infinite number) of contingent worlds are really possible; or logically possible in the 'Divine' sense that they are each compatible with the necessary existence of God but not compatible with each other.

The following simple argument, using the Divine sense of logical possibility, can then be constructed:

1. If x is logically possible, then it is necessarily true that x is logically possible. (Axiom)
2. No logically necessary truth is incompatible with any other. (Def.)
3. It is logically possible that a set of exclusively disjunctive states $(1-n)$ exists.
4. All contingent propositions exclude some others (minimally, their contradictories). (Def.)
5. It is necessarily true that $(1-n)$ is logically possible. (From 1 and 3)
6. God can do whatever is logically possible. (Axiom)
7. It is necessarily true that God can bring about $(1-n)$. (From 5 and 6)
8. If God creates 1, this excludes him creating all the members of $(1-n)$. (From 4 and 7)
9. It is not logically necessary that God creates 1. (From 2 and 8)
10. It is necessarily true that God can perform some contingent acts. (From 7 and 9)

To put it more briefly, if contingent worlds are really possible, God can create them; and therefore he can, necessarily, perform some contingent acts. If a contingent world is possible, it is necessarily possible. Then a God who lacks contingency lacks some necessary property. The proposition Thomas would have to dispute would be 3. He might say that contingent worlds are not logically possible; or that they may be logically possible, but they are not really possible; so that God may be logically able to bring them about, but he cannot in fact do so, being what he is. There is certainly room for argument here; but my inclination is to say that it cannot be demonstrated that anything excludes the existence of contingent worlds. So far as reason goes, we have to choose between making God absolutely necessary in every respect, and allowing alternative possible worlds. It looks as though we can coherently say that God is the subject of many necessarily true propositions; in fact that in some sense he is the subject of all necessarily true propositions. But this might actually entail that he is also the subject of some truly contingent propositions.

The point might be put by distinguishing two senses of 'contingent'. Augustine's God is contingent in some respects in·the sense that, though he cannot now do other than he does, there was a logically possible alternative to some of his acts (he need not have created this world). But a God who is temporal as well as eternal can be contingent in the stronger sense that he is at some time actually in a state when he can (when it is possible for him to) choose one of many alternative possibilities. If it is ever true of God that he can choose A or B, then two incompatible statements will be true of God—first, that he can choose A; and second, that he cannot choose A (because he has chosen B, and A and B are incompatible.). This incompatibility can only be resolved by introducing temporality into God; so that real choice between alternatives logically requires temporality. The classical tradition has to deny this sense of 'strong contingency'. But, as I have pointed out, even weak contingency must then really be denied of God, as being founded upon imperfect knowledge. A more elegant choice is to admit temporality and contingency into the Divine being, and thus qualify the classical view that God's being is necessary in every respect.

This account also allows of a more satisfactory notion of omnipotence than the classical idea that God cannot do anything other than he actually does. We can ascribe to God a dynamic and creative power, capable of an infinite number of new actions. An omnipotent being, we might say, is one that is capable of doing anything that a maximally perfect being can possibly do. If we suppose that such a being could possibly create any one of a disjunctive class of possible worlds, then any necessarily omnipotent being will be contingent in some respects. God will be immutable in everything that is necessarily true of him— including his capability of free creative action. The exercise of that capability, the consequent dependent knowledge he will accrue and the causal changes he will make in response, will all be contingent.

God will thus have some immutable knowledge and some mutable knowledge; he will be changeless in eternal bliss and changing by participating in the sorrow of creation. There is no more contradiction in this than in accepting that I always know that $2+2=4$, while I keep learning and forgetting the details of Godel's theorem. Or we might say that I know what sensations I am having in one way, and I know the truth of Godel's theorem in another. There is little difficulty in one being possessing two such different types of knowledge. Is it the *same* God who knows some things changelessly and others mutably, who experiences changeless bliss and transient sorrow? Yes; because it is that necessarily omnipotent God who must be capable of contingent action, and that necessarily omniscient God who must know to be true every contingent fact that is true. Any tension this view implies is surely less marked than the tension inherent in the classical doctrine of incarnation, which requires that the changeless and impassible God is identical with a being (Jesus) who changes and suffers.

If God is temporal, are we after all faced with Augustine's problem of why God created this world when he did? No; we can accept the definition of time as a relation between objects, measured by their change. But we can now speculate even more boldly than Augustine did, calling in aid the work of contemporary physicists. We can hypothesize that, as time is a relation between objects, there is no *a priori* reason why every temporal object should be temporally related to every other. There may be many times and spaces, temporally and spatially unrelated to one another. When and in so far as God is temporal, he enters into responsive interaction with these space-times; and he may so relate to many different space-times. That means God will indeed transcend time as we understand it. Must we think of him as inhabiting a super-time, in which all space-times must be located in relation to the successivity of the Divine being itself? Or can we suppose that God relates to this space-time as a whole, and relates to other space-times as a whole, though it cannot be said that he relates to us before, after or at the same time as he relates to the others?

Perhaps at this point we should repeat Augustine's words, 'This I thought to handle without affirming, that my readers may see what questions to forbear as dangerous, and not hold them fit for farther inquiry' (12.25). But at least we may see that to place God beyond our space-time, as its creator, does not entail the view that he is beyond all succession or change whatsoever. We may place God beyond the limitations and defects of time which we experience without subjecting him to the even greater defect of being unable to change, act, choose or respond. If we are to follow the Christian Fathers in affirming the ineffability of God, perhaps we should say, not that he is wholly immutable, but simply that he does not change as we do, by loss and decay. It glorifies God more to say that he is both changeless in wisdom and bliss and endlessly creative in loving response than to say that there is nothing more he can be than what he already is. At least, that is what we might expect a faith founded on belief in the incarnation of the eternal in time to say.

Foreknowledge and the Vulnerability of God

J. R. LUCAS

Elijah foretold evil for Ahab in the name of the Lord. 'I will bring evil upon you; I will utterly sweep you away, and will cut off from Ahab every male, bond or free in Israel' . . . but when he heard those words, he rent his clothes, and put sackcloth upon his flesh, and fasted and lay in the sackcloth, and went about dejectedly. And the word of the Lord came to Elijah saying 'Have you seen how Ahab has humbled himself before me? Because he has humbled himself before me, I will not bring the evil in his days, but in his son's days I will bring evil upon his house.'[1]

The natural reading is that God changed His mind. He did not speak mendaciously to Elijah the first time: rather, at that time He intended to sweep away the house of Ahab in his own lifetime so that he could appreciate his punishment, but later, in the light of his penitence, suspended part of the sentence for the remainder of his life. And He might have done more, had Ahab repented more. Suppose he had not merely fasted and put on sackcloth himself, but, besides giving back the vineyard to Naboth's heirs, had universalized the prescription, 'Let neither man nor beast, herd nor flock, taste anything; let them not feed or drink water, but let man and beast be covered with sackcloth, and let them pray mightily to God; . . . who knows God may then have repented and turned from his fierce anger, so that we perish not'.[2]

Such a possibility cannot be excluded *a priori*. In the Old Testament the story of Jonah makes the point explicitly: in the New Testament the goods news is that if we repent, we can wipe out the past, and escape the consequences of our ill-doing that would otherwise ensue. 'Unless you repent, you will all likewise perish.'[3] The clear picture is of a God who can change His mind, and is prepared to make prophecies made in His name and on His explicit commands come false.

Such a view accords with the natural reading of the Bible, preserves free will, and fits the highly human view of God that Jesus enjoins us to adopt. But it has been discountenanced by most theologians, partly on

---

[1] I Kings 21.17–24, 27–29 (RSV).
[2] Cf. Jonah 3.7–9.
[3] St Luke, 13.3, and 5.

logical, partly on the theological grounds. Logically, it has seemed impossible for an Omniscient Being not to know all truths, including those about future contingents; theologically, it has been felt to derogate from the perfection of God that He should change His mind.

I want to pursue this line of thought as it bears on the traditional issue of foreknowledge and free will. There are two problems, one a philosophical one about the logical grammar of the word 'know', the other a theological one about the nature of God.

The philosophical problem arises from our being over-scrupulous in the use of the word 'know'. In ordinary usage we can speak of knowing propositions about the future and many other dubious things, but under pressure from philosophers we tighten up our standards for knowledge until it is inappropriate to claim to know anything that might conceivably be wrong. Plato, Descartes, Locke, and in our own time A. J. Ayer, have been telling us that we do not really know all sorts of things we thought we did, but only probably believe them. I cannot know that Bush is President of the United States, because it is conceivable that in the last hour he has died of a heart attack, and Quayle has been sworn in instead. Such a line of argument is very attractive, particularly to the young, for shaking people out of confident complacency, but it is essentially introducing a new use of the word 'know'. Although it is incorrect, in ordinary parlance, to say 'I know that Senor Fanfani is President of Peru, but I may well be wrong', it is not incorrect to say 'I know that Bush is President of the United States', while admitting that I could conceivably be wrong. Plato's argument for the infallibility of knowledge is not an exegesis of ordinary usage, but a stipulation of a different sense of the word, what I shall call 'philosophical knowledge'. We cannot philosophically know anything that might conceivably be untrue, and so cannot philosophically know future contingent propositions. Not even God can philosophically know future contingent propositions, but this is no more a derogation of his Omniscience that His inability to know false propositions. Omniscience cannot mean knowing everything, but only knowing all there is to be known. And future contingent propositions are not there to be philosophically known, any more than false ones are.

Ordinary knowledge is, *pace* the philosophers, fallible. You knew I was going to be lecturing here today. But you could have been wrong. I might have got ill. I might have been murdered by an IRA terrorist. I might have become an Existentialist, and set off for Paris to begin a new, more authentic life there as an art critic or novelist. If this had happened, then you would have had to withdraw your previous claim to knowledge, and say 'I thought I knew, but I was wrong: he did not turn up but had gone mooching off to Paris, leaving us all in the lurch'. Provided I do turn up, you knew all along that I would, but if I had not, your perfectly reasonable claims to knowledge would be subject to retrospective withdrawal. Ordinary knowledge is in this sense defeasible. I have it in my power to alter what was the case in so far as your knowledge about my future actions is in issue. Up until the moment I begin to lecture, I can change my mind and decide not to. Although you are quite entitled to put forward knowledge claims about my future action, and say that you know that I shall be here, that I shall not start beating my wife, going gay in San Francisco, or setting up an art exhibition on the Left Bank, each one of those has an implicitly understood proviso attached—so long as I do not change my mind. There is no incompatibility, therefore, between ordinary foreknowledge and human free will. We regularly foreknow our own actions and those of others: life would be impossible if we could not say where we were going to have lunch, and know where others were to be at certain future times. But because this knowledge is subject to a proviso, it does not foreclose the freedom of the will. There is an escape clause, which acknowledges our continuing freedom to change our mind, and make what had seemed to be foreknowledge only mistaken, though well-grounded, opinion. We retain our ultimate freedom of action because the foreknowledge of what we shall do, however well-warranted, remains fallible and can be falsified in the event.

In the case of divine foreknowledge, such a let-out has seemed unavailable, because it seems to derogate from the perfection of God. If God foreknew that Ahab was coming to a sticky end, and then Ahab repented and escaped the fate that awaited him, we should have to say then that God had been mistaken in His foreknowledge, *quod*, says Boethius, *nefas judico*, I reckon a blasphemy.[4] But to be a blasphemy, it must impute a gratuitous imperfection to God, and the fallibility of ordinary, as opposed to philosophical, knowledge is inherent in the concept of ordinary knowing, not a gratuitous failure on the part of God. If we stipulate that it is conceptually impossible for God to be contaminated by fallibility, then we are saying that it is conceptually impossible for God to have ordinary, as opposed to philosophical, knowledge. God cannot know where I am going to have lunch, because the only sort of knowledge God can have is infallible, philosophical knowledge, and there can be no such knowledge of future contingents. By making more stringent the standards for divine knowledge, we restrict its range, and make God less, not more, knowledgeable. It is much the same as with power. It we insist that everything God tries to bring about must surely happen, we restrict the operation of the Holy Spirit, which works through human agents, and depends essentially on

---

[4] Boethius, *Consolations of Philosophy*, V, 3, ll.6–16; cf. St Augustine, *De Libero Arbitrio*, III, 2, 4; *City of God*, Bk. V, Ch. 9.

human co-operation. Many designated Jeremiahs have declined the office of speaking out the truth, because they were too young, too busy, too frightened, or had not been to the right school. Less spectacularly, we have all on occasion failed to do God's will. It is right on such occasions to say that God's will has not been accomplished as originally intended. To make out that since it was not accomplished, it cannot have been intended, is to deny that God could ever work through the willing co-operation of human agents, and thus once again to confine the power of the Deity to DIY jobs. If God, or any one of us, is to be able to work through the agency of other autonomous agents, it is inherent in the whole endeavour that the others may refuse to play, and He, or we, will be unsuccessful. But to say that we can never undertake anything unless we can be sure of succeeding is to diminish our range of power, not to enhance it. And the same holds for knowledge too.

Since ascriptions of ordinary knowledge are defeasible, they are 'Occamite', and susceptible to what is sometimes called 'Cambridge change', that is, ascriptions of ordinary knowledge are exceptions to the principle that we cannot alter the truth-value of apparently past-tensed propositions. In much the same way as I can make it true that Julius Caesar died two thousand and thirty years before I crossed the Rubicon—by taking care to cross the Rubicon myself exactly two thousand and thirty years after his death—so I can make it true that you knew that I should be lecturing today; and in much the same way as I can make it false that Julius Caesar died two thousand and thirty years before I crossed the Rubicon—by taking care not to cross the Rubicon myself exactly two thousand and thirty years after his death—so I can make it false that you knew that I should be lecturing today. Whether or not you knew it depends in part on what I shall do. Although 'knew' is, grammatically, in the past tense, logically it is not entirely past, but has some future reference too. In fact it changes its truth-value more radically than the standard examples of 'Cambridge change'. For in our ordinary way of speaking you already knew that I should be lecturing, if you had good reason to expect me to, *even before* the time when I could have made it false. If you had adequate justification for expecting me to lecture, you could have properly said that yesterday you knew that I would. You knew it, unless and until you were proved wrong in the event. So in that sense ascriptions of knowledge are exceptions to the general rule 'Once true always true'. That is to say, I may, quite justifiably, allow that it is true that I know that the sun will rise tomorrow, and yet be ready to withdraw that claim in the event of its not doing so. Equally, it is true that my pupils know that I shall be lecturing next week in Oxford, in spite of the fact that I—or an IRA terrorist—can in the intervening week make it false that they knew it. If I decide to slope off to Paris to manifest my autonomy, or a terrorist happens to lob a bomb at a shop in which I am buying a book, then I shall not lecture, and instead of having known it they will have falsely believed it. It is like the case of the employer who sacks an employee first thing on Monday morning, thereby making the previous Friday the last day the employee worked for him. On Friday it was not true that that was the last day of the employee's employment, but it was retrospectively made true by the employer's subsequent action. With ordinary, non-philosophical foreknowledge of the future free actions of free agents, the agents play the part of the employer, the foreknowers the part of the employee. The agent can Cambridgely bring it about that the foreknowledge of his actions was indeed foreknowledge or that it was not.

Cambridge change seems fishy. It does not enter into the ordinary nexus of cause and effect. A Cambridge change does not produce any other changes in its immediate spatiotemporal vicinity.[5] It can, on those grounds, be stigmatized as not being really real. But that is to claim too much. True, Cambridge changes are not *physical*. But we have no warrant for confining reality to physical reality. A legal analogy may help. In some circumstances one person can enter into a contract for another. A father can sign a lease for a grown-up son who is abroad, subject to the son's not repudiating it on his return. If the son repudiates it, then the contract is null and void. But if the son does not repudiate it, the contract is binding, and runs from the date when it was signed by the father, not from when the son implicitly approved it. The father's signing creates legal and moral obligations from that date, although no physical change in the vicinity, but only defeasibly. They can be subsequently annulled by the son's repudiating the contract. But unless annulled, they already exist, and are not created by the son's implicit approval of his father's action on his behalf.

The possibility that we can alter the past in respect of the way it ought to be described and evaluated is no new one. Aristotle in his discussion of responsibility makes disclaimers of responsibility conditional on *metameleia* regret; whether I did not really do something depends not only on the conditions obtaining at the time (that I acted under duress, *bia* or in ignorance, *di'agnoian*), but on subsequent attitude as well; if I am not sorry afterwards that my javelin hit a particular bystander, then I wounded him even though I had not intended to at the time I threw it. Two less happy examples, one from the Middle Ages and one from a contemporary dilemma illustrate the same point. Grosseteste, Bishop of Lincoln in the thirteenth century, had a dispute with King Henry II over the legitimization of illegitimate children. The king's court held that a child born out of wedlock was a child born out of wedlock, and no

---

[5] H. D. Mellor, *Real Time* (Cambridge University Press, 1981) 107–110.

subsequent action of the parent could alter that fact. The bishop, believing that marriage was a matter of intention more than of legal formality, held that the subsequent marriage of the parents provided that they were free to marry at the time of the child's birth, was effective in making the child legitimate all along.[6] In recent years we have been much exercised over brain death. In many tragic cases we are being led to conclude that a person is dead when the brain is dead, even if the heart is kept beating still by artificial means. But, of course, one cannot be absolutely sure. Miracles can happen, and men in deep coma may yet recover consciousness. We are being led, therefore, to say that the man is dead from the time that his brain stopped functioning, not from the time that the life support machine was switched off, but that IF a man did recover consciousness, then clearly he was not dead. The ascription of death is defeasible, and should be retrospectively withdrawn in the happy event of subsequent recovery.

Knowledge of the future free actions of a free agent is like a defeasible contract. If proved true in the event, it existed all along, from the time the warranted knowledge claim was first made: if, however, it proves false, then it never was knowledge, only justified but untrue belief. In ascribing knowledge, we are not merely stating something physical, but also evaluating the claim to know. There is no physical difference in the immediate vicinity between the case where someone knows what another will do and where he reasonably, but as it happens falsely, opines what he will do. The difference lies in the evaluation of the knowledge claim: in the one case it is vindicated by events, and in the other it is not and must therefore be withdrawn or retrospectively disallowed. Not only with employers sacking unsuspecting employees, but quite generally with the free actions of a free agent which anyone else is predicting, the agent has it in his power to bring it about that the knowledge of his actions was indeed foreknowledge, or that it was not. You know that I shall not let you down, but I still can let you down and make a fool of you all. And equally with God, we have it in our power to turn His prescience into nescience, and make it retrospectively the case that He did not know all along what we were going to do.

In spite of objections,[7] this solution to the problem of over-scrupulosity in our use of the word 'know' is adequate, so far as it goes. But it

[6] For Grosseteste's own example of our being able to alter the truth of statements about the past, see *Beitrage*, 165, 11.14–19 (main text), and 11.31–32 (alternative text). For an account of Grosseteste's quarrel with the king's courts, see R. W. Southern, *Robert Grosseteste* (Oxford University Press, 1986), Ch. 10, III, 2, 252–257.

[7] See, for example, Anthony Kenny, *The God of the Philosophers* (Oxford University Press, 1979), 60–61.

does not go far enough. For one thing, although it resolves the apparent difficulty of foreknowledge, it does nothing to ease the comparable one of forebelief: and more fundamentally, it does not touch the underlying question about the nature of God.

Although ordinary knowledge is Occamite, belief is not. I may have been able to bring it about that you did not know that I should be giving this lecture, but I could not have prevented you having had the confident expectation that I should. The announcement made last summer is a 'hard fact', which it was subsequently too late to alter. Equally with God, the word He sent by the mouth of Elijah the prophet could not be subsequently withdrawn. Elijah could revise the message sent to Ahab, but could not call back and unsay the words he had previously uttered. If we believe in a God who is actually concerned with what we do, and therefore thinks about what we are going to do, and sometimes intervenes to warn us or encourage us, then we are still faced with the fact that we are in a position to disappoint His expectations, and sometimes do. Once again we are imputing the possiblity of God's being mistaken in His predictions. We are thus still left with an ineliminable conflict between the perfection of God, as traditionally understood, and the freedom of the will, and this is not a problem of logic, but of theology and our understanding of the nature of God.

It is a weighty argument. It does seem to derogate from the greatness of God that He should change His mind. We are swayed by an argument of Plato, and claim that either His first thoughts were perfect, in which case the change of mind was for the worse, or that, if the change were for the better, then clearly His first thoughts were not all they might have been. But the argument proves too much. It proves the Impassibility of God, and leads not to a God who sent His Son to die for us, and who then raised him from the dead, but to an impersonal Neoplatonist Absolute, who never changes, never responds to prayers, never acts in this world at all. It is open to anyone to argue that such a being exists and is worthy of our worship. But it is not possible to make out that such a being is the Christian God, and difficult to make out that the Christian God is not a possible deity at all.

We need to distinguish two different counters to the argument from perfection, one concerned with the concept of perfection, the other based on the willing vulnerabilty of God. It is easy to say that God is perfect without pausing to think what the word 'perfect' means. Unthinkingly we assume that it must mean being the absolutely mostest in all respects, but this is absurd, because often the more one is in one respect, the less one is in another, so that maximal satisfaction of incompatible requirements is logically impossible. If we say that God cannot make a world so big that He cannot move it, we are revealing not the imperfection of God but the inconsistency of the predicate 'x makes a world so big that x cannot move it'. We need therefore to be wary of the theological superlative. If we take the *omni* of omnipotence and omniscience literally, we rapidly reduce these concepts to inconsistency, as Findlay, Kenny and Blumenfeld have pointed out.[8] Perfection cannot be construed as meaning being the mostest in all possible respects, and it is no derogation of God's greatness to acknowledge that there are things He cannot do—He cannot alter the past; He cannot sin—and things He cannot know. God cannot, in any sense of the word 'know', know what is false; God cannot philosophically know what He is going to do until He has made up His mind—else Divine omniscience would have foreclosed Divine freedom, and curtailed His omnipotence—and God cannot, so long as He has created us free and autonomous agents, philosophically know what we are going to do until we have done it.

Instead of construing omnipotence and omniscience as meaning being able to do absolutely everything and knowing absolutely everything, we should construe them negatively. I am not omnipotent because there are lots of things I cannot do, and it is a defect of mine that I cannot. I cannot write Greek elegiacs, I cannot jump over the moon, I cannot swim across the Bering Strait. But other people can, and it is only because I am not as good as they that I cannot. Equally, I am not omniscient: I do not know French, I do not know Twister theory, I do not know American history. Other people do, and I should be less ignorant if I did too. In other cases, however, it is no defect of mine that I cannot do, or do not know, something. I cannot make a flag that is red and green all over, not on account of any inadequacy of mine, but because it is a logically impossible task. It is no skin off my nose that I cannot alter the past—it is not something I ought to remedy, or could try to overcome with effort or careful attention to the teaching of Professor Dummett. Where the question 'Why can't you' or 'Why don't you know?' has to be met with a confession of inability or ignorance on my part, it is reasonable to look for God's not being subject to any such limitation. But where it is not due to an incapacity of the person but is in the nature of the case that something cannot be done or known, then it is no derogation from God that He cannot do it or know it either.[9]

[8] J. N. Findlay, 'Can God's Existence Be Disproved?', *Mind* 57 (1948), 108–118; Kenny, op. cit., David Blumenfeld, 'On the Compossibility of the Divine Attributes', *Philosophical Studies* 34 (1978), 91–103, reprinted in Thomas V. Morris (ed.), *The Concept of God* (Oxford University Press, 1987), 201–215.

[9] Compare Thomas P. Flint and Alfred J. Freddoso, 'Maximal Power', in Alfred J. Freddoso (ed.), *Existence and Nature of God*, reprinted in Thomas V. Morris (ed.), *The Concept of God* (Oxford University Press, 1987), 151. 'Therefore . . . there will be some state of affairs . . . which even an omnipotent agent is incapable of actualizing. And since this inability results solely

It may be allowed that perfection should not be construed as a simple minded slapping on of all possible superlatives, and yet doubted whether the limitations suggested here on God's foreknowledge are compatible with any doctrine of divine providence. Certainly it is incompatible with one traditional view, which ascribes every event to God's specific choice. But that is not the only account of God's providence we could reasonably give. God would be providing for us equally well if He confined Himself to securing generally beneficent conditions and redressing some of the ill consequences of our bad decisions. God's providence is shown not in the fact that everything happens as it does, but in some good things happening when they might well have not happened. It is perfectly possible to believe in a providential ordering of the world both because its general arrangements are conducive to our welfare and because setbacks, though real, can characteristically be overcome. Instead of thinking of God's providence as a sort of blueprint, with the inevitably Procrustean overtones of that metaphor, we should liken it to the Persian rug-maker, who lets his children work at one end while he does the other. The children make mistakes, but so great is his skill that he adapts the design at his end to take into account each error at the children's end, and works it into a new, constantly up-dated pattern.[10]

The greatness of God is understood very differently on this view from the traditional account of His absolute perfection. God is a father, first and foremost, and His Kingdom, power and glory are that of a father rather than an absolute monarch. He created us, but as children rather than artefacts, and therefore as being capable of independent action which He cannot completely control or infallibly foreknow. It does not follow that He is totally ignorant or completely impotent. God can know, albeit defeasibly and fallibly, what we are going to do, and take actions accordingly. Often, sadly, He can foresee our foolish and wicked actions. Like as a father pitieth his own children, He may try to dissuade us, but will not prevent or frustrate us absolutely. But also, like a father, having failed to dissuade us, He will then mitigate the consequences of our decisions, often through the actions of our own chastened selves or through those of others. For in seeing Him, as Jesus did, as a loving father, we see Him as suffering but not as completely

---

[10] I have tried to work out the analogy more fully in J. R. Lucas, *Freedom and Grace* (London: SPCK, 1976), Chs 4 and 5, esp. p. 39. See also Jacques Maritain, *God and the Permission of Evil*, cited by Flint and Freddoso, op. cit., 163, n. 30.

---

from the *logically necessary* truth that one being cannot causally determine how another will freely act, it should not be viewed . . . as a kind of inability which disqualifies an agent from ranking as omnipotent.'

powerless, or unable to bring it about that good does not succeed in the end, in spite of us. The world we live in is one that conduces to virtue and makes vice self-defeating. Human beings, though not the puppets of the Holy Spirit, are open to His counsels and admonitions, and some people have tried quite hard to carry out God's purposes in the world. Although it is a necessary condition of our freedom of effective action that laws of nature should be reliably regular, and miracles very much the exception, there are no sound arguments *a priori* against their occurring, and reasonable testimony for supposing that on some occasions God has intervened in the course of history, most notably in revealing His nature to us in sending His Son to live among us.

Once we cease imputing to the suffering God of the Christian religion the supposed perfections of the God of the philosophers, we can see how it is that God can be God without thereby depriving us of freedom and responsibility. God may have a fair idea of the way things are going, but is far more concerned to save us from perils ahead than to preserve His prescience. Other gods may be concerned to save their infallibility, but God who is prepared to sacrifice His own Son on the cross is not going to set much store on not being wrong in His prognostications.

But it is a different view of God, and not one we come to easily. It makes God out to be not only fallible, but vulnerable. The vulnerability of God is the peculiar characteristic of Christian teaching, the point on which it differs from other, more intellectually acceptable, religions. It follows from God's being an agent, and yet not omnipotent. To act is to choose to bring about some states of affairs in preference to others, and therefore to value them more highly, but not to be omnipotent is to allow that those other states of affairs may none the less come to pass. We can understand why it is that God should have chosen to limit His power, and create men with free will, able therefore to thwart His wishes, and to make a mess of things. But the price is high. Whereas the Buddhist portray the Buddha as impassive, the symbol of Christianity is the cross.

On Not Knowing Too Much About God

The Apophatic Way of the Neoplatonists and other influences from ancient philosophy which have worked against dogmatic assertion in Christian thinking

A. H. ARMSTRONG

Christianity stands out among the three great Abrahamic religions in its willingness to make extremely precise dogmatic statements about God. The Christians who make these statements have generally regarded them as universally and absolutely true, since they are divinely revealed, or divinely guaranteed interpretations of revealed texts. Of course from the beginning there has not been universal agreement (to put it mildly) among Christians about what statements should be so regarded and how they should be worded: and the seriousness with which this need for dogmatic precision has been taken is shown by the way in which the inevitable disputes did not only involve theologians but the general body of Christians, and have led to divisions of churches, long continuing and flourishing mutual hatreds, and an overwhelming amount of theoretical and, where opportunity offered (i.e. where a Church party could get a secular power on its side), practical intolerance.[1] Two areas of Church history which seem to me to provide particularly clear evidence of the incompatible verbal precisions demanded in dogmatic statements and the serious consequences of these demands are the Christological controversies of the fifth and sixth centuries and the *Filioque* dispute between East and West (though there is plenty of choice, and others may have other preferences). In both of these, theologians with a real and deep sense of the mystery of God often seem to an outside observer, in spite of their passionate assertions that this is not at all what they are doing and the rhetorical

---

[1] A grim comment on this, which became more and more manifestly true as the Christian centuries went on, was made very early in the period of Christian dominance by a fair-minded non-Christian observer, the historian Ammianus Marcellinus. Speaking of the Emperor Julian's advice to Christians of all parties (which he knew very well would not be taken) to live at peace with each other, observing their own beliefs freely, he says 'Julian knew from experience that no wild beasts are such enemies of humanity as most Christians are deadly dangerous (*ferales*) to each other' (Ammianus XXII, 5.4).

129

reverence of their language, to be arguing as if the God-Man or the Trinity were small finite objects which they had pinned down firmly in their theological laboratories and were examining under the microscope.

The difference in this way between Christianity on the one hand and Judaism and Islam on the other seems to be largely due to the greater influence of Hellenic philosophy on Christian thinking in the discussions which led to the formulation of authoritative statements of Christian doctrine. It is therefore interesting that this philosophy itself has provided Christians with some powerful means of overcoming their extreme addiction to the imposition of precise dogmatic statements as truths about God in which all must believe.

Hellenic philosophers were from the beginning in the habit of making extremely definite statements about everything, including the divine: and it was of course essential to their particular kind of activity that as soon as a statement, especially about something regarded as interesting and important, was made, someone else (or perhaps the same philosopher later, if he was properly self-critical) would challenge it and argue against it, and probably in the end make a counter-statement, which would then itself in due course be countered in its turn: and so on. Philosophy was for them, as it has generally remained since, intrinsically a conversational activity;[2] and, though vigorous attempts have sometimes been made to close the conversation on particular subjects (notably the subject of the divine) they have never, because of the very nature of philosophy, been successful, and philosophical conversations have continued to be obstinately open-ended. Of course, like all conversations, Hellenic philosophical conversation could take a number of different forms. It could be a discussion between friends, civilized, courteous, and moderately fair-minded, as Plato's earlier dialogues are and as the Seventh Platonic Letter says that any philosophical conversation which is to attain its end must be.[3] Or it could be viciously bad-tempered and unfair, as controversy between the different philosophical schools generally was: a horrid example is the anti-Aristotelian polemic of Atticus preserved by the Christian

---

[2] I prefer to use 'conversation', 'conversational' rather than the more technical and precise-sounding 'dialectic', 'dialectical' because 'dialectic', both in ancient and modern times, has had so many meanings, some of which in the present context would be unduly restrictive or misleading.

[3] Letter VII, 3448, 4–9, 'But by rubbing each of them strenuously against each other, names and definitions and sights and perceptions, testing them out in kindly discussions by the use of questions and answers without jealous ill-will, understanding and intelligence of each reality flashes out, at the highest intensity humanly possible' (trans. A.H.A.).

church historian Eusebius.[4] But very much greater philosophers than Atticus, e.g. Aristotle or Plotinus, are not at their best in inter-school controversy. And there is of course plenty of conversation, of a sort, in the ancient as well as in the modern philosophical world, in which the 'dialogue' consists of a series of monologues in which no speaker pays the slightest attention to what the others have said.

At least a smattering of this sort of conversational and controversial philosophy was part of the education of the Christians in the early centuries of our era who thought out and formulated the authoritative Church statements of Christian doctrine, simply because it was part of the higher education of everyone in the very small minority of the population who received any in the Graeco-Roman world. And, since that education was predominantly rhetorical (the old quarrel between philosophers and rhetoricians was long since over), such philosophy as entered and formed the minds of educated Christians generally tended to do so in a somewhat rhetoricized form: that is, with the issues over-simplified and contrasts sharpened, and any tendencies to agnosticism, tentativeness, and serious attempts to understand opposing points of view minimized.[5] It is easy to understand the effect of this sort of philosophico-rhetorical training of the mind on people like the early Christians who already had a deep religious anxiety about words because the divine relevation in which they believed was given in verbal form, as a body of Scriptures claiming divine authority.[6] By noting that this effect was adverse, I do not at all intend to range myself with the de-Hellenizers in the long controversy about the influence of Greek philosophy on Christianity.[7] I believe this to have been on the whole beneficial, and on many points am more inclined to advocate the re-Hellenization rather than the de-Hellenization of Christianity. But for this very reason I think it important to note adverse effects of philosophy, or of particular philosophies, on Christian teaching and practice when I see them. The attempts to express the essential con-

---

[4] Eusebius, *Praeparatio Evangelica* XI, 1–2; XV, 4–9; 12F: Atticus, *Fragments*, ed. E. Des Places (Paris: Les Belles Lettres, 1977).

[5] On philosophy, rhetoric and education in antiquity see I. Hadot, *Arts Liberaux et Philosophie dans la Pensée Antique* (Paris: Etudes Augustiniennes, 1984).

[6] Cf. James Hillman, 'On Paranoia', *Eranos* **54** (1985; Frankfurt: Insel, 1987), 269–324.

[7] The works of E. P. Meijering, notably his books on Von Harnack, *Theologische Urteile uber die Dogmengeschichte* (Leiden: Brill, 1978), and *Die Hellenisierung des Christentums im Urteil Adolf Von Harnacks* (Amsterdam, London and New York: North-Holland Publishing Co., 1985), are to be recommended to those unfamiliar with this predominantly Lutheran-inspired controversy. I agree generally with his conclusions.

tents of the Word of God, which may be better understood as poetry and myth, in terms of systematic philosophical definition do seem to me to have played an important part in developing that distinctive ferality which has marked the attitude of most Christians to others who disagree with them till very recently.

But, of course, to describe Hellenic philosophy in this way is to give a very inadequate idea of it. There was a great deal more to it than the disputes of the schools. We should never forget that aspect of it as 'spiritual exercise', as a quest for enlightenment and liberation, a seeking to attain such likeness to the divine as may be possible for humans, to which Pierre and Ilsetraut Hadot have recently called our attention.[8] And this might often be closely connected with the deep sense of diffidence[9] which is apparent at least in some philosophers from the beginning, which expresses itself in a tendency to self-critical examination in which the principal questions are 'How much, if anything, can we really know, especially about the divine? Isn't wisdom the attribute of the gods? Can we humans ever be more than lovers of and seekers after wisdom (*philosophoi*)?' This is particularly evident in Plato, and this is important for our purposes, as it was Platonism in the early centuries of our era (as perhaps it has always been since) which exercised the deepest influence on Christian thought of any kind of Hellenic philosophy. The figure of the Platonic Socrates, with his continual profession of ignorance, became for later generations the paradigm of what a philosopher should be. And the Seventh Platonic Letter, in its philosophical digression (342A–344D) expresses with great force the inadequacy of language in dealing with transcendent realities. (The question of the authorship of this is not relevant to our present purposes. In the period with which we are concerned it was accepted as by Plato, and was a text of great authority for Platonists.) And, whatever Plato himself may have intended, there is a great deal in the Dialogues the reading of which can strengthen this tendency to diffidence and encourage the readers to develop it in various ways. It could also, of course, develop independently of any reading or influence of Plato, as a disposition engendered by philosophical reflection on philosophical

---

[8] P. Hadot, *Exercices Spirituels et Philosophie Antique*, 2nd edn, revised and extended (Paris: Etudes Augustiniennes, 1987). I. Hadot, 'The Spiritual Guide', in A. H. Armstrong (ed.), *Classical Mediterranean Spirituality*, Vol. 15 of *World Spirituality* (New York: Crossroad, 1985), 436–459. Cf. A. H. Armstrong, *Expectations of Immortality in Late Antiquity* (Milwaukee: Marquette University, 1987), 22–23.

[9] A. H. Armstrong, 'The Hidden and the Open in Hellenic Thought', *Eranos* **54** (1985), 96–99.

encounters, a philosophy, if you like, of philosophical conferences: this was probably the case with Pyrrho.

There are two developments from this original diffidence which, I think, have done something in the past to correct the addiction of Christians to thinking they know and saying much too much about God and may do considerably more in the future, now that the hold of absolute and clear-cut certainties on the minds of religious people is, for a variety of good reasons, steadily weakening and likely to continue to do so in spite of conservative reactions. These are the Apophatic way or Via Negativa of the Neoplatonists and the ancient traditions of Scepticism, the Pyrrhonian and that which developed in Plato's school at Athens, the Academic. The two belong to quite different periods in the history of Hellenic philosophy, the Sceptical to that immediately after Aristotle which it is convenient to call Hellenistic as long as this is not taken to imply too precise a date for its ending, and the Apophatic, which really begins with Plotinus in the third century of our era, to late antiquity. And their main influence on Christian thought has also been exercised at different periods, the Apophatic in patristic and medieval times and the Sceptical from the Renaissance onwards. In view of their common origin in diffidence, their common insistence on the importance of not knowing, and the way in which they can work together harmoniously, in some circumstances, in the minds of religious people, it is tempting to look for some signs of influence of the earlier tendency, the Sceptical, on the later, the Apophatic. But there is little evidence of this, and I do not think that a search for more is likely to get us very far. The dogmatic Platonists of the Roman Empire generally found the sceptical interlude in the history of their school something of an embarrassment, and it seems to me unlikely that Plotinus ever applied his mind seriously to Scepticism in any of its forms, though the possibility cannot be excluded. The following statement by the late Richard Wallis, who before his untimely death had been doing a good deal of research in this area, seems to me to go as far as is reasonably possible in drawing attention to resemblance and suggesting some degree of influence:

> How far Pyrrhonism influenced Neoplatonic views on divine unknowability (as later Scepticism certainly influenced Plotinus on other points) remains uncertain. But at least two of its principles are echoed by the Neoplatonists. First, statements about Ultimate Reality are mere expressions of our own attitude thereto; second, negations used of the Supreme must in turn be negated.[10]

[10] A. Wallis, 'The Spiritual Importance of Not Knowing', in *Classical Mediterranean Spirituality* (above n. 8), 465. I have not yet been able to see Wallis's 'Scepticism and Neoplatonism', to be published in *Aufstieg und*

This certainly indicates that it is worth while taking Scepticism as well as the negative way of the Neoplatonists into account in considering the desirability of not knowing too much about God, and I shall attempt to do so to some extent. But I shall concentrate attention mainly on the Neoplatonic way. This is in accordance with the original intention of this series of lectures and the limitations of my own competence. It is only from the Renaissance onwards that there is any real evidence of serious influence of the ancient Sceptical traditions on Christian thought (as distinct from the polemical trick, very common in early as in later Christian writers, of using Sceptical arguments from the disagreements of philosophers as sticks to beat other people's dogmas while maintaining an ultra-dogmatic stance themselves: this I do not find very important, interesting, or attractive). This period lies rather outside our terms of reference, and I know just enough about the Christian thinkers of the sixteenth and seventeenth centuries and later on whom Sceptical influence has been detected to know how little I know.

The Negative Way

That way of thinking towards God which is usually referred to as the 'negative' or 'apophatic' way begins as a serious way of thinking which exercised a strong and deep influence on people who were seriously religious, with Plotinus (205–270CE). There had been anticipations of it in the revived dogmatic Platonism and revived Pythagoreanism of the two centuries before Plotinus, and something like it is to be found in the Gnostics of the same period. There are assertions of the absolute unity and supreme transcendence and unknowability of the first principle of

---

Niedergang der Romischen Welt (Anrw), W. Haase and H. Temporini (eds), II, 36.2. David T. Runia, 'Naming and Knowing: Themes in Philonic Theology with special reference to the *De mutatione nominum*', in R. van den Broek, T. Baarda and J. Mansfeld (eds), *Knowledge of God in the Graeco-Roman World* (Leiden: Brill, 1988), 69–91, has a very interesting discussion (iv, 82–89) of Philo's theological use of the rhetorical term *katachresis*, the 'abusive' or 'improper' use of language, in which he cites a somewhat analogous use of the word in Sextus Empiricus (*Outlines of Pyrrhonism* I, 207). Though the word *katachresis* is rare in philosophical authors of the first three centuries CE (as Runia notes), and nobody else exploits it theologically as Philo does, the discussion does suggest at least the possibility that there may be some sceptical influence detectable in Plotinus's frequently expressed conviction that all our ways of speaking about the One are improper (particularly evident in VI, 8 (39), 13–18, where he uses the most strongly positive language to be found anywhere in the *Enneads*: cf. also, for the way in which we can use language about the One, VI, 9 (9), 4, 11–14).

reality, sometimes placing it above real being (the Platonic Forms) and/or the divine mind which created the universe. Much of the exegesis of the Dialogues of Plato on which Plotinus relies seems to have originated in this period, notably the fantastic explanation of the second part of the *Parmenides*—probably a complete misunderstanding of the intentions of Plato, but one which proved remarkably fruitful. But what made the apophatic way important for later religious thought was the thinking through again, bringing together and developing of these earlier, rather inchoate, ideas by Plotinus, under the pressure of an intense experience of the presence of that which he knew he could not think or speak of, but had to go on trying to do so to keep the awareness awake in himself and wake it in others so that they could share it. In my attempts to speak about this way in its original Hellenic[11] form I shall rely mainly on Plotinus, though without neglecting the developments and clarifications of his thought which are to be found in the later Hellenic Neoplatonists.

The Neoplatonic Negative Way is often described as a way of thinking about God in which it is considered preferable in speaking about him to say what he is not than what he is. Denial gives a better approach to the divine than affirmation. This is true as far as it goes, but rather over-simplified, and can lead to misunderstandings. To understand it better the first thing we need to do is to distinguish between the underlying experience and the intellectual approach to God which it stimulates, and which helps to establish and strengthen it. (It will probably begin to be noticed here that I am rather carefully avoiding the word 'mystic'; and I do not intend to refer to 'ecstasy'. This is in accordance with Plotinus's own usage[12] and will avoid various entirely inappropriate and misleading associations which the words have nowadays.) It is important, however, not to make the distinction too sharp and not to suppose that the experience and the proper following of the intellectual way can be disjoined. This would be anachronistic and misleading. In the Christian tradition, before the disjunctions and

---

[11] Instead of the rather silly and in intention derogatory word 'pagan', I prefer to use in this context 'Hellene', 'Hellenic' which were used both by the philosophers and their Christian opponents during the period of conflict between Christianity and the old religion when referring to the adherents of the latter and their beliefs and practices.

[12] The adverb *Mustikōs* is used once in the *Enneads* (III, 6 (25), 19, 26), referring not to anything like 'mystical union' but to the secret symbolism of ordinary Greek mystery-rites: the adjective *Mustikos* and the substantive *Mustēs* do not occur at all. *Ekstasis* may be used once (VI, 9 (9), 11, 23) in the sense of 'being out of oneself' in speaking of union with the One: but here there is a good deal to be said for an emendation of Theiler's which would eliminate the word (see my note ad. loc. in the Loeb Plotinus).

separations of the high Middle Ages, and later, in the West which have led to our being inclined to make very sharp distinctions, first between theology and philosophy, and then between theology and 'spirituality', religious experience and theology went very closely together, as they still do in the Christian East. And for the Hellenes, for whom of course no separation between philosophy and theology was possible, philosophy, and especially that part of it which they called *Theologia*, was always, as has already been said (above p. 132), a 'spiritual exercise', a quest for transforming enlightenment and liberation, a movement towards assimilation to or union with the divine.

The experience which underlies and provides the driving force for the negative way from its beginning and is increasingly realized as it goes on is of course, according to the accounts given of it by those who follow that way in East and West, ineffable, and it is therefore obviously desirable to say as little as possible about it. It would be preferable not to say anything, but it is rather difficult to write a paper about the Negative Way without doing so. Of course it should be made clear at this point that anything I say is second-hand. I do not claim the experience of a true apophatic contemplative like Plotinus, but at most the sort of dim awareness of what he and others are talking about which is necessary for anyone who tries to write or speak about him and which may in fact be quite common: he himself thought that it was universal.[13] What must be said, to avoid a common misunderstanding, is that this growing experience is of something immeasurably positive and that the realization as one follows the negative way to its proper end in the negating of all the negations, that all thought and language is inadequate is immensely liberating and indeed glorifying, because it points on to something that our minds cannot contain. This is why most Neoplatonists[14] retain some positive terms for their goal, above all 'One'

[13] '. . . all men are naturally and spontaneously moved to speak of the god who is in each one of us as one and the same. And if someone did not ask them how this is and want to examine their opinion rationally, this is what they would assume, and with this active and actual in their thinking they would come to rest in this way, somehow supporting themselves on this one and the same, and they would not wish to be cut away from this unity' (VI, 5 (23), 1, 2–8; trans. A. H. Armstrong). It is worth reflecting on the fact that Plotinus regards this as commonplace and generally acceptable. It does something to illustrate the closeness in some ways of Neoplatonic thought to that of India, and the change made by centuries of Christianity in the kind of religious statements we regard as obvious and commonplace, whether we believe them or not.

[14] Iamblichus in the fourth century and Damascius and Simplicius in the sixth separated the absolutely transcendent Ineffable from the One/Good. But Proclus (fifth century), the greatest and most precise systematizer among the

and 'Good', though they know very well how inadequate they are. 'One' indicates for them the impossibility of applying to the First the divisions, distinctions and separations which alone make discursive thought and discourse possible, and 'Good' acts as a kind of direction-finder or signpost, indicating that what we are travelling to along the way is more and better, not less and worse, than anything we can conceive. This preserves that consonance between religious and moral convictions which seems necessary to prevent any religious reflection from becoming perniciously insane.

This emphasis on the positive power of the experience which generates and is strengthened by the negative way leads necessarily to a consideration of the attitude of negative theologians to the positive or Kataphatic theology which makes affirmative statements about God. This cannot be one of simple exclusion or rejection, for two reasons. The first is that if one is following a way of negation one has to have something solid to negate: a negative theology needs a positive theology to wrestle with and transcend. And if the negation is to be done properly, one has to understand what one is trying to negate: and 'understand' here must be taken in a serious sense, as involving a great deal of hard study and intellectual effort, and some respect for and good will towards the people who make the positive statement one is trying to negate. This of course applies to negations in general, whether one is following the way of negative theology or not. A really good negation cannot be just polemical or journalistic.[15] The second reason, perhaps, goes rather deeper. The great negative theologians, from Plotinus onwards, are always aware as they follow the negative way that in the end they must negate their negations:[16] if not, they will arrive in the end at an empty space neatly fenced by negative dogmas, which is not at all

[15] Cf. Mary Midgley, 'Sneer Tactics', *Guardian* (Wednesday, 7 October 1977): an excellent comment on negation by flippant dismissal.

[16] There is a good account of the negation of negations at the end of the part of the *Commentary on the Parmenides* of Proclus which survives only in Latin:

> Parmenides, then, is imitating this and ends by doing away both with the negations and with the whole argument, because he wants to conclude the discourse about the One with the inexpressible. For the term of the progress towards it has to be a halt; of the upward movement, rest; of the arguments that it is inexpressible and of all knowledge, unification. . . . For by means of a negation Parmenides has removed all negations. With silence he concludes the contemplation of the One (*Plato Latinus* III, trans. Anscombe and Labowsky (London: Warburg Institute, 1953), 76–77).

Hellenic Neoplatonists, does not find this necessary: and Plotinus, I believe, would have thought that it showed an insufficient understanding of the odd, flexible, paradoxical, detached use of language which becomes necessary at this level.

where they want to be. So if the negative theologian finds himself becoming captivated by his negations he will immediately negate them vigorously while continuing to bear them in mind and keep them in balance and tension with the positive statements he is impelled to imply in negating them. (At this point one can see how close negative theology can come to ancient Scepticism, as Wallis noted (above p. 133): though I still think the two should be distinguished.) These reasons account for the vast amount of positive theology which is to be found in the works of the great negative theologians, Hellenic and Christian.

What has just been said leads, I think, naturally to a consideration of a kind of description of the Neoplatonic way often used, especially by Christian theologians, as an 'intellectual' or 'philosophical' way. (This is usually intended to be derogatory: 'merely' is either explicitly said or implied.) This is true in a sense, but requires some explanation and qualification. It is true in the sense that those who follow the negative way of Plotinus know that they can only get beyond thought by thinking with the highest possible degree of intensity and concentration through a long course of critical and self-critical reflection and argument. (In the later Hellenic Neoplatonists the position is complicated by their acceptance of a 'theurgic' way deemed to be in some sense superior to the philosophical. But when they follow the philosophical way this still remains true of them.) But what I said earlier about ancient philosophy as spiritual exercise, and the closeness of the way and the underlying experience, should indicate that one has to broaden the meaning of 'intellectual' considerably and use 'philosophical' in a wide and loose way of which a good many present-day philosophers would not approve. Very hard thinking is certainly going on, but it is by some standards decidedly peculiar thinking. One should never in reading Plotinus forget that the experience is primary and that it is apprehended by him and the other Neoplatonists as something given, light from above, voices from on high, a power given in our nature by the Good as our source which impels or lifts us to the Good as our goal. And we go the way it drives and use what it puts in our way, poetry and myth and symbol and paradox as well as straightforward argument.

There is another limitation on the intellectualism of the Hellenic and traditional Christian, Jewish and Muslim Neoplatonists which must also be taken into account. The positive theologies with which they wrestle and which they seek to transcend are of course the theologies of their own traditions, and they take them as they find them. And the intellectual world in which Neoplatonism developed and passed to Christian thinkers was strongly traditionalist in the sense that the authority of whatever one regarded as the authentic tradition was absolute.[17] This remains true even of a thinker as original and indepen-

[17] Cf. A. H. Armstrong, 'Pagan and Christian Traditionalism in the First

dent-minded as Plotinus. He does not think it right to disagree know-ingly with Plato. Of course ancient methods of exegesis, as illustrated by the Fathers of the Church expounding the Scriptures or Proclus expounding Plato's *Timaeus* and *Parmenides*, made it much easier to combine traditionalism with considerable freedom of thought. But the intellectual limitation remained, and did a good deal to hamper some possible developments of the negative way. Its influence was real, powerful, and widespread in the Christian patristic and medieval tradi-tion. It is by no means confined to the Dionysian writings and those influenced by them in East and West. It can be observed in the fourth-century Greek Fathers and in predominantly kataphatic thinkers of the West, most notably Augustine and Aquinas. But it does not affect their theology as pervasively as might be expected. It does not make them more tentative about traditional dogmas, or even their own expositions of them, or more tolerant of dogmatic disagreement. (The same is true of Proclus and other late Hellenic Neoplatonists.) I shall return to this briefly in my conclusion.

The attitude of those who follow the way of negation to the external observances of religion, to sacred rites and sacraments and images, can be a good deal more positive than is sometimes supposed. Plotinus himself had little personal use for or interest in them, and perhaps most apophatic contemplatives become more and more independent of them as they advance on the negative way. But he had no objection to his closest associate Amelius being much concerned with external obser-vances, as long as he himself was not required to take part in them.[18] He recognizes their sacredness and value for the vast majority of human beings who need them, and his occasional references to them in the *Enneads* are always respectful. And at least once he shows himself as ready as his pupil, the great anti-Christian controversialist Porphyry, to defend the whole Hellenic inheritance of cult and myth against the growing assaults of Christianity.[19] He is no more detachable from or

[18] Porphyry, *Life of Plotinus* 10, 33–37. On the significance of this story in the context of what we are told in the *Life* about the position of Amelius in the group see A. H. Armstrong, 'Iamblichus and Egypt', *Les Etudes Philos-ophiques* **2–3** (1987) 182–183 and 188.

[19] *Enneads* II, 9 (33), *Against the Gnostics*, 9: the key sentence is 1.35–39. 'It is not contracting the divine into one but showing it in that multiplicity in which God himself has shown it, which is proper to those who know the power of God, inasmuch as, abiding who he is, he makes many gods, all depending upon himself and existing through him and from him' (trans. A.H.A.). I have tried to bring out the full significance of this in 'Plotinus and Christianity', to be published in a volume of essays in honour of Edouard des Places.

Three Centuries A.D.', in *Studia Patristica* **XV**, No. 1, E. A. Livingstone (ed.) (Berlin: Akademie-Verlag, 1984), 414–431.

hostile to his Hellenic religious environment than most great Christian contemplatives who have followed the negative way have been from the rites and sacraments of their churches. And the later Hellenic Neo-platonists, in the period of increasingly intolerant Christian domination, were passionate and committed defenders of their whole religious inheritance against the new religion.

This seems to lead naturally to a consideration of another characteristic often attributed to the negative way, to some extent rightly, its interiority, One does indeed advance on the way indicated by Plotinus by an intense introspection. One must seek the principle and goal of one's existence, the Good, within oneself. But Plotinus, who very well knows the inadequacy of all such spatial metaphors, prefers to speak of each lower stage which one passes through on the quest as within the higher, so that Soul and its work, the material cosmos, are in the Divine Intellect and Intellect is in the Good. The Good is immediately present at every level, containing and pervading them all, so that the apprehension of it is always not only of it as discovered in, beyond and containing the self but as in, beyond and containing all things, imparting to them, each in their degree, such reality as they have. The supreme moment of union is indeed one of extreme interiority and complete unawareness of self and all else. But this is rare and attained by few. And because of this intimate and immediate presence of the Good in and containing all things, the heightened awareness of it given by the ultimate experience or such communication of it as is possible makes those who have undergone it, or had it fruitfully communicated to them, more aware of this supreme divine presence not only within themselves but in all external and material things, which makes them each and every one theophanies or icons, and as such holy and lovable. It is a constantly recurring experience of those who study Plotinus that he teaches us to love the world: not in a way which makes us want to possess or exploit the things in it, which would be contrary to the whole spirit of Hellenic philosophy, and also, I believe, of authentic traditional Christianity, but in contemplative enjoyment of the light of the Good shining in and on its beauty. This 'iconic' awareness and understanding of the world is one of the most powerful and pervasive legacies of Neoplatonism to the Christian world, apparent in its art and poetry as much as, or more than, its theology and spiritual teaching.

Ancient Scepticism

I shall now try to say something about the ancient Sceptical traditions and the kind of influence they can exercise on religious thinking. This will be very brief for reasons already indicated, and mainly directed to showing both the differences between Sceptical religious thought and

the Negative Way and the possibility, in some circumstances, of their
working harmoniously together to mitigate dogmatic fanaticism. I shall
concentrate on trying to present Scepticism as an attitude or temper of
mind rather than on discussing the details of, and differences between
the more highly organized, systematic and coherent forms of Sceptical
thinking, the Academic Scepticism of Arcesilaus and Carneades and
the Neo-Pyrrhonism inaugurated by Aenesidemus.[20] It would of course
be absurd and contrary to the intentions of the ancient Sceptics to
present any form of Scepticism as a system, or even a collection, of anti-
dogmatic dogmas supported by conclusive arguments: for Sceptics all
arguments, including their own, are inconclusive: the investigation
must always be pursued further. And there may be a subsidiary reason
for presenting Scepticism in the way which I have chosen. In spite of
the extent to which the Neo-Pyrrhonian Sextus Empiricus was read and
used by Christian thinkers in the Renaissance, I am inclined to think
that the most pervasive Sceptical influence in the Christian West has
been that of the rather weak and watery Scepticism (as it appeared to his
contemporaries and to later connoisseurs of the Scepticality of Scepticisms) of Philo of Larissa, as transmitted by the very widely read and
influential Cicero. And this urbane, tentative Philonian or Ciceronian
Academic Scepticism certainly transmitted itself as an attitude or temper of mind rather than as the tidy parcel of knock-down arguments so
efficiently provided by Sextus Empiricus.

The most important thing to understand about ancient Sceptics and
those in later times who have been influenced by them is that they do try
to remain genuinely open-minded. Their suspense of judgment is real,
and does not conceal a negative certainty. This should be remembered
when considering Sceptical views on religion and influence on religious
thought. When confronted with a metaphysical or religious dogma (as
with any other kind) they do not simply deny or reject it: they enquire
into it as long as there are any questions to be asked, but at no stage deny
that there is something to enquire into (though they do not, of course,
affirm this either). If they are Pyrrhonians they may pursue the enquiry
only sufficiently far to rest in inconclusiveness and so ensure their own
tranquillity. If they are Academics, who really enjoy arguments and are
not particularly interested in tranquillity, they will pursue the enquiry
indefinitely. In practical, every-day religious life this Sceptical temper
is a strong defence against the fanaticism which is so easily bred by

[20] The precise study of ancient Scepticisms from Pyrrho to Aenesidemus has
now been made very much easier by the admirable source-book recently
produced by A. A. Long and D. N. Sedley, *The Hellenistic Philosophers*, 2
vols (Cambridge University Press, 1987). Their documentation and discussion of the varieties of Scepticism is particularly full, exact and illuminating.

dogmatic certainty. It will often, especially in its more Pyrrhonian forms, tend to conformism. In Christian terms, the Pyrrhonian will tend to be a conservative churchgoer who does not actually believe anything, or, quite often nowadays, a conservative non-churchgoer who thinks that the services which he does not attend should remain in all respects unchanged. This conformism is what the ancient Pyrrhonians explicitly recommend.[21] But Academics who follow Carneades in regarding probability as an adequate guide in everyday life and are capable of enthusiasm may find it quite compatible with strong support for radical reform and even revolutionary change in religious matters.[22]

The main reason for introducing Scepticism into this paper was that it can provide an alternative means to the Negative Way by which Christians can avoid the temptation to know too much about God. It seems therefore important for clarity to distinguish the ways in which they can affect the religious mind. The Negative Way is a very passionate business. It is the awareness of a supremely powerful and attractive presence which drives one on to go beyond the limited statements of dogmatic theology to that which cannot be thought or spoken. Sceptics have their own passions and their own sense of enlightenment and liberation, but these are different from those of the Negative Way. Pyrrho intensely desired, and probably attained, that liberation and peace of mind which comes from the dismissal from the mind of theoretical conclusions (not of course in favour of practical conclusions but in favour of not arriving at any conclusions at all). The Academics had a passion for argument for its own sake, and delighted in showing their skill, as Carneades did so well, by arguing excellently on both sides of a question, thereby satisfying themselves and demonstrating to others that all the arguments anyone can think of are inconclusive and the matter requires further investigation and discussion, so that they can pursue their favourite occupation indefinitely. All Sceptics operate entirely on the level of discursive reason, which the followers of the Negative Way are trying to get beyond. But these are well aware that they must continually be active on this, as on all, levels. So they may find the Sceptics and their arguments a great help in dealing with those who would set up dogmatic blocks to their further progress. And the

[21] Cf. Sextus Empiricus, *Outlines of Pyrrhonism* II, 2. 'In the way of ordinary life we affirm undogmatically that the gods exist and we give them honour and affirm that they exercise providence but against the headlong rashness of the dogmatists we have this to say': . . . there follows a very full statement of the reasons which make it impossible to be certain that anything is the case about the gods.

[22] There is a good statement of the difference indicated here, of course from the Neo-Pyrrhonian point of view, in Sextus Empiricus, *Outlines of Pyrrhonism* I, 228–231.

Sceptics, if they are true Sceptics in the ancient Greek style, though they may not share the faith of the followers of the Negative Way, may be open to it if it comes to them because they have no dogmatic blocks. They may help each other to provide some corrective to Christian dogmatic fanaticism, though how effective this will be will depend very much on the religious circumstances of the place and time and the character of the prevailing kataphatic dogmatism, which the Sceptics need in order to criticize it as much as the followers of the Negative Way need it to wrestle with and transcend.

How far in fact did the two tendencies ever work together after the full development of the Negative Way by Plotinus in the third century? There does seem to be one way of thinking in which it may be possible to detect the influence of both, though I would not be too dogmatic about the Sceptical side. This is the tolerant pluralism of the Hellenic intellectual opposition to the new Christian domination in the fourth century, so well expressed by Symmachus (who certainly read Cicero) and Themistius (an independent-minded philosopher-orator, of predominantly Aristotelian tendency, who might well have known something of the Sceptics).[23] This, however, is hardly relevant to our main subject, as it was furiously rejected by the leaders of Christian thought at the time, and the rejection was maintained throughout the centuries of Christian domination, as it still is by conservative theologians. It is tempting at first sight to see some Sceptical influence in a way of Christian thinking very much more germane to our main concern, the idea of Eriugena, powerfully developed by Cusanus, that our knowledge of God never attains more than the *Verisimile*, is always *Coniectura*.[24] This, however, I think would be a mistake. It is historically most unlikely, and the development can be adequately accounted for by that deep Platonic and pre-Platonic diffidence about the possibility of adequate and expressible knowledge of the divine about which I spoke earlier (p. 132), which is still powerfully apparent in Plotinus. This is of course the starting-point of the Negative Way, of which Eriugena is one of the greatest Western Christian exponents. Its development by Nicholas of Cusa is worth noting, as his influence on the Christian Platonism of the sixteenth and seventeenth centuries was considerable, and it is here that we can see the strong beginnings of an effective

[23] Symmachus, *Relatio* III, 10; Themistius, *Oration* 5, and the summaries of his lost speech on tolerance before the Emperor Valens in the church historians (Socrates IV, 32, and Sozomen VI, 6–7): cf. Henry Chadwick, 'Gewissen', *Reallexikon für Antike und Christentum* **X** (1978), viii d, col. 1101–1102; A. H. Armstrong, 'The Way and the Ways', *Vigiliae Christianae* **33** (1984), 8–11.

[24] W. Beierwaltes, 'Eriugena und Cusanus', in *Eriugena Redivivus* (Heidelberg: O. Winter, 1987), 328–338.

tentativeness about our knowledge of God, effective in the sense that awareness that 'truth is bigger than our minds', that God is beyond our knowledge, is leading, in a way new in the history of dominant Christianity, to the belief that we should be less dogmatic about our own dogmas and more tolerant and kindly to those who disagree with them. We should, however, observe that negative theology is very much in the background in Renaissance Christian Platonism, when it is there at all, especially in England. The Cambridge Platonists are very uneasy with radical negations.[25] Their admirable tolerance was more directly inspired by a moderate, subtle and flexible Scepticism which seems to derive from the Ciceronian–Philonian Scepticism of which I spoke earlier (p. 141).[26]

On the whole it seems that in the earlier period of Christian history, down to and including the Reformation, the Negative Way, though often powerfully present and with a strong influence on the spirituality and thought of individuals, was always kept very much under control and rather in the background. Apophatic theology was very much dominated by Kataphatic, with which, as I have said, its relationship can never be simply hostile or dismissive. The reasons for this are various.[27] But perhaps the most important is that Christian thought throughout this period was traditionalist in the sense which I indicated above (pp. 138–9) and traditionalist in a particularly rigid, exclusive and authoritarian way. It was only when it began to be considered permissible to disagree with the sacred authorities, the Church and the Bible, that the full possibilities of the Negative Way could develop, and in particular that what Jean Trouillard[28] called the 'critical value of

---

[25] R. Cudworth, *True Intellectual System of the Universe*, I.4.36, 558. Cudworth was consciously opposed to Scepticism and to the tolerant pluralism of the fourth-century Hellenes: cf. I.4.26, 434–433 and 446–447. The weakening of dogmatic absolutism, especially among the clergy, had not gone very far in his time. There is, however, much more positive attitude to Scepticism in Benjamin Whichcote's *Select Notions (Aphorisms)* I.7.

[26] Cf. Margaret L. Wiley, *The Subtle Knot* (London: Unwin, 1952; reprinted New York: Greenwood Press, 1968); *Creative Sceptics* (London: Unwin, 1966).

[27] I have attempted to suggest and illustrate some of them in a contribution, 'Apophatic-Kataphatic Tensions in Religious Thought from the Third to the Sixth Centuries A.D.', to a volume of essays to be published in honour of John O'Meara.

[28] J. Trouillard, 'Valeur critique de la mystique Plotinienne', *Revue Philosophique de Louvain* 59 (August 1961), 431–434. Trouillard has influenced my personal understanding of the *Via Negativa* greatly; my memorial tribute to him is in 'The Hidden and the Open in Hellenic Thought', *Eranos* 54 (1987), 101–106.

mysticism' could become manifest. Before that, it might mitigate dogmatic fanaticism by continually leading those who follow it on to a God
beyond the dogmas, but it remained compatible with a rigid dogmatism
because it took the kataphatic theology which it wrestled with and
sought to transcend at its own valuation as the one exclusively true
statement at the level of discourse and definition of what had been
divinely revealed. The undermining and eventual overthrow of this
sort of kataphatic absolutism, in so far as it has been undermined and
overthrown, as for many of us it irrevocably has, in recent times, has
been due not so much to the following of the Negative Way as to
disciplines and ways of thinking which derive from that Hellenic tendency to continual critical questioning which found its clearest theoretical formulations in ancient Scepticism. It is for this reason that in our
present situation, when more and more even of those who retain a deep
and strong religious faith feel that they know less and less about God, it
has seemed to me important to distinguish the parts played by the
Negative Way of the Neoplatonists and the ways of the Sceptics in
leading towards a salutary and liberating ignorance in which faith rests
on the Unknowable and is nourished by silence.

'Where Two are to Become One': Mysticism and Monism

GRACE JANTZEN

I

(1) If you would know God, you must not merely be *like* the Son, you must *be* the Son yourself.[1]

With these words Meister Eckhart encapsulates the aim of Christian mysticism as he understood it: to know God, and to know God in such a way that the knower is not merely *like* Christ but actually *becomes* Christ, taken into the Trinity itself. Eckhart speaks frequently of this in his sermons.

> The Father bears his son in the inmost part of the soul, and bears you with his only begotten Son, no less. If I am to be the Son, then I must be Son in the same essence as that in which he is Son, and not otherwise.[2]

In another sermon he discusses further the connection between knowing God and being the Son of God. Because the Christian is taught by God, it is possible for such a person to say that God's knowing has become her own.

> And since his knowing is mine, and since his substance is his knowing and his nature and his essence, it follows that his essence and his substance and his nature are mine. And if his substance, his being and his nature are mine, then I am the son of God . . . Note *how* we are the Son of God—by having the same essence that the Son has.[3]

Nor is this participation in the essence of the Son merely a matter of likeness. Eckhart is quite clear that he is talking about more than likeness: he is talking about being *one* with God.

> Where two are to become one, one of them must lose its being. So it is: and if God and your soul are to become one, your soul must lose her being and her life. As far as anything remained, they would

[1] *Meister Eckhart: Sermons and Treatises*, 3 vols, trans. M. O'C. Walshe (London: Watkins, 1979–87), Vol. I, 127.

[2] Ibid., 148.

[3] Ibid., 66.

indeed be *united*, but for them to become *one*, the one must lose its identity and the other must keep its identity: then they are one.[4]

Eckhart was trained and later became a teacher in the University of Paris just after the time of Thomas Aquinas and Albert the Great, his fellow Dominicans, and he was fully conversant with scholastic philosophy. His words cannot therefore be taken as effusions of mystical emotion. They are, rather, representative of his efforts to explain and lead his hearers into knowledge of God, and they have often been taken as some of the most explicitly monistic of Christian mystical writing.[5]

(2) Meister Eckhart, however, is by no means the only medieval mystic from whose writings can be gleaned statements that support the view that mysticism involves monism. St Bernard of Clairvaux uses the metaphor of eating to explain the way in which we become one with God.

> I am chewed as I am reproved by him; I am swallowed as I am taught; I am digested as I am changed; I am assimilated as I am transformed; I am made one as I am conformed. Do not wonder at this, for he feeds upon us and is fed by us that we may be the more closely bound to him. Otherwise we are not perfectly united with him.[6]

Bernard goes on to explain the Biblical Johanine concept of mutual indwelling of God and the believer by extending the eating metaphor:

> If I eat and am not eaten, then he is in me but I am not yet in him. But if I am eaten and do not eat, then he has me in him, but it would appear that he is not yet in me; and in neither case will there be perfect unity between us. But he eats me that he may have me in himself, and he in turn is eaten by me that he may be in me, and the bond between us will be strong and the union complete, for I shall be in him and he will likewise be in me.[7]

(3) A different sort of metaphor is used by St John of the Cross to explicate mystical union; yet it too is consistent with monistic interpretation. John speaks of the soul as a log or a coal enkindled and burning with the living flame of love that is God. When the log is first

---

[4] Ibid., 52.

[5] From the papal bull which denounced him, *In Agro Domino*, to Evelyn Underhill.

[6] Bernard of Clairvaux, *On the Song of Songs,* 4 vols (Kalamazoo: Cistercian Publications, 1977–1980), Serm. 71.

[7] Ibid.

exposed to the flame, the log and the flame can be identified separately as the flame gradually heats and purges the log. Once the wood catches fire, however, the flames shoot forth from within it. It glows and is one with the flame.

> Hence we can compare the soul . . . in this state of transformation in love to the log of wood that is ever immersed in fire, and the acts of this soul to the flame that blazes up from the fire of love. The more intense the fire of union, the more vehemently does this fire burst into flames . . . As a result all the acts of the soul are divine, since the movement toward these acts and their execution stems from God.[8]

According to John, the transformation is so complete that in this union of love between God and the soul, the activity that results can be said to be divine. It would be impossible to separate out which aspects are contributed by God and which by the person so united to God.

John suggests that we can think of the soul as consisting of many layers, like rings in a log of wood, each of which in turn must be purged and enkindled with the living flame of love until its deepest centre is reached.

> We can say that there are as many centres in God possible to the soul, each one deeper than the other, as there are degrees of love of God possible to it . . .
>
> The soul's centre is God. When it has reached God with all the capacity of its being and the strength of its operation and inclination, it will have attained to its final and deepest centre in God, it will know, love, and enjoy God with all its might.[9]

Like Eckhart and Bernard, John's chief aim in writing is to assist his readers in their own growth to union with God; and it is clear that such union is considered by all of them to be the goal and summit of the mystical life. From passages such as these, it has been held that mysticism requires monism as its underlying metaphysic, a unity of substance or essence between God and the soul, in which all things are one, and the distinction between subject and object is lost in unity.

II

(1) Such a view has regularly been accepted by theologians and philosophers analysing mysticism. Sometimes this has been held to the credit

---

[8] John of the Cross, *The Living Flame of Love* in *The Collected Works of John of the Cross,* trans. Kieren Kavanaugh (Washington, DC: Institute of Carmelite Studies, 1973), 580.

[9] Ibid., 583.

of mysticism, and sometimes to its debit. In German Protestant theology there have been some particularly vociferous condemnations of mysticism on the grounds of its alleged monism. One of the most influential of these voices was that of Adolf von Harnack, who argued in *What is Christianity?*[10] that the original Gospel of Jesus of Nazareth has been obscured by centuries of dogma and tradition. The core of the Gospel is the understanding of God as Father, the worth of the human soul, and the ethical ideal of the kingdom of God. It is utterly misguided to seek or to claim union with God on the basis of mystical experiences. Such ideas are a perversion of the Gospel of Christ arising from the attempt to accommodate Christianity to Greek culture. Mysticism represents the 'greatest triumph' of Neoplatonism in assimilating Christianity into itself, and is to be altogether deplored.[11]

Harnack considers mysticism to be always pantheistic in its basic outlook. God, nature, and the human soul are of one substance: the many are a part of the One, and there is a merging of each and All.[12] Even the Trinity is ultimately an inadequate conception. God must be conceived of as One, beyond the Trinity: Harnack cites the teachings of Eckhart as a significant instance of this position.[13]

Mystical union is therefore seen by Harnack as the conscious merging with or absorption into this One, into a realized monism. For this to be possible, the soul must be stripped of all hindrances, especially those involved in ownership of property and sexuality,[14] and live a life of purity and devotion. Harnack sees all such stripping of hindrances as a variation of the theme of trying to curry favour with the divine by means of good works.[15]

> The [Roman] Catholic character of this elevation shows itself most plainly in this, that with repentance, faith, and love to Christ, the process is not concluded; man must become entirely nothing; he must pass out of himself, in order, finally, to be merged into the Godhead . . . God is all and the individual is nothing, freedom can only be considered as absorption into the Deity.[16]

Both content and phrasing show that here as elsewhere Harnack had Eckhart particularly in mind: his words echo the passage from Eckhart already quoted:

[10] *Das Wesen des Christentums* (Leipzig, 1900; English trans. London, 1901).
[11] *History of Dogma*, 7 vols (English trans. London, 1894–1899), Vol. I, 359.
[12] VI, 97.
[13] VI, 105.
[14] III, 109.
[15] VI, 110.
[16] VI, 105.

Where two are to become one, one of them must lose its being. So it is; and if God and your soul are to become one, your soul must lose her being and her life.[17]

According to Harnack, such misguided ideas about merging with the divine are implicated in the Chalcedonian definition of Christ as having two natures in one person. Because men and women believed themselves to have direct experience of merging with God and hence of being identical with God in mystical union, Christ too had to be taken as both human and divine, the prototype of such mystical union.[18] Harnack considered such Christology hopelessly confused, and made even more appalling by the development of doctrines of the Eucharist in which people tried to find the real presence of Christ, the union between God and the physical elements of bread and wine mirroring the mystical union of God and the soul.[19] Instead of a simple service of remembrance of Jesus' teaching and his death, the Eucharist could then be seen as an occasion of actually participating in the divine, literally taking Christ into one's mouth. In Harnack's view, such ideas turn faith into barbarity; and the fault lies squarely with mystical monism.[20]

Even worse is to come. If God has become human, and if Christ can be born again in us, then we can be reborn in him—we can become divine. Harnack's words reveal his belief that such union is both religiously perverse and philosophically misguided, because it seeks to overstep the limits of human knowledge as articulated by Kant.

But if the soul is capable, through rapture, of such a flight from its nothingness to God, if God can enter into its inmost depths, then— here is the necessary inversion of the view—the soul itself includes, in its innermost being, a deeply hidden divine element. Pantheism is transformed into self-deification. The divine is at bottom the capacity of the soul to abstract and emancipate itself from all that is phenomenal . . .[21]

Harnock holds that such a capacity is illusory: the phenomenal is the boundary of our knowledge and experience. Supposing ourselves to transcend it only leaves us preoccupied with our own souls rather than soberly doing our duty by following the precepts for right living and social justice as good Christians—and good Kantians—should.

The reference to Kant is not incidental: I shall argue later that the view of mysticism as monism and the sense of outrage which it evokes in

[17] Eckhart, Vol. I, 52.
[18] Harnack, Vol. V, 280.
[19] V, 305; cf. 291; IV, 270–282.
[20] IV, 271–272.
[21] VI, 106.

Harnack and many others with him have more to do with Kantian epistemology than with medieval mystics. A significant clue in that direction comes from the curious fact that subsequent theologians, among them Emil Brunner and Karl Barth, who utterly repudiated many of Harnack's views, nevertheless did not question his account of mysticism. Barth, for instance, thought that Harnack was quite wrong to reject the Chalcedonian definition of Christ, and strongly affirmed the real presence and voice of Christ in the Word of proclamation; yet he said that mysticism is 'esoteric atheism'.[22] As we saw, according to Harnack it was mysticism that was largely responsible for the Chalcedonian formula. Is it not odd that Barth totally disagrees with Harnack about the formula itself, and yet never pauses to reconsider either Harnack's account of mysticism or his evaluation of it?

Fundamental to Barth's theology is a strong distinction between Creator and creature, a gap that can only be bridged by God's self-revelation through God's word. Accordingly, Barth holds that the knowledge of God must always be objective knowledge: God is distinct from human beings who are knowing subjects. Accordingly Barth repudiates

> all those ideas of knowledge of God which understand it as the union of man with God, and which do not regard it as an objective knowledge but leave out the distinction between the knower and the known.[23]

Such ontological merging Barth, like Harnack, characterizes as mystical.

(2) Philosophers have been as confident as theologians that mysticism and monism are interconnected. William James speaks in *Pragmatism* of the attraction of monism to 'mystical minds', the recognition, through discipline, that at bottom all is One, 'melted into oneness'.

> In the passion of love we have the mystic germ of what might mean a total union of all sentient life. This mystical germ wakes up in us on hearing the monistic utterances, acknowledges their authority, and assigns to intellectual considerations a secondary place.[24]

Although as the passage continues James goes on to dissociate himself from mysticism and monism, he does not question the identification of the two.

[22] Karl Barth, *Church Dogmatics*, 4 vols (English trans. T. & T. Clark, Edinburgh, 1975–1977), Vol. I.2, 319.

[23] II.1, 10; cf. 57; III.4, 190.

[24] *Pragmatism* (New York: Longmans, Green & Co., 1907), 151–155.

In his more extended discussion of mysticism in *The Varieties of Religious Experience*, which is still standard undergraduate reading and has incalculably influenced subsequent philosophical study of mysticism, he goes even farther. He asserts that mystical states, in spite of being strictly untheoretical, 'assert a pretty distinct theoretic drift' and 'point in definite philosophical directions. One of these directions is optimism, and the other is monism.'[25] And he argues that although those who have never experienced such states may legitimately remain sceptical, 'mystical states . . . have the right to be absolutely authoritative over the individuals to whom they come'.[26] Although James does not explicitly say so, it is a consequence of his position that those who experience mystical states are entitled to adopt a monistic philosophical stance.

Walter Terence Stace goes still farther. He distinguishes between 'two types of mystical consciousness, the extrovertive and the introvertive'.[27] The extrovertive mystic experiences what Stace calls 'the Unifying Vision', in which all things are seen as One; but the ego, though in blissful harmony with this totality, still remains differentiated from it. The introvertive mystic, by contrast, experiences not just harmony but unity, the falling away of all distinctions.

> . . . the individual self which has the experience must lose its individuality, cease to be a separate individual, and lose its identity because lost or merged in the One, or Absolute, or God.[28]

This introvertive experience in which all distinctions are overcome is according to Stace the paradigm of all mysticism: the extrovertive experience is 'on a lower level . . . it is an incomplete kind of experience which finds its completion and fulfilment in the introvertive kind of experience'.[29]

Whereas for Harnack and Barth this alleged monism is a reason to deplore mysticism, for Stace it provides the essential element required for a universal core of religion, even though often in tension with organized religious systems of doctrine and ethics. To be accurate, Stace in a later chapter makes clear his preference for 'pantheism' rather than 'monism' as the term which best describes the mystics' view of reality, on the grounds that as he defines it monism is the view that the relation between God and the world is 'pure identity with no dif-

---

[25] *The Varieties of Religious Experience* (Glasgow: Fontana, Collins, 1977), 401.
[26] Ibid., 407.
[27] *Mysticism and Philosophy* (London: Macmillan, 1960), 131.
[28] Ibid., 111.
[29] Ibid., 132.

ference'.[30] Stace points out that if this were taken literally it would make a nonsense of the mystics' struggle to *overcome* difference and achieve unity. Nevertheless, the mystical experience as Stace understands it is a merging into One; and Stace urges that this experience is

> not merely subjective, but . . . in very truth what the mystics themselves claim, namely a direct experience of the One, the Universal Self, God.[31]

If this is correct, it would seem that all the theologians' worst fears are confirmed.

III

Many other examples could be given of theologians and philosophers who join Harnack and Barth, James and Stace, in the view that mysticism entails a view of reality in which distinctions are lost in a conscious merging with the One.[32] In spite of the chorus of assent, however, some niggling doubts might already present themselves. In the first place, a good deal more needs to be said about exactly what this alleged monism comes to. Is it the case that the mystic is seeking to achieve an undifferentiated unity which was not there before? That is, does the mystical experience *bring about* monism? That idea hardly makes sense if we are using the term 'monism' in its traditional sense of the oneness or unity of all reality, or even its more specific sense of the absolute identity of mind and matter. If monism is true then surely it must be true whether people have mystical experiences or not, and could hardly be something that the having of such experiences could bring about.

Accordingly, it might make more sense to suggest that the mystic is learning to *recognize* what has been true all along. On this view the mystical experience does not bring about a change in reality but a change in perception. But this again is inadequate, not least because of the unexamined assumption that perception and reality are neatly separable. In any case, the quotations from Eckhart, Bernard and John make clear that what is needed is more than a change of view. Increasing union with God is seen by them as a change in how things *are* at a fundamental level; not merely a change in how things are perceived. Thus it begins to appear that the whole way of setting the question

---

[30] Ibid., 219.

[31] Ibid., 207.

[32] Theologians of the stature of Tillich, Brunner, Nygren, and Underhill give voice to variations of this theme; joined by philosophers like O'Hear, Staal, and Smart.

needs more thought: the simplistic dilemma generated by the assumption that mystical experience either brings about monism or else merely recognizes it cannot but result in inadequate treatment of both monism and mysticism.

A further consideration arises from the fact that all three mystics cited, in common with the Christian mystical tradition generally, see union with God not as an all-or-nothing experience, but as something which can develop and increase. Contrary to what one might have expected from reading James or Stace, the mystics do not speak of union with God as though it were a state of subjective consciousness which is either achieved or not, but rather as a gradual transformation of the personality in response to the love of God, until the actions arising from such a personality are indistinguishable from divine *caritas*: remember John of the Cross's metaphor of the living flame of love slowly warming and purging the log until the log glows indistinguishably from the flame. The whole manner of speaking is of a different order from the one we would expect if the union in question were the attainment or recognition of a state of metaphysical monism: those do not seem to be the issues at stake.

It becomes apparent when we begin to ask questions of this sort that it is necessary to probe more deeply into what the mystics actually mean by union with God. What exactly is it that is united? Is it a union of love and affectivity, or of intellect, or of will, or of all of these put together? Or, if it is a union of substance or essence, how are those words to be understood? Eckhart, who as we saw spoke of union in terms of substance and essence, is using those terms within the technical precision of Northern European scholasticism: we must look more closely at their meaning before assuming that he is implying metaphysical monism.

It is also worth bearing in mind that Bernard, Eckhart and John were all members of Christian religious orders, and indeed in positions of leadership within those orders. As such they were immersed in Scripture and tradition, and well aware of the doctrine of Creation which, in all the variants of its interpretation, affirms a basic distinction between God as Creator and all other things as creatures. All of them were explicit about their loyalty to the teaching of the Church. Given that this is so, it is surely no more than prudent to be very cautious about interpreting them as denying a Creator–creature distinction; one should move to such an interpretation of them only if all other possible ways of understanding them fail. This in turn requires careful attention to the context of their utterances, first of all within the texts from which they are quoted and also more broadly within their social and political and ecclesiastical settings.

Yet theologians and philosophers have been notoriously unwilling to investigate the actual texts and contexts of mystical writing. Harnack was famous as a historian of dogma, and Barth was very well versed in patristic writing; both were perfectly competent to carry out the necessary historical study. Yet they make very little effort to check the accuracy of their comments about mysticism against a range of actual mystical writings. Even when they do cite instances (which in the case of Barth is infrequent), the citations are fitted on to a monistic Procrustean Bed rather than examined in depth.

The same is true of James and Stace. Both these philosophers sprinkle their writings with quotations from mysical writers; but once one's suspicions are alerted, it is impossible not to feel that they are using these quotations rather like a fundamentalist might pepper an argument with passages from the Bible, using them as proof texts without regard for their literary or historical context. By careful selection of texts such as those at the beginning of this lecture it is perfectly possible to 'prove' that mystics are monists, just as it is possible to select verses from the Bible that 'prove' the inferiority of women: from whence follows neither the one nor the other, but rather some acid comments about the poor scholarship involved, and its ideological origins.

IV

(1) In fact, it does not take inordinate effort to show that when the quotations from Bernard and John of the Cross are placed in context, they lend no support whatever to a monistic interpretation of union with God, and that even in the case of Eckhart an alternative interpretation is at least available. The passage from Bernard in which he discusses mystical union under the metaphor of eating and being eaten is followed immediately by a discussion of how this union of the soul and God differs from the union with one another enjoyed by the members of the Trinity. Bernard says explicitly that the mutual indwelling of the Father and the Son is not the same as the mutual indwelling of God and the soul. The latter is an indwelling of charity, a harmony of love. The former is a unity of substance.

> The Father and the Son . . . are one, because they have and are one substance, since they have not each separate substance. On the contrary, since God and man do not share the same nature or substance, they cannot be said to be a unity, yet they are with complete truth and accuracy, said to be one spirit, if they cohere with the bond of love. But that unity is caused not so much by the identity of essences as by the concurrence of wills.[33]

33 Bernard, Serm. 71.8.

The union with God to which human beings are invited is an immersion in the love of God to such an extent that there is 'a communion of wills and the agreement in charity'. But the union between the Father and the Son cannot be described in terms of communion or agreement, because

> there must be at least two wills for there to be agreement, and two essences for there to be combining or uniting in agreement. There are none of these things in the Father and the Son since they have neither two essences nor two wills.[34]

By making a distinction between even the most complete union with God possible for human beings and the union between the Father and the Son, Bernard cuts the ground out from a monistic interpretation of his work.

Or does he? Surely this raises again the fundamental question of how monism should be understood. If monism is the doctrine that God and the soul are an undifferentiated unity, and mystical experience is the consciousness of such Oneness, then Bernard cannot be used to support it: he makes very clear that the merging of God and the soul is a union of charity and will, not a merging of substance. But what does he mean by substance? It is anachronistic to read this in the post-Cartesian or post-Deist sense, as though there is physical stuff and mental stuff, or world stuff and God stuff, and Bernard is denying that these are the same. Without pretending that medieval writers were monolithic, it is a fair generalization to point out that they held to a much stronger sense of God as the continuing source and support of all things. As Julian of Norwich summed it up,

> God is essence in his very nature; that is to say, that goodness which is natural is God. He is the ground, his is the substance, he is very essence or nature, and he is the true Father and the true Mother of natures.[35]

The modern interpretation of creation *ex nihilo* which sees the distinction between God and the world in terms of difference of stuff would be foreign to them. The stuff of the world flows out from God and is sustained in being by God's Being; it is not something independent of God in either origin or continuation.[36]

The real distinction between Creator and creature is rather a distinction arising from the autonomy given to creatures, particularly to

---

[34] Op. cit., 71.9.

[35] *Showings*, trans. E. Colledge and J. Walsh, *Classics of Western Spirituality* (New York: Paulist Press, and London: SPCK, 1978), Long Text 62.

[36] Cf. my *Julian of Norwich, Mystic and Theologian* (London: SPCK, 1987), 128–149.

human beings, who in virtue of our individuation are able to think and feel and will as independent entities. This independence is obviously not absolute or self-generated, but is ours by the generosity of God who sustains our being even while fostering our selfhood.[37] When out of our autonomous selfhood we respond to the *caritas* of God and are thereby united with God, the union is a union of human and divine will. Bernard makes clear that it is this which differentiates the union of God and the soul from the union of the Father and the Son. In Bernard's terms, we may experience *union*; the members of the Trinity form a *unity*. By contrast with this unity,

> we think of God and man as dwelling in each other in a very different way, because their wills, and their substances are distinct and different; that is, their substances are not intermingled, yet their wills are in agreement; and this union is for them a communion of wills and an agreement in charity.[38]

When Bernard says 'their substances are not intermingled' he does not mean merely that God and human beings are made of different kinds of metaphysical stuff which do not mix well together. Rather, he is referring to what we might call the essential selfhood of each, the autonomy in virtue of which we are human, and which enables us to find beatitude in free communion of will with the will of God.

It is clear from this that the question of whether or not this is monistic is much too narrowly conceived. Bernard is at pains to preserve the Creator–creature distinction even—or especially—in mystical union; on the other hand that distinction does not rest on the question of how many kinds of metaphysical stuff we can count, but on created autonomy of will. It is no accident that Bernard, in company with many others in the Christian mystical tradition, uses erotic imagery to depict mystical union: the merging of wills and affections in loving sexual encounter is enhanced, not undermined, by the strength of personhood of each participant, and each bring their full selves to the partnership and are cherished in it. If the personhood of either partner is diminished by the union, the relationship is sick. In a healthy relationship, there is not obliteration of distinction, or a merging of subject and object, but a glad nurturing of the selfhood of each. If this is the model of mystical union, it can hardly be called monistic.

(2) John of the Cross similarly makes it perfectly clear that an interpretation of mystical union which denies the Creator–creature distinction cannot be sustained from his writings. In his comparison of union

---

[37] Bernard, Serm. 71.10.
[38] Ibid.

with God to the log and the flames of fire, he does indeed say, as already quoted, that the acts of such a person 'are divine'. In fact, he actually says that 'in this state the soul cannot make acts because the Holy Spirit makes them all and moves it toward them'.[39] Taken on its own, this sounds as though the soul's individuality and freedom are lost in the mystical union, as though only God acts and the soul is passive or even helpless.

As soon as we look at the passage in its entirety, however, it becomes clear that this cannot be what John means. John is speaking, not of diminishment of human freedom, but of its fullness, indeed of such total liberation that the quality of action can be compared to nothing less than the freedom of God. He continues the passage,

> It seems to a person that every time this flame shoots up, making him love with delight and divine quality, it is giving him eternal life, since it raises him up to the activity of God in God.[40]

According to John of the Cross, eternal life is the very life of heaven, and our participation in it will be the fulfilment of all desires and the perfection of our freedom. To be enabled to act in this life out of that eternal wellspring of liberation is given to those who are in union with God.

This union comes about, as we have seen, by the elimination of impurity and response to love: in the terms of John's metaphor, the flame of love first warms and purges the log before the log itself catches fire. But it would trivialize John's teaching if this were to mean no more than that would-be mystics must become very nice people. What John means by purgation is the stripping away of self-deception—not least religious self-deception—in thought and action, so that we increasingly 'come to ourselves', own ourselves in freedom in response to the love of God.

> Love is the soul's inclination, strength and power in making its way to God, for love unites it with God. The more degrees it has, the more deeply it enters into God and centres itself in him . . . A stronger love is a more unitive love.[41]

This love, however, is not simply a feeling or emotion directed towards God; it is rather a liberation of all aspects of the human personality, so that the person becomes capable of acting out of this centredness with profound social consequences. The liberated soul seeks the liberation of the world: the love of God is a love turned *towards* all God's

[39] Kavenaugh, 580.
[40] Ibid., 581.
[41] Ibid., 583.

creatures, not away from them. Speaking of the consummation of this loving freedom, John says,

> Once it has attained the final degree, God's love will have arrived at wounding the soul in its deepest centre, which is to transform and clarify it in its whole being, power, and strength, and according to its capacity, until it appears to be God.[42]

The picture is not of an ecstatic state of consciousness which renders the person incapable of coherent thought or action, but rather of all the human capacities at full strength, clarified, integrated, and centred, so that action can be effectual, mirroring the free and creative action of God.

Lest there be any misunderstanding, John completes the passage by using another metaphor which shows more clearly than the log and flame picture the union and yet the distinction between God and the soul.

> When the light shines upon a clear and pure crystal, we find that the more intense the degree of light, the more light the crystal has concentrated within it and the brighter it becomes; it can become so brilliant due to the abundance of light it receives that it seems to be all light. And then the crystal is undistinguishable from the light, since it is illumined according to its full capacity, which is to appear to be light.[43]

The picture is not one that lends credence to a monistic interpretation if by that is meant a submerging or erasure of the distinction between God and the soul. The soul is, we might say, increasingly *itself*, free from self-deception and clutter, and able to rejoice to the limits of its capacities.

> This is like saying: O enkindled love, with your living movements you are pleasantly glorifying me according to the greater capacity and strength of my soul, bestowing divine knowledge according to all the ability and capacity of my intellect, and communicating love according to the greater power of my will, and rejoicing the substance of my soul with the torrent of your delight by your own divine contract and substantial union, in harmony with the greater purity of my substance and the capacity and breadth of my memory![44]

(3) This reference to substantial union, however, may raise again the spectre of monism, the obliteration of distinction. Even if it is clear

[42] Ibid., 584.
[43] Ibid.
[44] Ibid., 585–586.

from the passage as a whole that this meaning cannot be attributed to John of the Cross, there is no denying that Eckhart says things which sound exceedingly like monism: 'Where two are to become one, one of them must lose its being'. Taken literally and out of context, this sounds as though the human soul must be annihilated and replaced by God. Again, however, this is not the most plausible interpretation. The immediate context of this quotation is a discussion of the Trinity, in which there is unity precisely *without* obliterating the distinction between the persons: this should already warn us against any interpretation which eliminates distinctions altogether.

More generally, it seems to me that major distortions of interpretation of Eckhart (and of Christian mysticism in general) have resulted from an inadequate philosophy of language on the part of theologians and philosophers, which is incapable of doing justice to the function of Eckhart's teaching of hyperbole, paradox, metaphor, and *perspektivenwechsel*, the deliberate adoption of points of view in dialectical tension with one another. Such dialectical tension is necessary, in Eckhart's view, because of the limitation of human thought and language about God. Since God cannot be captured in human concepts and logic, every sort of metaphor and perspective must be brought to bear to stretch our capacity and open our imagination, even while recognizing that God is beyond all that we can think or speak. 'Therefore the "Name that is above every name" is not unnameable but "omninameable".'[45]

Eckhart was a master of language; and in his sermons he used startling and hyperbolic forms of speech to focus attention on what union with God involves. When in his scholarly Latin works he seeks to elucidate his understanding of the relationship between God and creatures, he says,

> You should know that nothing is as dissimilar as the Creator and any creature. In the second place, nothing is as similar as the Creator and any creature. And in the third place, nothing is as equally dissimilar and similar to anything else as God and the creature are dissimilar and similar in the same degree.[46]

The explanation he gives is as follows. Creatures are utterly dissimilar from their Creator, because the Creator has/is being, while creatures have no being whatever in their own right: in Thomistic terms,

[45] Commentary on Exodus 35, in *Meister Eckhart: Teacher and Preacher,* Bernard McGinn (ed.), Classics of Western Spirituality (New York: Paulist Press, and London: SPCK, 1986); cf. Frank Tobin, *Meister Eckhart: Thought and Language* (Philadelphia: University of Pennsylvania Press, 1986), esp. 52–56.

[46] 'Comm. on Ex. No. 112'.

creatures are wholly contingent. On the other hand, creatures are similar to their Creator in that the being which they have is not an alienated being; all creatures are created and sustained by God and exist only by God's gift to us of being. Eckhart holds in common with the medieval tradition that our being is not ultimately from a source other than God. Finally, this tension between having no being of our own, and hence being utterly dissimilar to God, and yet having the very being of God by God's creation of us, makes both the dissimilarity and the similarity between God and creatures greater than that between any two created things: we are simultaneously both more like God and more unlike God than we are like or unlike one another. It is obvious that thought and language are being stretched to their limits in an effort to be open to the mystery of God; it is also obvious that Eckhart cannot possibly be slotted into a neat category labelled 'undifferentiated monism'.

Most helpful for clarifying his position is his metaphor of the mirror and the sun. When a mirror is turned to the sun, its whole being is the sun,

> and yet it is what it is. So it is with God. God is in the soul with his nature, with his being, and with his Godhead, and yet he is not the soul. The reflection of the soul in God is God, and yet she is what she is.[47]

But of course a mirror must be turned to the sun in order to reflect it; and it is also possible for it to be turned elsewhere and to reflect other things. The same is true of the soul: it can focus upon and hence be filled by all manner of lesser things. But when the soul is fully turned to God, then there is a sense in which the substance of God and the soul are one, as the substance of the mirror and the sun are one when the mirror fully reflects the sun, 'and yet she is what she is'.

Eckhart points out that any image that is *in* the mirror is not an image *of* the mirror; a mirror can image anything but itself.[48] In this sense the mirror has no being of its own; it takes on the being of whatever it reflects. Yet this does not obliterate its reality as a mirror, but rather fulfils it. With this metaphor in mind, Eckhart's saying that 'where two are to become one, one of them must lose its being', has an altogether different connotation. The loss of identity is not the loss of the soul's selfhood, but the deliberate openness to the mystery of God, cleansed from self-preoccupation and distraction. And we need to remember that the metaphor of the mirror has had a long run in Christian thought: already in the New Testament are the words,

[47] Walshe, Vol. 2, 81.
[48] Ibid.

We all reflect as in a mirror the splendour of the Lord; thus we are transfigured into his likeness, from splendour to splendour; such is the infuence of the Lord who is the Spirit.[49]

Anyone who is tempted to label Eckhart a monist or pantheist will have a job to show why St Paul should not be similarly classified.

Eckhart specialists continue to debate about whether or not he overstepped the boundaries of orthodoxy, even while agreeing that the trial to which he was subjected was grossly unfair.[50] (It is worthy of note that in the course of his trial Eckhart frequently denied that he meant his account of the union of God and the soul to be understood in a way at variance with Christian orthodoxy.) Still, Eckhart is a complicated thinker, and it would be foolish to suppose that I have resolved all the problems of his understanding of the relationship between God and the soul. What does seem to me to be quite clear, however, is that given the available alternatives, it creates far more problems than it solves to treat Eckhart as a monist who believed in the obliteration of distinction between God and the soul in mystical union.

V

I conclude, therefore, that at least in the cases of Bernard, Eckhart, and John of the Cross, the standard theological and philosophical categorization of mysticism as monism is simplistic and incorrect. There are of course many other mystics in the Christian tradition; but given the paradigmatic status of these three, it would be romping in territory where angels fear to tread if one were to claim that they are in this respect exceptional, and that the general thesis that mysticism is monism can still be retained.

But now a new problem presents itself. How is it that scholars of the calibre of Harnack and Barth, Stace and James, and the many others whom they represent, are so easily taken in? It has not taken vast quantities of time or any special erudition to show their mistake in the case of these three representatives of Christian mysticism: surely they could have discovered it themselves? It is instructive to ponder briefly why they did not.

One obvious suggestion, at least in the case of Harnack and Barth, is that they stand in a self-consciously Protestant position, and set themselves against what they see as Roman Catholic error. Now all three of

---

[49] II. Cor. III.18.
[50] Cf. Richard Woods, *Eckhart's Way* (London: Darton, Longman and Todd, 1987); Oliver Davies, *God Within* (London: Darton, Longman and Todd, 1988), Ch. 2.

the mystics we have considered, and many others, lived and wrote in a monastic context. This at once made them suspect to post-Lutheran thinkers, who tended to see the monastic and ascetical side of mysticism as an effort at self-righteousness, and union with God as an attempt to bypass faith in the revelation of God in Christ.[51]

Yet Harnack and Barth were both well able to challenge assumptions and received ideas in other respects; indeed each of them is noted for his radical rethinking of what Christianity is. Although they may have identified mysticism with monasticism, and monasticism with self-righteousness, this hardly explains why they were content not to explore the matter further.

One of the reasons was undoubtedly the simple fact that the view that mysticism and monism are interlinked was received as truth by almost everyone in post-Kantian philosophy and theology. Reacting against Kant's strictures on the possiblity of knowledge or experience of God, Schleiermacher in his *Speeches* located religion in immediate feeling or consciousness. He alleged that in this primal consciousness objective content is not discriminated from subjective participation; it is therefore preconceptual and prelinguistic. Nevertheless it is the source of any true religious knowledge. Furthermore it is in some sense *given* to our experience; we are passive in reception of it, and can retain it only for fleeting moments. Most significant for our purposes, Schleiermacher alleges that in the immediacy of the experience the subject or self is absorbed, just as the object also is: the self is lost or annihilated in the Infinite, merged with it in a unity preceding discursive thought.[52]

This idea of religious experience as immediate consciousness preceding doctrine or morality found a ready audience among Romantics like Schelling, in whose hands it was specifically identified with mysticism.[53] Although the close connection between James and the Romantic movement is seldom noted, it is easy to see its influence on his characterization of mysticism as ineffable, having a noetic quality, passive, and transient, and his unquestioning acceptance of its affinities with monism.[54] Reinforcing this view of mysticism for many thinkers from Schleiermacher onwards was the consideration made more urgent by the awareness of world religions, that such immediate consciousness might be seen as a core of religion, shared across cultures and doctrinal

[51] Cf. Karl Barth, *Church Dogmatics* I.1, 391–392; II.1, 10; III.4, 59.

[52] *On Religion: Speeches to its Cultured Despisers* (English trans. New York and London: Harper Torchbooks, 1958), esp. Speech 2.

[53] Cf. *History of Modern Philosophy*, in K. F. A. Schelling (ed.), *Schellings Sämmtliche Werke* (Stuttgart and Augsburg, 1860), Vol. X, 190–192.

[54] *Varieties*, Lecture XVI; cf. my 'Mysticism and Experience', in *Religious Studies* (forthcoming).

systems, which are only stammering attempts at articulating the ineffable. It is clear that for Stace this was a major attraction of mysticism; while for Barth it was a reason to reject mysticism as 'religious' rather than Christian: as we have seen, neither of them questioned the underlying assumption of monism.

But even allowing for the pervasiveness of the view, it is still incredible that so many scholars simply parrot the same assumptions, when even moderate acquaintance with the primary sources would have been enough to challenge those assumptions at their root. Even James, who makes much of facts and empirical observation, drew the quotations on which he based his case largely from a compilation made by his friend Edwin Starbuch, without reference to their original context. How was it that so many competent scholars failed to study their sources? The work of Michel Foucault, among others, has taught us that when there is a mistake of such pervasiveness, which could have been corrected quite easily, we should suspect that there is more at stake than meets the eye. I wish in conclusion to explore this suspicion, and to offer some suggestions toward the deconstruction of the prevailing theological and philosophical attitude toward an account of mysticism.

In the first place, the suspicion is reinforced by what I see as a series of classic reversals. For instance, Stace openly speaks of the mystic as confused, as 'often enough, a poor logician, a poor philosopher, and a poor analyst',[55] and therefore gullible in the interpretation of mystical experience. But from what we have seen in this paper, surely we need to ask who it is that is being gullible? Bernard, Eckhart, and John of the Cross are all at great pains to eliminate self-deception; indeed a will to integrity can be seen as central to the Christian mystical tradition.[56] Had there been as much caution on the part of philosophers and theologians in their analysis of mysticism, this paper would have been unnecessary.

Again, the writings of mysticism and spirituality are widely considered to be 'not serious scholarship.' Serious about *what*? There can be no doubt about the seriousness of the mystics' desire for God, and their efforts to stretch their minds and hearts to the limits of understanding of the divine, whatever the cost in lifestyle or labour. Yet in current theological curricula the study of Christian mystics is at best on the margin. Thus even in the study of theology, which purports to seek understanding of the divine, there is little engagement with mystical writings on the grounds that they do not fit into the categories of academic scholarship. And it is indeed true that it is virtually impos-

---

[55] Ibid., 306.
[56] Cf. my 'Conspicuous Sanctity and Religious Belief', in Abraham and Holtzer (eds), *The Rationality of Religious Belief* (Oxford, 1987).

sible to take the writings of the mystics seriously without radically questioning these categories and with them the academic ideal of disengaged objectivity: if these are the characteristics of scholarship, then one should indeed be wary of the mystics! But it is difficult to avoid the suspicion that theologians all too often would rather retreat to academic neutrality than expose ourselves to the vulnerability called for by engagement with mystical writing; and we disguise our own failure of seriousness by attributing it to the mystics.

These reversals have all the hallmarks of pervasive self-deception. But why should philosophers and theologians collude in such self-blinkering? What are we afraid of? I offer only one suggestion among many. It is a matter open to observation that when philosophers and theologians make reference to mysticism as monism they also very frequently refer to the sexual imagery used by mystics to describe the union of God and the soul; and take this sexual imagery to imply the complete loss of self, the submergence of the soul in God. Now as I have already pointed out in the discussion of Bernard, sexual union does *not* mean loss of self, submergence of one person in the other. Or does it? When this interpretation of the submergence of the self is coupled with the fact that the soul is always spoken of as feminine and God as masculine, it is hard to resist the idea that theologians and philosophers, predominantly male, have seen sexuality *precisely* in terms of the submergence of the female, her loss of name and self and any power of her own as a consequence of her union with the male. Is it possible that the consistent identification of mysticism with monism, and the persistent failure to read the mystics properly, is because taking them seriously would radically undermine patriarchal ideas of sexuality and power?

Faith and Goodness

ELEONORE STUMP

Introduction

Recent work on the subject of faith has tended to focus on the epistemology of religious belief, considering such issues as whether beliefs held in faith are rational and how they may be justified. Richard Swinburne, for example, has developed an intricate explanation of the relationship between the propositions of faith and the evidence for them.[1] Alvin Plantinga, on the other hand, has maintained that belief in God may be properly basic, that is, that a belief that God exists can be part of the foundation of a rational noetic structure.[2] This sort of work has been useful in drawing attention to significant issues in the epistemology of religion, but these approaches to faith seem to me also to deepen some long-standing perplexities about traditional Christian views of faith.

First, if there is an omniscient and omnipotent God, why would he want human relationships with him to be based on faith? Why wouldn't he make his existence and nature as obvious and uncontroversial to all human beings as the existence of their physical surroundings is?[3] Second, why should having faith be meritorious, as Christian doctrine maintains it is? And why should faith be supposed to make acceptable to God a person whom God would otherwise reject?[4] Finally, why is it

---

[1] Richard Swinburne, *Faith and Reason* (Oxford: Clarendon Press, 1981).

[2] See, for example, Alvin Plantinga, 'Reason and Belief in God', in Alvin Plantinga and Nicholas Wolterstorff (eds), *Faith and Rationality: Reason and Belief in God* (Notre Dame University Press, 1983), 16–93.

[3] As an answer to this sort of question, it is sometimes suggested that if it were indubitable to all of us that God exists, we would be overwhelmed by him, and our capacity to use our free will to make significant choices would be undermined. (See, for example, Richard Swinburne, *The Existence of God*, (Oxford: Clarendon Press, 1979), 211–212.) But this answer cannot adequately serve as a defence of Christian views of faith. According to traditional Christian doctrine angels who stood in the presence of God were nonetheless able to make the significant free choice of rebelling against him.

[4] For an interesting answer to these question, different from the one I will pursue in this paper, see Robert Adams, 'The Virtue of Faith', reprinted in *The Virtue of Faith and Other Essays in Philosophical Theology*, (Oxford University Press, 1987), 9–24. Adams answers the questions I raise here by

that epistemological considerations seem to play so little role in adult conversions? Anecdotal evidence suggests that in many cases conversion to religious belief is not at all the result of the judicious weighing of evidence or a consideration of the requirements of rationality. We might be inclined to account for this state of affairs by supposing there to be some sort of epistemological inadequacy or defect on the part of those being converted. But such a quick and familiar assessment seems blind to an interesting feature of some kinds of conversion stories with which we are all familiar: it isn't the case that the person undergoing the conversion weighs epistemological considerations insufficiently or confusedly; rather the person undergoing the conversion doesn't take epistemological considerations into account at all.

These questions suggest that epistemological considerations alone do not do justice to the nature of faith, that more than epistemology is needed to complete the account. Such an additional element in faith was commonly discussed in the works of medieval philosophers and theologians. In this paper I want to look at Aquinas's account of the nature of faith in order to show something about this other, often unexamined side of faith. At first hearing, Aquinas's account of faith may strike us as implausible and philosophically problematic. I will first present his account and then go on to discuss some of the problems it raises. After that I will consider the sort of response Aquinas's account provides to the questions concerning faith just raised.

Aquinas's Understanding of the Will

Because Aquinas's account of faith assigns an important role to the will, it is helpful to begin with a brief discussion of Aquinas's understanding of the nature of the will. Aquinas's conception of the will is different from the one most of us take for granted. He understands the will not as the neutral steering capacity of a person's psyche, but as a particular bent or inclination. On his view, the will is an innate hunger, a natural appetite, for goodness. By 'goodness' here, Aquinas means goodness in general and not this or that specific good thing. Determining that this or that *particular* thing (or event or state of affairs) is in fact good is not the business of the will but rather of the intellect.[5] The intellect

---

[5] Those who are uncomfortable with the apparent hypostatization of medieval terminology here may recast the discussion in the more fashionable terms of either programs or modules. For example, talk about the will in this context

arguing that some involuntary cognitive failures are none the less blameworthy and that sometimes the rightness of beliefs is the feature of them which occasions praise.

presents to the will as good certain things or states of affairs, under certain descriptions. (It is important to emphasize that these representations of the intellect need not be explicit or conscious. They may be only tacit or implicit, and not in any way conscious, and still count as the reason for a person's willing what she does, if she would refer to those representations in explaining her act of will.) The will wills the things represented as good by the intellect because the will is an appetite for the good and they are apprehended as good. For this reason, the intellect is said to move the will not as an efficient cause moves but as a final cause does, because what is understood as good moves the will as an end.[6]

(This line of approach may strike some people as implausible, perhaps in part because their introspection seems to them to reveal more of a unity than Aquinas's division into intellect and will suggests. Introspection is, of course, a notoriously unreliable guide when it comes to the details of cognitive organization or functioning. That the capacity for semantics and the capacity for syntax are not part of one and the same cognitive capacity is not something readily noticeable on the basis of introspection, for example, and yet that they are not is indicated by the radical difference between Broca's aphasia and Wernicke's aphasia. Having said so much, however, I should also make clear that Aquinas stresses the unity of the agent. Just as neither Broca's area nor Wernicke's area of the brain is sufficient by itself for full functioning as regards language, so neither will nor intellect by itself can function as a person does. Rather, will and intellect are components of a single person, whose functioning as a person is dependent on the joint and interactive functioning of both will and intellect. As long as we are clear on this score and not inclined to identify will and intellect with inner homunculi, we can with equal appropriateness speak of a person's willing something or his will's willing that thing, of a person's understanding or of his intellect's understanding. In this respect we will be in line with current linguistic convention which permits such locutions as 'The hippocampus constructs, stores, and reads cognitive maps'.)

On Aquinas's view, the will wills some things by necessity. Because it is a hunger for the good, whatever is good to such an extent and in such

[6] See ST IaIIae q.6 a.4 ad 1; Ia q.82 a.1, q.83 a.1, and q.82 a.4.

---

can be recast in terms of the module responsible for what neuropsychologists sometimes call 'the executive function'. The particular claim of Aquinas's at issue here can then be understood in this way. The module which is responsible for the executive function is organized in such a way as to be activated by the recognition of goodness, but some other module, some component unit of what Aquinas calls intellect, is responsible for processing the recognition of goodness and passing it on to the module which corresponds to what he calls will.

a way that a person cannot help but see it as good, the will wills by natural necessity. One's own happiness is of this sort, and so a person necessarily wills her own happiness. But even those few things (such as obedience to God's commands, on Aquinas's view) which, independent of circumstances, have a necessary connection to happiness are not for that reason alone willed necessarily. The willer might not be cognizant of their necessary connection to happiness,[7] or it might be the case that they could be thought of under descriptions (such as unenlightened fundamentalism, in the case of obedience to God's commands) which obscure the connection to happiness. And something of the same sort can be said for the things a person might *mistakenly* suppose to have a necessary connection with her happiness (such as winning a figure-skating competition she has trained many months for). Because these things are in fact not necessary for happiness, they can always be thought of under other descriptions (such as distraction from her long-term goal of becoming a doctor) which sever their connection to happiness. They are therefore not willed necessarily either. Consequently, except for happiness and those things so obviously connected with happiness that their connection is overwhelming and indubitable, the will is not determined to one thing because of its relation to the intellect.

What the intellect determines with respect to goodness is somewhat complicated because the intellect is itself moved by other things. In particular, the will moves the intellect as an efficient cause, by willing it to attend to some things and to neglect others.[8] (The psychological act accompanying the common locution 'I don't want to think about it' is an example of what Aquinas has in mind here.) Secondly, the passions, such as wrath and fear, can influence the intellect, because in the grip of such a passion something may seem good to a person which would not seem good to him if he were calm.[9] The intellect, however, is not compelled by the passions in any way but can resist them,[10] for

---

[7] ST Ia q.82 a.1 and a.2. To those who suppose that cases of suicide are an obvious counterexample to Aquinas's account here, Aquinas might reply that the action of a suicide, and the despair in which it is done, can be explained precisely by assuming that in the view of the suicide, the closest he can get to happiness is the oblivion of death. He chooses the evasion of unhappiness as his nearest approach to happiness.

[8] Cf. ST IaIIae q.17 a.1. Of course, on Aquinas's theory, the will does so only in case the intellect represents doing so at that time, under some description, as good. Every act of willing is preceded by some apprehension on the part of the intellect, but not every apprehension on the part of the intellect need be preceded by an act of will. (See ST Ia q.82 a.4.)

[9] ST IaIIae q.9 a.2.

[10] Cf. ST Ia q.81 a. 3 and ST IaIIae q.10 a.3.

example, by being aware of the passion and correcting for its effects on judgment, as one does when one decides to leave a letter written in anger until the next morning rather than mailing it right away.

On Aquinas's view, the will cannot in general be constrained to move in a particular way by something outside the willer, because (with the exception of one's own happiness and divine goodness as seen in the beatific vision) no matter what object is presented to the intellect, it is open to the intellect to consider it under some description which makes it seem not good. So, for example, the further acquisition of money can be considered good under the description *means of sending the children to school* and not good under some other description, such as *wages from an immoral and disgusting job*. On the other hand, it is still possible for the will not to will even things which are clearly and obviously good, because it is always in a person's power not to think of such things and consequently not to will them actually. That is, it is open to the will not to will such things by willing that the intellect not attend to them. (Of course, if the will does so, on Aquinas's account, it is in virtue of some representation on the part of the intellect that doing so is good, at that time, under some description.)

It is apparent, then, that on Aquinas's account of the will, it is part of a complicated feedback system, composed of will, intellect, and the passions, and set in motion by the nature of the will as a hunger for the good.[11]

Aquinas's Account of Faith

On Aquinas's view of the relation between intellect and will, intellect clearly has a role to play in all acts of the will. But he also holds that will has a role to play in most, though not all, acts of intellect. That this is so can be seen just from his account of the nature of the will, where he maintains that the will can command the intellect to attend or not to attend to something. But will also enters into acts of intellect in another way, because cognitive assent (that is, acceptance of a proposition or set of propositions) is part of many intellectual acts, and assent of certain sorts pertains to the will.[12]

According to Aquinas, intellectual assent can be brought about in different ways. Assent to a proposition (about the existence of an entity,

---

[11] I discuss Aquinas's theory of the will and his account of the will's freedom more fully in 'Intellect, Will and the Principles of Alternate Possibilities', in Michael Beaty (ed.), *Christian Theism and the Problems of Philosophy* (Notre Dame, Ind.: Notre Dame University Press, forthcoming).

[12] See ST IIaIIae q.2 a.1; De veritate q.14 a.1.

the occurrence of an event, or the obtaining of a state of affairs) can be produced by the object of the intellect (the entity, event, or state of affairs being cognized), either because that object is known directly, as when one assents to first principles, or because it is known on the basis of other propositions, as when one assents to the conclusions of demonstrations.[13] In either of these sorts of cases, the object of the intellectual act moves the intellect by itself and by itself produces intellectual assent to one thing rather than another. So, for example, whether she wants to do so or not, a mother may find herself assenting to the proposition that the judge dislikes her son's performance in the piano recital because of the way the judge behaves as he listens, his movements and facial expression. In other cases, however, intellectual assent is obtained in a different way, because the intellect is moved to assent not by its object but by the will, which elects to assent to one proposition rather than another on the basis of considerations sufficient to move the will but not the intellect. So, for example, the mother might believe that the judge takes bribes, and her belief might result not from overwhelming evidence against the judge but from some evidence combined with her dislike of the man.

It is important to point out that where the object of the intellectual act is sufficient to move the intellect by itself, there is no room for will to have a role of this sort in intellectual assent. If the evidence that the judge takes bribes is outweighed by evidence that he does not, and if this evidence is sufficient by itself to move the mother's intellect, then it will not be possible for her to form the belief that the judge takes bribes, no matter how much she dislikes the judge. Nothing in Aquinas's view about the relations between intellect and will contravenes the common view that we do not in general have voluntary control over our beliefs. But in cases where the object of the intellect is *not* sufficient to move the intellect by itself, then it is possible for will to have an effect on intellectual assent to propositions. In cases of this sort, acts of will enter into the attitudes of believing, forming an opinion, and having faith.[14]

That will can affect intellectual assent in such cases is widely recognized, for example, in science, where experimenters frequently must design their experiments to take account of the fact that their desire to have results turn out a certain way may influence their readings of the

[13] ST IIaIIae q.1 a.4.
[14] See, for example, ST IIaIIae q.5 a.2; cf. also De veritate q.14 a.1. Aquinas's example illustrating the role of the will in intellectual acts involves belief based on the testimony of another, as in the case of someone who sees a prophet raise a person from the dead and consequently comes to believe the prophet's prediction about the future. This example, however, does not make clear just how the will is supposed to contribute to the act of the intellect.

data. (I have in mind, for example, the sort of case double-blind experimental design is meant to exclude.) In cases of this kind, Aquinas tends to talk about the will's commanding or directing the intellect to assent; we are more likely to explain the situation in terms of desires influencing beliefs. But in spite of the different terminology, the point is fundamentally the same: in cases where the object of the intellect is not sufficient to move the intellect by itself, that is, where the evidence does not compel belief, it is possible that some desire of the will's is primarily responsible for a person's holding a certain belief.

The sorts of cases in which will enters into belief that are most likely to occur to us are those in which someone acts badly, as in the example above in which the mother believed the worst of the judge. But it is also possible to think of examples in which a belief based on both will and intellect has something admirable about it. In George Eliot's *Middlemarch*, when Dorothea Casaubon finds her friend and admirer Will Ladislaw in a compromising embrace with the wife of one of his friends, she does not immediately believe the worst of him. Although it is possible (and in the novel is true) that there is an exonerating explanation of Ladislaw's conduct, the evidence available to Dorothea, though not sufficient to determine that Ladislaw's behaviour merits disapprobation, is none the less strongly against him. But because of her commitment to him, Dorothea, in spite of the evidence, cleaves to her view that Ladislaw is not a scoundrel and a traitor to his friend.[15]

We can spell out this case a little more, using Aquinas's theory of the will, by saying that Dorothea wants to maintain her belief in Ladislaw's character and that her intellect in consequence assents to the exoneration of Ladislaw. Dorothea may have had moral reasons for this position; she may have thought that loyalty to friends prohibited adopting a harsh view of them if it could possibly be avoided. Or she may have had more self-interested reasons; if Ladislaw turned out to be a scoun-

---

[15] We might suppose that this is just a case in which Dorothea is weighing evidence, the evidence of what she has seen against the evidence of her knowledge of Ladislaw's character, and coming down on the side of the evidence based on her knowledge of his character. If this were a correct analysis of the case, then it would not constitute an example of will's effecting assent to a belief. But, in fact, I think this analysis is not true to the phenomena in more than one way. In the first place, Dorothea does not deliberate or weigh evidence. Although she reflects on what she has seen, her tendency from the outset is to exonerate Ladislaw. Futhermore, this analysis by itself cannot account for Dorothea's standing by Ladislaw. A dispassionate weighing of the evidence cannot yield the conclusion that Ladislaw was not acting the part of the scoundrel, no matter how virtuous his past behaviour was. Sad experience teaches us that no one, however splendid his character has been, is immune from a moral fall.

drel, then Dorothea would have lost the good of a relationship with a man who admired her and whose character she could respect. Either way, although her intellect is not sufficiently moved by its object to determine it to one or another view, her will is; and her belief that Ladislaw is not treacherous to his friend constitutes intellectual assent in which will has a crucial role.

According to Aquinas, will plays a similar role in faith. Considered in its own right, the object of faith is God himself, but since (in this life) our minds cannot comprehend God directly or immediately, the object of faith, considered from the point of view of human knowers, is not God but propositions about him.[16] On Aquinas's view, assent to the propositions of faith lies between knowledge and opinion. In faith, the intellect assents to propositions believed, as it does in knowledge or opinion, but the assent of faith is not generated by the intellect's being sufficiently moved by its object, as it is in the case of knowledge. Rather, in faith assent is generated by the will, which is moved by the object of faith sufficiently to command the intellect to assent. In this respect, faith is like opinion, in which will also has a role in the generation of assent. On the other hand, unlike opinion, faith holds to its object with certainty, without any hesitation or hanging back; and in this respect faith is like knowledge.[17]

The contribution of will to the intellectual assent in faith occurs in this way. By nature, the will is moved by considerations of goodness. The ultimate end of the will can be thought of in either of two ways. On the one hand, it is the happiness of the willer; and, on the other hand, it is God, who is himself the true good and thus the perfect happiness of the willer. The propositions of faith, entertained by the intellect, describe the combination of both these ultimate goods, namely, the beatitude of eternal life in union with God, and present it as available to the believer. By themselves, the propositions of faith, together with whatever else is known or believed by the intellect, are not sufficient to move the intellect to assent to the propositions of faith.[18] But the will is drawn to the great good presented in the propositions of faith, and it influences the intellect to assent, in the sort of way familiar to us from

[16] ST IIaIIae q.1 a.2.

[17] ST IIaIIae q.1 a.4, q.2 a.1 and a.2.

[18] Some propositions of faith, such as the proposition that God is one substance but three persons, might seem to some people sufficient to move the will to *dissent* from them. For considerations of space I leave such propositions of faith and their problems to one side. But for an example of what can be done even in such cases to disarm the claim that some propositions of faith are repugnant to reason, see Peter van Inwagen, 'And Yet They are Not Three Gods But One God', in Thomas Morris (ed.), *Philosophy and the Christian Faith* (University of Notre Dame Press, 1988), 241–278.

science, where the design of experiments is often tailored to rule out just this kind of influence of will on intellect. In the case of faith, on Aquinas's view, will does and should influence the intellect to assent to the propositions of faith. For faith, then, a motion is required both on the part of the intellect and on the part of the will. Furthermore, in consequence of this influence of will on intellect, intellect and will cleave to the propositions of faith with the sort of certainty normally found only in cases of knowledge.[19]

This description of Aquinas's conception of faith, however, does not yet distinguish between the faith of committed religious believers and the faith of devils. The devils also believe, and tremble (James 2:19). On traditional Christian doctrine, of course, for some of the propositions of faith, devils have knowledge, and not faith; the proposition that God exists is a prime example. But for some of the propositions of faith, such as that the man Jesus is the incarnate Son of God, the promised redeemer of the world, or that Christ will come again to establish the kingdom of heaven on earth, the devils must rely on belief rather than knowledge. Nothing in their experience of God or the supernatural realm (at least up to a certain time, such as the time of the harrowing of hell or the second coming) puts them in a position to know that that particular human being is God's chosen means of saving the fallen human race or restoring the earth. With regard to such propositions, on Aquinas's account, the difference between devils and religious believers is not that believers have faith and devils do not, but rather that devils (or any others who are convinced of the truth of Christianity and hate it) do not have what Aquinas calls formed faith, while believers do.

The will can move the intellect to assent in two different ways, according to Aquinas. In the case of believers, the will is drawn by God's goodness to move the intellect to assent to the propositions of faith. This way of having the will move the intellect in faith is called 'formed faith' because in it the intellectual assent to the propositions of faith takes its form from the love of God's goodness which animates the will. In the case of the devils, however, the faith they have is unformed by charity and remains perfectly consistent with malice. Even though the devils do not see for themselves the truth of what the church teaches, their will commands the intellect to assent to the teachings of the church, Aquinas says, because they see manifest signs that the doctrine of the church is from God.[20]

This point of Aquinas's is not clear. Why should belief based on evident signs testifying to the truth of what is believed count as a case of

---

[19] Cf. ST IIaIIae q.4 a.1; De veritate q.14 a.1 and a.2.
[20] ST IIaIIae q.5 a.2.

will influencing intellectual assent? Why shouldn't it count instead as a case in which the object of the belief is sufficient by itself to move the intellect? And how does this description of the devils' belief distinguish their sort of faith from the faith of believers? The first part of the answer to these questions comes from noticing that the manifest signs aren't evidence for the propositions believed but rather evidence for the authority of the people and institutions promulgating those propositions. The example of unformed faith Aquinas gives in this connection is one where belief in a prophet's prediction arises from seeing that prophet raise a person from the dead. This example suggests that what Aquinas means by manifest signs inclining the devils to belief is a demonstration of superhuman power which seems attributable only to God. If this is right, then the manifest signs testify to the authority of those promulgating what is believed, and so indirectly to the truth of what is believed, because they indicate that the authority of God supports those who teach the beliefs in question.

If we now take seriously Aquinas's claim that what distinguishes diabolical from human belief in God is the kind of contribution made by the will to the intellectual assent, we will have a clearer understanding of the distinction between formed and unformed faith. The act of faith on the part of committed believers is formed by charity, or love of God's goodness; and their faith is a virtue, a habit which contributes to perfecting a power or capacity. Since both will and intellect are involved in faith, for faith to be a virtue it has to contribute to perfecting a capacity of the will as well as an intellectual capacity. Now, for Aquinas, the intellect is perfected by the acquisition of truth; and since the propositions of faith are in his view true, the beliefs accepted in faith are perfective of the intellect. In this respect, there is no difference between diabolical and human faith. The act of will on the part of a committed believer, however, takes the form it does because of the charity she has, that is, because of her love of God's goodness. What inclines her will to move her intellect to assent to the propositions of faith, then, is the goodness represented by them. What inclines the will of the devils, on the other hand, is not the goodness of God perceived in the claims of faith but their perception of God's power—power to be envied, hated, or sought for oneself—allied with those teaching the faith. Power considered just in its own right, however, is not a moral good; and so in being moved by considerations of power alone, the will is moved by an apparent, rather than a real, good. In this way, the devils' act of faith is unformed by charity or love of God's goodness and does not count as a virtue, because it leaves the will unperfected, and the will is one of the two powers involved in the act of faith.[21]

---

[21] ST IIaIIae q.4 a.1, a.4, a.5; q.7 a.1; De veritate q.14 a.2, a.5, and a.6.

On Aquinas's account of faith, then, the propositions of faith entertained by the intellect are not sufficient to move the intellect to assent;
but the will, which is a hunger for goodness, is drawn by them because
of the good of eternal life in union with God which the propositions of
faith taken together present. Because the will is drawn to this good, it
moves the intellect to assent to the propositions of faith; and it moves
the intellect in such a way that the consequent intellectual assent has the
kind of certainty ordinarily found only in cases of knowledge. It is clear
that this account raises many questions; I want to focus on just three of
them.[22]

Objection 1. The role Aquinas assigns to the will in faith seems to
imply (a) an acknowledgment that faith is without justification and (b)
a concession of the sorts of charges Freudians often level against faith,
namely, that faith is simply another case of wish-fulfilment belief. (a) If
a believer's intellectual assent to the propositions of faith results primarily from her will's being drawn to the good represented in those
propositions, there seems to be no reason for supposing that the propositions of faith are *true* or that her belief in them is justified. (b) On the
other hand, if there is some way of warding off this sort of objection,
then it seems as if precisely analogous sorts of reasoning ought to

[22] Somewhat different analyses of Aquinas's account of faith are given in the
following works: Terence Penelhum, 'The Analysis of Faith in St. Thomas
Aquinas', *Religious Studies* **13** (1977), 133–151; Louis P. Pojman, *Religious
Belief and the Will* (London: Routledge and Kegan Paul, 1986), esp. 32–40;
Timothy Potts, 'Aquinas on Belief and Faith', in *Inquiries in Medieval
Philosophy: A Collection in Honor of Francis P. Clarke* (Westport, Conn:
Greenwood Publishing Co., 1971), 3–22; James Ross, 'Aquinas on Belief and
Knowledge', in Girard Etzkorn (ed.), *Essays Honoring Allan B. Wolter* (St
Bonaventure, NY: Franciscan Institute, 1985), 245–269; and James Ross,
'Believing for Profit', in Gerald D. McCarthy (ed.), *The Ethics of Belief
Debate* (Atlanta, Georgia: Scholars Press, 1986), 221–235. My objections to
the interpretations of Aquinas in the work of Penelhum and Potts are given in
effect in my own analysis above; and the problems they raise for Aquinas's
account in my view either are solved or do not arise in the first place on the
interpretation of Aquinas presented here. Although there are some superficial
differences between my interpretation of Aquinas and that argued for by Ross,
my account is in many respects similar to his, and I am indebted to his papers
for stimulating my interest in Aquinas's view of faith. Ross insists on rendering
'*cognitio*' as knowledge and thus making faith a species of knowledge for
Aquinas. In my view, this insistence is more confusing than helpful. Aquinas's
criteria for knowledge are much stricter than contemporary standards, which
allow as knowledge much that Aquinas would have classified under dialectic
rather than demonstration. To render both '*cognitio*' and '*scientia*' as knowledge is to blur what is a distinction for Aquinas and to make his epistemology
sound more contemporary than it is.

support as true or justified any belief a person wants to be true, such as Cromwell's false but firmly held belief during his last illness that he would be completely restored to health and continue to lead the nation.

Objection 2. Since the certainty of faith seems based at least largely on the action of the will, when the object of faith is not sufficient by itself to move the intellect to assent, why should faith be thought to have any certainty? The certainty of a set of beliefs seems to be or be dependent on some epistemic property of those beliefs. But on Aquinas's account, the certainty of faith stems from the *will's* being moved by the object of faith. Why would he suppose that an act of will is even relevant to the epistemic properties of beliefs?

Objection 3. Aquinas thinks that the way a human believer believes in God is preferable to the way devils believe. But why should he think so? Wouldn't it be better if human intellectual assent were obtained on the basis of considerations which by themselves moved the intellect sufficiently for assent, as in cases of knowledge, or, at least, if assent to beliefs were (like the assent of the devils) based on grounds sufficient to establish the authority of those promulgating the beliefs? There is something apparently inappropriate about obtaining intellectual assent by attracting the will to goodness rather than by moving the intellect, the sort of inappropriateness there is, for example, in using a sewing machine to join two pieces of cloth by gluing the two pieces of cloth together and using the machine as a weight to hold them in place as the glue dries. Aquinas takes God to be the designer and creator of the intellect. Since God is omniscient and omnipotent, he could easily provide the sort of object for the intellect which would enable the intellect to function in the way it was made to do, either by making the propositions of faith so evident that they move the intellect to knowledge, or at least by providing for human beings the sort of evidence which according to Aquinas inclines devils to believe in some propositions of faith on the authority of the church. Why, then, should Aquinas think it is better for belief in the propositions of faith to be generated by the will's inclining to goodness?

Aquinas's Account of Goodness

Aquinas's understanding of the nature of goodness provides an important part of the basis on which to reply to these objections, especially to Objection 1(a), that faith is unjustified since it is based on the will's hunger for goodness.

The central thesis of Aquinas's metaethics is that the terms 'being' and 'goodness' are the same in reference but different in sense.[23] This

[23] ST Ia q.5 a.1; De veritate q.21 a.1 and a.2. Aquinas's metaethics is

claim is likely to strike us as obscure and peculiar, at least in part because we equate being with existence in the actual world, and it is quite clear that goodness is not to be identified with existence in the actual world. But Aquinas's concept of being is much broader than our concepts of existence. By 'being', Aquinas has in mind something like the full actualization of the potentialities a thing has in virtue of belonging to a natural kind; and this is what both 'being' and 'goodness' refer to, though they refer to it under two different descriptions. The expressions 'being' and 'goodness' are thus analogous to the expressions 'morning star' and 'evening star' in referring to the same thing but with different senses.

Aquinas takes the specifying potentiality of human beings to be reason, and he understands the actualization of it to consist in acting in accordance with reason. By converting the specific potentiality of humans into actuality, an agent's actions in accordance with reason increase the extent to which that agent has being as a human person. Given the connection between being and goodness, such actions consequently also increase the extent to which the agent has goodness as a human person. So human goodness, like any other goodness appropriate to a particular species, is acquired in actualizing the potentiality specific to that species. The actions that contribute to a human agent's moral goodness, then, will be acts of will in accordance with reason.[24] Since on Aquinas's view, whatever actualizes a thing's specifying potentiality thereby also perfects the nature of the thing, his view about goodness can be summarized by saying that what is good for a thing is what is natural to it, and what is unnatural to a thing is bad for it. As for human nature, since it is characterized essentially by a capacity for rationality, what is irrational is contrary to human nature and so also not moral.[25] Virtues, on this account, are habits disposing a person to act in accordance with essential human nature; vices are habits disposing a person to irrationality and are therefore discordant with human nature.[26]

[24] See, e.g., SCG III 9.1 (n. 1928); ST IaIIae q.18 a.5.
[25] SCG III 7.6 (n. 1915); ST IaIIae q.17 a.1.
[26] ST IaIIae q.54 a.3.

---

discussed in detail in Eleonore Stump and Norman Kretzmann, 'Being and Goodness', in Thomas Morris (ed.), *Divine and Human Action: Essays in the Metaphysics of Theism* (Ithaca, NY: Cornell University Press, 1988), 281–312; see also Jan Aertsen, *Nature and Creature. Thomas Aquinas's Way of Thought* (Leiden: E. J. Brill, 1988). For the medieval tradition before Aquinas, see Scott MacDonald, *The Metaphysics of Goodness in Medieval Philosophy Before Aquinas* (unpublished PhD dissertation, Cornell University, 1986).

Aquinas's attempt to ground a virtue theory of ethics in a metaethical claim relating goodness and being raises many questions and objections; but because I have discussed them elsewhere,[27] I will leave them to one side here and add just one point about the relation of Aquinas's metaethics to his theology. Aquinas takes God to be essentially and uniquely "being itself". Given his metaethical thesis, it is no surprise to discover that Aquinas also takes God to be essentially and uniquely goodness itself. This theological interpretation of Aquinas's thesis regarding being and goodness entails a relationship between God and morality that is an interesting alternative to divine command theories of morality, which connect theology to morality by making morality a function of God's will or God's commands. Like divine command theories, the relation between God and morality Aquinas adopts entails that there is a strong connection between God and the standard for morality. The goodness for the sake of which and in accordance with which God wills whatever he wills regarding human morality is identical with the divine nature. But because it is God's very nature and not any arbitrary decision of his that thereby constitutes the standard for morality, only things consonant with God's nature could be morally good. The theological interpretation of the central thesis of Aquinas's ethical theory thus provides the basis for an objective religious morality and avoids the subjectivism which often characterizes divine command theories.

The Relation of Faith to Goodness

On the basis of this sketch of Aquinas's account of goodness and the preceding description of Aquinas's theory of the will, we can consider the objections to Aquinas's view of faith.

Objection (1) has two parts. Objection 1(a) is that the propositions accepted in faith are unjustified, because it is the will's inclining to the good presented in them, rather than the intellect's being sufficiently moved by its object, which is primarily responsible for intellectual assent to those propositions. Objection 1(b) is that this way of justifying beliefs held in faith seems to justify wish-fulfilment beliefs in general.

In order for a belief to be justified, there are certain criteria the belief must satisfy. It must have been acquired by a reliable method, or it must cohere in the right sorts of ways with our other beliefs, or something else of the sort. In one or another of these ways, depending on the epistemological theory we adopt, we suppose that a belief is

---

[27] 'Being and Goodness', op. cit.

justified and that a believer may have some reasonable confidence in supposing that what he believes is in fact true. If a belief does not meet such criteria, we regard it as unjustified, or irrational. In general, Aquinas shares such views; he espouses a version of Aristotelian epistemology, and he is often careful to distinguish the epistemological status of the propositions in arguments he is considering. But in the case of faith, epistemological considerations seem not to play a major evaluative role at all for Aquinas. What, then, keeps faith from being unjustified or irrational?

The answer lies, I think, in the connection Aquinas makes between being and goodness. Since 'goodness' and 'being' are the same in reference, where there is being there is also goodness, at least goodness in some respect and to some degree. For that reason, on Aquinas's account, even the worst of human beings, even Satan in fact, is not wholly bad, but has some goodness in some respect. But the relationship between being and goodness also holds the other way around. The presence of goodness entails the presence of being. Now since, as we saw, Aquinas does not take being to be identical to existence in the actual world, this claim does not entail that any good thing we can imagine actually exists. Oedipus in Sophocles's *Oedipus Rex* is basically a good person but may be an entirely fictional character who never existed in reality. The sort of being Oedipus has in that case is just the sort of being appropriate to fictional characters (however exactly we explain that sort of being). Aquinas is not a Meinongian; he does not suppose that characters such as Oedipus have existence, even existence of some peculiar or attenuated sort. So in the case of any limited good, however we explain the attribution of being to it, on Aquinas's account the being it has will also be limited and need not include actual existence.

In the case of perfect goodness, on the other hand, things are different. The sort of being entailed by perfect goodness is perfect being, and Aquinas maintains that perfect being not only exists but exists necessarily. At this stage we can simply take this claim about the necessary existence of perfect being as a stipulation on Aquinas's part. But, in fact, the motivation for it is fundamental to his metaphysics. For Aquinas, *perfect* being is being that is whole and complete, without defect or limit. But to be entirely whole and without defect, on Aquinas's view, is to be without any unactualized potentiality. Perfect being, then, is altogether actual. Anything which is altogether actual, however, must have its existence included within its essence; otherwise, according to Aquinas, there would be in it the potential for non-existence. But if perfect being has its existence as part of its essence, if it has no potential for non-existence, then it is necessarily existent.[28]

---

[28] See, e.g., ST Ia q.3 a.4: 'Secundo, [in Deo est idem essentia et esse] quia

Considerations of this sort lie behind his view that perfect being necessarily exists. Those who are unmoved by them, however, may for present purposes just take this claim as a stipulation of his theory. What is important to notice here is that since perfect being is entailed by perfect goodness, if perfect being necessarily exists, then perfect goodness is also necessarily exemplified.

What these further reflections on Aquinas's claim about the connection between being and goodness show us is this. If the will hungers for a certain good thing whose goodness falls short of perfect goodness, and because of that hunger moves the intellect to assent to the proposition that that thing exists, the resulting belief will be unjustified or irrational. This is so because, while it follows from Aquinas's basic metaethical thesis that any particular good thing which is limited in goodness has being of some sort, it does not follow that it actually exists. On the other hand, if the will hungers for goodness which is perfect and unlimited, and on that basis moves the intellect to assent to the proposition that what is hungered for exists or obtains, the resulting belief will not similarly be unjustified, for where there is perfect goodness, there is perfect being; and perfect being necessarily exists.

Since Aquinas identifies perfect being with God, someone might object at this point that if we do not take Aquinas's claim about the necessary existence of perfect being as a stipulation but follow his reasoning from the nature of perfect being to that conclusion, we have an attempt at a proof—a peculiar variation on the ontological argument—of God's existence, so that what Aquinas maintains about perfect goodness can be admitted only by those willing to accept such a proof and its conclusion. But this objection is just confused. The premises of this putative proof are such that they would only be accepted by someone who already accepted the conclusion, so that the putative proof would be blatantly question-begging. Aquinas's reasoning, then, does not constitute a proof for God's existence; it is rather a clarification of two standard divine attributes and their interrelations.

Nonetheless, Aquinas's clarification of the interrelation of being and goodness does serve to explain why a belief formed on the basis of the will's hunger for God's goodness is not unjustified. Does his reasoning in that case not constitute some sort of argument for (at least some of)

---

esse est actualitas omnis formae vel naturae . . . Oportet igitur quod ipsum esse comparetur ad essentiam quae est aliud ab ipso, sicut actus ad potentiam. Cum igitur in Deo nihil sit potentiale, ut ostensum est supra, sequitur quod non sit aliud in eo essentia quam suum esse. Sua igitur essentia est suum esse.' For a defence of Aquinas's account of divine simplicity, see Eleonore Stump and Norman Kretzmann, 'Absolute Simplicity', *Faith and Philosophy* **2** (1985), 353–382.

the propositions of faith? It is helpful here to distinguish between what we might call the metaphysical and the epistemological strands of an account of the justification of beliefs. The epistemological strand gives us criteria for determining which beliefs of ours are justified and which are not; for any individual belief, such criteria (at least in theory) enable us to tell whether we are justified in holding that belief. The metaphysical strand, on the other hand, provides an account of the nature of human knowing or of the world and our epistemic relation to it, or something of this sort, which explains the fact that some of our beliefs are justified, but it may do nothing to enable us to differentiate justified from unjustified beliefs in individual cases. Another way of getting at the same point is to think in terms of levels of justification. We can distinguish between S's being justified in believing p, on the one hand, and S's being justified in believing that S is justified in believing p, on the other. S might be justified in believing p without being in a position to know, or even to believe justifiedly, that he is justified in his belief that p.[29] (As we shall see, Aquinas himself makes a distinction somewhat similar to this one, in distinguishing between the certainty of a belief and the subjective certainty of the believer who holds that belief.)

The explanation of the justification for the propositions of faith provided by Aquinas's account of being and goodness contains only the metaphysical strand. It gives reasons for thinking that a believer is justified in believing the propositions of the faith, but not for thinking that a believer is in a position to know that he is so justified. Aquinas's views explain what it is about reality and our relation to it which accounts for the justification of beliefs held in faith. In ordinary cases, as in the kinds of cases good experimental design is intended to prevent in science, beliefs stemming primarily from the will's moving the intellect to assent to something because of the will's hungering for some good would not have much (if any) justification. Because goodness supervenes on being, limited goods have limited being, in some sense of the word 'being'; but they may or may not actually exist. Perfect goodness, however, supervenes on perfect being; and, according to Aquinas, perfect being, which has no potentiality but is altogether actual, necessarily exists. If the will moves the intellect to assent to the existence of a thing on the basis of the will's hungering for the good of that thing, and if the good of that thing is not some limited good but perfect goodness, then in that case, on Aquinas's account, the resulting belief in the existence of that thing will have a great deal of justification.

[29] See, for example, William Alston, 'Level Confusions in Epistemology', *Midwest Studies in Philosophy* **5** (1980); reprinted in his *Epistemic Justification: Essays in the Theory of Knowledge* (Ithaca, NY: Cornell University Press, 1989).

What is *perfectly* good not only is something which exists but in fact something which exists necessarily, since it supervenes on perfect being, which exists necessarily. Given this metaphysical theory, that is, given the supposition that goodness and being have the characteristics this theory ascribes to them, the beliefs held in faith are justified.

But, of course, we might not have a good argument for (or we might not even accept) some or all of the metaphysical theory in question here; or we might accept it but not believe that any goodness or any being is perfect, so that the will's hungering for the good represented by the propositions of faith is just another instance of the will's hungering for a limited good, which may or may not exist. And Aquinas's account gives us no certain procedure for deciding whether a good that the will hungers for is a perfect or a limited good. For these reasons, Aquinas's account constitutes only the metaphysical and not the epistemological strand of a theory of justification for the beliefs held in faith. His account tells us what justifies the beliefs held in faith but not how we can *tell* with any high degree of probability *that* they are justified. Without an epistemological strand, however, his account does not constitute an argument for the propositions of faith. Furthermore, as we shall see, it is important to Aquinas that there should not be such an epistemological strand in his account of faith.

As I have developed the reply to Objection 1(a), that on Aquinas's account beliefs held in faith are unjustified, it has implicit within it also a reply against Objection 1(b), that Aquinas's account of faith warrants wish-fulfilment beliefs in general. In wish-fulfilment beliefs, such as the belief of a lazy, untalented student that he has done well on the exam he did not study for, the will moves the intellect to assent to the truth of a proposition asserting the existence of some good because of the will's desire for that good. But since for Aquinas limited goods may fail to exist, nothing in the will's hungering for limited goodness constitutes a reason for supposing that such a proposition is true; and so the belief that results from this process is unjustified. But since what the will hungers for in the case of faith is perfect goodness, there is not the same disconnection between the good hungered for and the existence of that good in the case of faith as there is in the case of wish-fulfilment. For this reason, the beliefs held in faith are not in the same camp as wish-fulfilment beliefs.

But there is perhaps one other thing to say about the objection that Aquinas's account of faith warrants wish-fulfilment beliefs. Besides the worry about the epistemological status of wish-fulfilment beliefs, we are inclined to find such beliefs objectionable because we think allowing will to guide intellect as it does in the case of wish-fulfilment beliefs is bound to lead to frustration or disappointment on the believer's part (or, as in the case of Cromwell, on the part of one's friends or followers). Without taking anything at all away from such commonsensical objections to wish-fulfilment beliefs, I want to point out that on Aquinas's account of the will there is another side to the story. According to Aquinas, a person necessarily wills her own happiness, and happiness is the ultimate end for the will; but a person's true happiness consists in her uniting with God. Therefore, the hunger of the will is not stilled until the willer is either in union with God or on the road to union with God, with the other desires of the will in harmony with that final goal. As Augustine puts it, addressing God, 'Our hearts are restless till they rest in thee'. But in that case, following the lead of the will, while frustrating or otherwise inadequate and deficient in the short run, is not an obstacle to human flourishing in the long run, if the process of following the will's hunger is carried on to its natural conclusion. If a person does not give up prematurely and settle for something ultimately unsatisfactory, following the desires of her heart, on this account, does end not only in her flourishing but also in the fulfilment of her heart's desire.

These replies to Objection (1) may serve only to exacerbate the worry embodied in Objection (2), that nothing in Aquinas's theory can account for the certainty he ascribes to those who have faith. As I argued above, Aquinas's account of the will as a hunger for the good and his conception of goodness and being provide the metaphysical strand of a theory of justification of belief but not the epistemological strand. They explain what it is about the world which, on Aquinas's view, makes the beliefs held in faith justified, but they do not put us in a position to determine with any great degree of probability that those beliefs are in fact so justified. What, then, allows Aquinas to say that believers have certainty with regard to the propositions of faith?

In fact, Aquinas concedes the main point of this objection. In a distinction analogous to the one I drew above between the metaphysical and the epistemological strands of the justification of belief, or between levels of justification, Aquinas says we can think of certainty in two different ways: either in terms of a cause of the certainty of the propositions' truth or as a characteristic of the person believing those propositions. The cause of the certainty of the propositions of faith is something altogether necessary, namely, the divine nature. Considered with regard to the cause of the certainty of the propositions' truth, then faith is at least as certain as any other true beliefs entertained by human reason. That is, given the divine nature, the propositions of faith are as certain as any propositions can be. On the other hand, however, if we can consider the certainty of faith with regard to the person who believes, then the certainty of faith is considerably less than the certainty of many things about which human beings have knowledge, because (at least some of) the propositions of faith are beyond human reason.[30] In other words, with regard to the proposition of faith, human intellect is not in a position to be moved to assent by the object of intellect alone but is moved instead by the will; the propositions of faith do not by themselves or in conjunction with other things known compel the intellect to believe them. The certainty of faith, then, is a certainty based on the cause of the certainty of the propositions' truth and not a certainty which is a characteristic of believers.

Aquinas's position here may strike us as lame or defeated. He begins with the bold claim that the *propositions* of faith have the same sort of certainty as mathematical propositions known to be true, and ends with the disappointingly weak claim that, even so, *believers* cannot be anything like as certain about the propositions of faith as mathematicians can be about mathematical truths. Does Aquinas's position undermine what is generally seen as a key characteristic of faith, namely, the deep confidence of believers in the truth of the propositions believed? The answer to this question is complicated.[31]

On Aquinas's account of faith, we can explain the assurance and confidence a believer has in the truth of the propositions believed in faith in two ways, based on the twofold role of intellect and will in faith. As regards intellect, a believer might not be in a position to know, or even to have a great deal of justification in the belief, that his belief in the propositions of faith is justified. But if he thinks of the propositions of faith as Aquinas does, as based on the immutable nature of God, then he is in a position to believe justifiedly that if his belief in the propositions of faith is justified at all, it is justified with the maximal justification possible for human beliefs. On the other hand, as regards the will, while a believer may not *know*, or even have a great deal of justification in the belief, that his belief in the propositions of faith is justified, he is in a position to know that if the propositions of faith are true, then his happiness can be achieved and the deepest desires of his heart can be fulfilled only by adherence to the propositions of faith. This way of looking at the believer's position helps us, I think, to understand the

[30] ST IIaIIae q.4 a.8.

[31] As everyone must recognize, a believer's adherence to the propositions of faith has a manifold basis, which includes religious experience, participation in a religious community such as a church, and so on. I certainly do not intend to ignore the importance of such elements in forming or sustaining adherence to faith. But what is of concern to me here is just that part of the explanation of a believer's adherence to the propositions of faith which is provided by Aquinas's account of goodness and being and his theory of the nature of the will, and so I will say nothing here about religious experience or Christian community. For an account of the importance of religious experience in forming and sustaining belief in God, see William Alston, *Perceiving God*, forthcoming.

commitment of believers to the propositions of faith; and it explains Aquinas's claim that although in the case of faith the object of the intellect is not sufficient to move the intellect by itself, it none the less inclines the will to move the intellect to the sort of unwavering assent given in cases of knowledge.

These replies to Objections (1) and (2) seem only to sharpen the point of Objection (3). Why would Aquinas think that the will's moving the intellect to assent to the propositions of faith is the way such assent ought to be obtained? He clearly supposes that basing assent to the propositions of faith on the will's desire is preferable to the way intellectual assent is obtained in the case of knowledge, when the object known is sufficient by itself to move the intellect, or to the way intellectual assent is produced in the case of the devils who, he thinks, see God's power working in those promulgating the faith and accept some of the propositions of the faith because of their concern with power. An omniscient, omnipotent God could make the propositions of faith so manifest that intellectual assent would be generated without any intervention on the part of the will. And we might be inclined to join Bertrand Russell in charging God with having provided 'not enough evidence'. But Aquinas is so far from supposing that God ought to have provided sufficient evidence that he plainly takes it to be an important feature of faith that the object of intellect in the case of faith is not enough by itself to move the intellect, that, instead, the intellect has to be moved by the will, which is drawn to the good represented in the propositions of faith.

To understand why Aquinas takes this position, it is important to see what he thinks the point of faith is. Both intellect and will have a role in faith, but we tend to assume unreflectively, as Russell clearly did, that the first and most important effect the acquisition of faith produces in the believer is a change in intellectual states. Consequently, we might suppose, the *immediate* point of faith is some alteration of the intellect.[32] If we think of the efficacy of faith in this way, it is certainly understandable that we should feel some perplexity. Why would an omniscient, omnipotent God, himself the creator of the intellect, arrange things in such a way that certain crucial states of intellect must be brought about by means which by-pass the natural functioning of the intellect? Aquinas, however, sees the role of faith differently, and in his position there is the solution of this difficulty. On Aquinas's view, the most important immediate point of faith is not its influence on the intellect, but its operation on the will. Of course, given the kind of connection Aquinas postulates between intellect and will, it is plain that whatever has an effect on the will first operates on the intellect (in the

---

[32] The *ultimate* point of faith is, of course, salvation.

way I have described in the first part of this paper). But, on Aquinas's view, the purpose of the changes in intellect brought about in the acquisition of faith has to do with the consequent and corresponding changes in the will.

On traditional Christian doctrine, which Aquinas accepts, all human beings are marred by original sin. Original sin entails, among other things, that a post-fall person tends to will what he ought not to will, that he tends to will his own immediate pleasure and power over greater goods, and that this inborn tendency of will results sooner or later in sinful actions, with consequent moral deterioration. In such a state a person cannot be united with God in heaven but is rather destined to be left to himself in hell. God in his goodness, however, has provided salvation from this state, which is available for all, although not all avail themselves of it. The story of how this salvation is brought about has two parts, one the doctrine of the atonement, which is outside the scope of this paper, and the other the doctrine of justification by faith.[33] Justification is the process by which the inborn defect of the will is corrected and in which God brings a person from the state of sin to a state of justice. In faith the will desires the goodness of God, which is what the propositions of faith taken together show the will. This desire for God's goodness naturally carries with it a repugnance for what is incompatible with God's goodness, and so for one's own sins. When a believer has such a love of God's goodness and hatred of her own sins, then God can carry on the work of fixing the bent will of the believer without violating her free will and turning her into a sort of robot. In loving God's goodness and hating her own sins, the believer in effect wants to have a will which wills what is good; and so by working to cure her will of its evil, God is giving her the sort of will she herself wants to have.[34] Without the believer's act of will in faith, however, God could not act on her will to fix it without violating the very nature of the will he was trying to make whole. Since it is also a central part of Christian doctrine that the believer cannot fix the defect in her will herself,[35] it is

---

[33] I discuss the doctrine of the atonement in 'Atonement According to Aquinas', in *Philosophy and the Christian Faith*, op. cit., 61–91; and I consider justification by faith in more detail in 'Atonement and Justification', in Ronald Feenstra and Cornelius Plantinga (eds), *Trinity, Incarnation, and Atonement: Philosophical and Theological Essays* (University of Notre Dame Press, forthcoming).

[34] For elaboration of this point, see my paper 'Sanctification, Hardening of the Heart, and Frankfurt's Concept of Free Will', *Journal of Philosophy* **85** (1988), 395–420.

[35] For some explanation and argument in support of this view, see my 'Atonement and Justification', op. cit.

clear that on traditional Christian views the act of will in faith is essential to salvation.

But if the act of will in faith has the importance it does in the scheme of salvation, then since on Aquinas's theory the will is moved by the intellect's representing certain things as good, the point of Objection 3 seems only sharpened. In view of all that has just been said, a proponent of this objection might hold, is it not clear that a good God ought to make the propositions of faith manifest to everyone, either by making the object of the intellect sufficient by itself to move the intellect or by making the authority of those promulgating those propositions evident, so that everyone would naturally form the act of will requisite for salvation?

On Aquinas's account of the way faith works, a believer's will is drawn by the goodness represented in the propositions of faith, although her intellect is not sufficiently moved by its object to assent to the propositions of faith. That is, the goodness of God is made manifest through the propositions of faith, but the truth of those propositions is not. Suppose now, however, that a person were to see manifestly and evidently either the truth of the propositions of faith or the authority of those promulgating such propositions. Then what such a person would know is that there exists an entity of unlimited power, the ruler of the universe, who draws human beings into union with himself through the redemptive power of the incarnate Christ. If such a person were then to ally herself with God, it might be because of an attraction to God's goodness, or it might also be because of a hunger for power.

Since, on the doctrine of original sin, human beings are already marred by a tendency to prefer their own power to greater goods, a tendency which faith is precisely designed to cure, there is consequently a great danger in allowing the things asserted in the propositions of faith to be overwhelmingly obvious. There would be a danger in trying to attract overweight people to Weight Watchers' meetings by promising to begin the meetings with a lavish banquet; but it would be a limited danger, because one could plan more ascetic meetings for later. Eventually, then, one could decouple the excessive desire for food and the desire for the good of temperance represented by Weight Watchers' meetings, so that the former desire would be diminished and the latter enhanced. But in the case of God, if it once becomes overwhelmingly obvious that an omniscient, omnipotent, perfectly good God exists and has a redemptive plan of the sort presented in the propositions of faith, then it also becomes overwhelmingly obvious that endless power is necessarily co-exemplified with perfect goodness and that human beings can be on the side of power in allying themselves with goodness. In that case, however, it ceases to be possible to decouple the desire for power and the desire for goodness, so that the former is diminished and the latter is enhanced. What these sketchy considerations suggest is that the failure to provide sufficient evidence for all the propositions of faith and the requirement that intellectual assent be produced by the will's attraction to goodness not only are no embarrassment for Aquinas's account of faith but in fact constitute an important means of furthering the purpose he takes faith to have, namely, the moral regeneration of post-fall human beings.

Conclusion

There is, then, another way of thinking about faith, which sees the main and immediate purpose of faith in its role in the moral life of the believer, rather than in its influence on the intellect. On this way of thinking about faith, the justification for faith is different from that for most other sorts of belief, because it is grounded not primarily in some relation of the intellect to its object, but rather in the will's relation to its object, where the nature of the will is understood as Aquinas takes it. Aquinas's understanding of faith does not enable us to *know* what is believed in faith (in his sense of knowledge), but it can nonetheless explain how what is believed in faith is certain. Furthermore, this approach to faith has the advantage of explaining why an omniscient, omnipotent, perfectly good God would let the epistemic relation of human beings to himself rest on faith, rather than knowledge, and why a person's having faith should be thought to be meritorious in any way, because it holds faith to be the beginning of a moral reform of the will, of a kind that simple knowledge of the propositions of faith by itself could not bring about. And, finally, this way of thinking about faith accounts for the common conviction that epistemological considerations play little role in initiating most conversions. On Aquinas's account of faith, what is happening in such cases (or, at any rate, in the case of true conversions) is not that the intellect is weighing and judging epistemological considerations but that the will is drawn to a love of God's goodness and in consequence moves the intellect to assent to the propositions of faith.

It is important to say explicitly and emphatically that nothing in this position of Aquinas's denies reason a role in the life of faith. In a tradition going back at least as far as Augustine, Aquinas takes *understanding* the propositions of faith to be the outcome of a process for which faith is a necessary condition. Having once acquired faith in the way spelled out here, the believer is then in a position to reflect philosophically on the propositions of faith, to engage in the enterprise of natural or philosophical theology.[36] But on Aquinas's view it would

[36] For a discussion of the role of reason in the life of faith and a consideration between the different states of acquiring faith and reflecting on it, see Norman Kretzmann, 'Evidence Against Anti-evidentialism', forthcoming.

be a mistake to suppose that faith is *acquired* by such an exercise of reason. While reason may clear away some intellectual obstacles which bar the believer's way to faith, assent to the propositions of faith is initially produced by the will's hungering for God's goodness and moving the intellect in consequence. And the point of this proceeding on the part of the intellect and will is not a peculiar acquisition of certain states of intellect but the moral regeneration of a post-fall human being from his tendency to prefer his own power and pleasure to greater goods.

With this understanding of faith, then, it is possible to see a solution to some long-standing puzzles about faith and to integrate the justification for faith with general Christian views about the role of faith in the scheme of salvation.[37]

[37] I am grateful to Norman Kretzmann for many helpful comments and suggestions on an earlier draft of this paper.

Hope

STEWART SUTHERLAND

I. Introduction

Most of us have probably heard Samuel Johnson's witticism about the reported proposal of an acquaintance to enter into a second marriage—'the triumph of hope over experience'. Whatever that tells us about his friend's previous marriage, it tells us quite a bit about the popular understanding of hope. A similiar point was implied by J. B. Priestley when he referred to whisky distillers marketing faith and hope at twelve shillings and sixpence per bottle, and not for the first time G. K. Chesterton got it superficially wrong in defining hope as 'the power of being cheerful in circumstances which we know to be desperate'.

Johnson's comment neatly separates the springs of hope from the world of empirical experience. Priestley underlines the view that hope can be artificially and indeed manipulatively created and Chesterton seems to reduce hope to the power of positive feeling. The humour of Johnson and Priestley presupposes, even if it does not necessarily share, a number of popular prejudices about the nature of hope. On such a view hope is generally thought to belong to the far-fetched, pie-in-the-sky territory of which Benjamin Franklin warned us when he wrote:

He that lives on hope will die fasting.

Such impressions of *religious* hopes as is implied in these various comments were built formally into the respectively different accounts of religion offered by Freud and Marx. Freud identified religion with, in his technical use of the word, 'illusion'. The primary characteristic of illusion is, he asserted, wish-fulfilment, or what we desire to be the case. Of course, as he pointed out, sometimes the poor maiden who pines by the roadside for Prince Charming to marry her, is rewarded (though the chances are much higher if she is from the upper-middle classes), but it is not a very good basis for planning and living a satisfactory and healthy life. Such hopes, wishes and dreams, he argued, are essentially illusory.

Marx also stressed the delusions of religious hopes although his analysis for their origins was radically different from the account offered by Freud. Perhaps he was unintentionally re-focused by Priestley, for Marx thought of religion *as* the opiate of the masses, not as something manufactured *by* the opiate of alcohol. None the less, however otherwise divergent, Marx and Freud both characterized religious hope as detached from true and well-founded readings of the experienced world. The popular conceptions of hope as at best discountable luxury and more probably distortion and distraction, are at least in the religious sphere given the accolade of supporting theoretical structures.

How surprising it might seem therefore to find hope, according to St Paul, included along with faith and charity as descriptive of the essence of the Christian life. Of the three the Epistle to the Corinthians characterizes charity as the 'greatest': faith, as we know, is considered by philosophers and theologians to lie at the core of Christianity and men and women have died rather than set it aside. What, however, of hope? Can we justify the place given to it in this religious trinity? And even if it were possible to do so in the past, is it possible to do so today?

Immediately we are faced with the dual problem of the set of contemporary popular attitudes to the very idea of hope illustrated above, and the distinct lack of help offered by English-speaking philosophy this century. Until the recent *A Philosophy of Human Hope* by Joseph J. Godfrey[1] the attention paid to hope by philosophers writing in English was sparse indeed. For example, in Britain there are only three attempts by empirically directed philosophers to analyse hope in the last forty years or so, to which I can draw your attention, and I shall discuss these in due course.

Continental thought has been dominated, unequally, by two sources. Ernst Bloch's massive three volume work recently translated into English as *The Principle of Hope*,[2] has had powerful influence upon philosophers influenced by Marx, as well as upon a range of theologians including Moltmann and MacQuarrie. From French and Roman Catholic circles Gabriel Marcel's writing on this topic[3] merits closer attention than it has been given by Anglo-Saxon philosophers.

Our first task must be to locate hope in its proper conceptual surroundings which are, I shall argue, rather different from those of the popular accounts implied above. Equally if religious hope is to be commended, as it is by St Paul, then it must be grounded in structures rather different from those proposed by either Marx or Freud.

---

[1] Martinus Nijhoff, 1987

[2] Published first in German in 1959. Translated into English by Neville Plaice, Stephen Plaice and Paul Knight (Oxford: Basil Blackwell, 1986).

[3] See *Homo Viator* (London: Victor Gollancz, 1951).

II. Hopes, Beliefs and Desires

Those philosophers who have discussed 'hope' have been few but in some cases, extremely important. Kant gave to the question 'What may I hope?' a significance and centrality without equal in serious philosophy. He rightly identified its importance in part as lying in its combination of the practical and the theoretical. Of the question he writes that it is

> at once practical and theoretical, in such a fashion that the practical serves as a clue that leads us to answer the theoretical question, and when this is followed out, to the speculative question.[4]

He offers great insight here into the importance of the concept of hope in its dual role. It is practical in that it directs our behaviour: it is theoretical in that it incorporates *beliefs* whose articulation gives us the concepts necessary for the description of our decision and deeds. The possibility of certain acts (involving as they do *intentions*) depends upon the availability of the ideas which structure our intentions to act and the characterization of those actions. No deed can be properly described, for example, as even partially 'realizing the kingdom of God on earth' unless we have the hope that such is possible—and so on. The concept of hope is in that sense 'Janus faced': it incorporates beliefs about what might be, and it gives sense to patterns of deciding and doing which require the intelligibility of such beliefs for their articulation, and which are goal-directed towards desires for relevant ends.

Amongst British philosophers of recent decades there has been one major point of agreement about the concept of hope and one major point of disagreement. Both of these are relevant to answering the question of the nature of religious hope and both, if well-founded, help redirect our minds from the popular characterization of hope as merely feelings of desire for what experience denies. The three British philosophers to whom I shall refer are H. H. Price, Jonathan Harrison and J. P. Day, and the point of agreement which they share is that hope is not simply a feeling of desire or wish, but that it also contains elements of belief.

H. H. Price, for example, writes:

> If we hope that x will happen, we must at least believe it possible that x will happen;

and adds,

> there is another belief-factor in hope: the valuational belief that it will be a good thing if x happens . . .[5]

[4] *Critique of Pure Reason*, trans. N. Kemp Smith, A805/B833.
[5] H. H. Price, *Belief* (London: Allen and Unwin), 268 and 269.

Jonathan Harrison is also quite explicit in pointing to those dual elements in hope:

Hoping that something is so implies two things, wanting it to be so . . . and neither believing that it is inevitable . . . nor impossible.[6]

J. P. Day accepts the same duality but presses for a much firmer belief content:

'A hopes that P' entails and is entailed by 'A thinks that P is probable and A wishes that P'.[7]

In each of these accounts hope is analysed into a combination of wishes or desires on the one hand, and beliefs on the other.

As we consider these statements in context, however, it becomes clear that there is significant disagreement about the belief content of hope. At one end of the spectrum Day insists that 'hope involves the belief that P is probable'; at the other Harrison argues that hope involves the belief that P is not inevitable, but on the other hand that it is not impossible. Between these two polarities we find Price insisting that

We must at least believe that it is possible that x will happen . . . to abolish our hope, it is enough to be convinced that what was hoped for is *logically* impossible . . . But if our hope is to be retained, we must believe that the thing hoped for is causally possible also. I may be very fond of the sunflower in the garden but I cannot very well hope that it will say 'Good morning' to me. It is no doubt logically possible that a sunflower should speak, but I do not believe that it is causally possible.

The issue is far-reaching and will in the end be quite determinative of the answer to Kant's question: What may I hope? However, that it is an issue is quite contrary to the account of hope which, to quote Chesterton, sees hope as 'the power of being cheerful in circumstances which we know to be desperate'.

Must I believe that what I hope for is 'probable' (Day), or simply 'neither inevitable nor impossible' (Harrison), or both 'logically and causally possible' (Price). If one thinks of some possible objects of hope, religious and secular, then we may see the implications of these differences.

For example, one may hope for a good examination result, or, for 'peace in our time', or for life everlasting. It is not obvious to me that in any of these cases it is necessary to believe that the desired object is

[6] 'Christian Virtues', *PASS* (1963), 86.
[7] 'Hope', *American Philosophical Quarterly* (1969), 95.

probable (as Day would insist). If in fact a good examination result is probable, then surely hope begins to shade into belief. Equally someone who hoped for peace in our time only when it was probable might well be thought to lack consistency of moral vision or ideal, and to have unduly constricted the limits of the possible to the current appearance of the actual. Hope for life everlasting or for heaven raises additional questions to which I shall turn shortly.

Ought we then to delimit the possible objects of hope to what is 'logically and causally possible' (Price)? Clearly this would include hope for a good examination result and also for peace in our time. There could, however, be difficulties in the hope for life everlasting and the hope for heaven. I understand what it would mean to agree or disagree that these are logically possible, and indeed Price made distinguished contributions to the discussion of relevant philosophical issues. It is not clear to me, on the other hand, what it would mean to agree or to disagree about the causal possibility of these objects of hope. On one account of these objects of hope—that they are for what transcends this world and what is not part of our history—then these are not causally possible in the empirical sense which Price gives to that expression. The reason for this is that if we can give a clear account of causal relations then these relations will presuppose temporal sequence and will be part of the history of this world which we inhabit. If the heaven, or life everlasting, for which we hope transcends this temporal world then that sort of causal possibility would seem to be ruled out.

However, even if one hoped for a heaven or an everlasting life which is a temporal extension of this world, it would be unduly harsh to make a precondition of the acceptability of such hopes, the ability to give an account of the causal possibility of such a heaven.

This leads me to prefer Harrison's proposal that the objects of hope should be found amongst those which we believe to be neither inevitable nor impossible. Thus it would be odd to hope for a good examination result if we already knew that it was inevitable. (The final mark of A+ was already known to us.) Equally someone could not properly hope for a good examination result if the impossibility of that (failure) was known.

The implication of all this is we have not characterized hope as involving beliefs about the objects of hope—that they are neither inevitable nor impossible—and desires for those objects. The latter point about desires is easily made, for although death by slow torture, or lectures which drearily extend for four hours, are neither inevitable nor impossible, they are not normally counted among the objects of human hopes. The reason, of course, is that they are not desired by normal human beings.

All of this takes us some way from the 'popular' or degenerate views of hope used by Johnson and Priestley to make jokes, or implied by Chesterton's attachment to cheerfulness as hope's defining characteristic. None the less it does leave us with an account which I would regard as unsatisfactory and my unease can be clarified by recalling Mr Micawber whose basic 'philosophy' was to hope that something turned up. It was certainly not inevitable that something would turn up and it could not be regarded as impossible that, for example, he might find a guinea in the street, or meet a nice chap. Indeed if he were asked he would certainly say that he would *like* either of those to 'turn up'. Do we find ourselves then with an account of hope which would rest content with Micawber as its most typical example? I fear that we do. Some of the reservations which are instinctively felt may be clarified by moving from Britain to France, from the philosophical world of Price, Day and Harrison to that of Gabriel Marcel.

III. Hopes and Values

The first point of distinction is drawn forcibly by Marcel as he distances what interests him on the topic of hope—what has 'roots in the very depth of what I am'—from what is,

> Merely a calculation concerning certain chances. I am considering a practical little problem of probabilities.[8]

Whether we find congenial the tradition of philosophy which writes in this way, there is no doubt that it is very different in character, both in general terms and in its analysis of hope, from a tradition, which in the words of Price insists,

> Hopes 'of' and 'for' are quite easily reduced to hopes 'that'.[9]

In the end the matter is one of the intensional object of hope. There are two questions which arise. The first is whether hope must inevitably have an object and the second is how, if that is so, we characterize or describe that object. However, before we tackle the second question which is a most important issue, we may note the initial difference between the tradition represented by Price, and that which formed Marcel.

There are, that is to say, those who with *prima facie* common sense, insist that all legitimate hope is hope *that*, which in some sense involves beliefs *that*, for example, x is neither inevitable nor impossible. On the other hand there are those represented by Marcel who are very reluc-

[8] *Homo Viator*, 29.
[9] Op. cit., 273.

tant to accept all of the implications which follow from such an analysis. I should not myself support a view that it is false to insist that hopes for involve hopes that, nor have I found any who have explicitly adopted that view. However Marcel, amongst others, has reservations about the clear, straightforward and unqualified reduction of the analysis of all well-structured 'hope-statements' to 'hope that' statements. It will be instructive to clarify the nature and content of those reservations.

Marcel offers two main arguments which would, if accepted, lead us away from such an analysis. Underlying this is his reluctance to give a detailed characterization of the objects of hope. The underlying premise is that if we analyse statements of hope into statements of hope that, then that involves providing an adequate description or at least characterization of the object of hope. This premise is implicit in the accounts of hope given by Day, Price and Harrison for we cannot answer the question of whether x is possible, probable, not inevitable, etc, unless we can characterize x in some way. Equally, although Mr Micawber might hope *generally* for something to turn up (=that something will turn up) he would speedily be able to reject or accept specific examples of what will constitute a satisfactory characterization of x. Thus whereas 'that he find a guinea' is an acceptable exemplification of x, 'that the debt-collector turns up' is not.

Marcel's point relates to the dangers which he believes arise from being preoccupied with giving a detailed characterization of the objects of hope. He believes that this may lead to giving substance to the view of Freud among others:

> It is here no doubt that we must remember the distinction between 'to hope' and 'to hope that'. The more hope tends to reduce itself to a matter of dwelling on, or of becoming hypnotized over something one has represented to oneself, the more the objection we have just formulated will be irrefutable. On the contrary, the more hope transcends imagination, so that I do not allow myself to imagine what I hope for, the more this objection seems to disappear.[10]

Marcel's argument which at face value sounds less than completely plausible, is that to fill in, even imaginatively, the particular content of religious hope is to stray towards the dangers of hope becoming illusion.

Why does he, and why would he want to argue for such a conclusion? The first point is that he overstates his case. Marcel apparently believes that there is an inevitable connection between wishing for something ardently and 'representing it to myself very distinctly' (op. cit., 44). He also believes that such distinct representation will lead one to 'believe it

[10] Op. cit., 45.

is actually going to happen'. This is a Freudian account of wishing/hoping for a religious object as wish-fulfilment, without the Freudian substructure. As I say, I believe that this overstates the situation. None the less I do believe that there is an important point in the midst of this which lies at the heart of my unease with what for shorthand I call 'the Anglo-Saxon' account of hope, allowing as it does Mr Micawber to be a typical example.

I do not think that, granted the above reservations, I am being over-compensating if I suggest that Marcel is here reminding us that in the case of religious and metaphysical hope, the relationship between hope and its content is a particularly subtle one. Central to such hope is not, as he insists, the detailed calculation of belief about what is or is not empirically possible, let alone probable. Rather, what is involved is vision of what might be, and in fact I should want to argue further that at the core of such hope is moral vision.

If one accepts the 'Anglo-Saxon' account of what is minimally necessary for any analysis of hope—desire coupled with belief—then Marcel's concern is that we become preoccupied with filling in the contours of that hope in such detail that we become obsessed with the tree of desire and delusion at the expense of the vision of the forest. If he were to add that hope has no specifiable content, which he does not, then there would be comparable dangers. My own proposal is that the essential content of hope is a moral vision of what might be. This account is one way of beginning to give content to the hope, for example, for heaven whether in this life or the life to come, or utopia, without the terrible difficulties which any such view confronts.

Let us consider the implications of the characterization of the content of religious hope as vision. There are, I believe, four important points to be noted initially.

The first is that one is dealing in pictures rather than empirical predictions and descriptions of future states of affairs. Thus for example one may have hopes for this world or, if such there be, the next, structured by the vision of the lamb lying down with the lion. Here we have a picture, with a deeply symbolic structure which gives clear content to hope but does not readily lend itself to the interrogation of detail. Someone who responds to the hope expressed in such a vision by asking literally, 'How many policemen do you expect in such a future society and will any of them carry truncheons?' would betray a deep misunderstanding of that hope. I do accept, however, that such a question could be asked in non-literal (e.g. ironic) terms precisely to bring out or cast doubt on the credibility of such a hope. However, I shall return to this point in due course.

The second point is that hope founded on vision pays due regard to the degree of uncertainty which is essentially part of hope. To use the term of Anglo-Saxon analysis, in such a hope, one is venturing the view that the object of one's hope is neither inevitable nor impossible. One is certainly not claiming that it is *probable* that the lamb will lie down with the lion, and again it seems conceptually ill-fitting to proceed beyond the claim that it is not impossible, to the more detailed assertion that it is causally possible. The point is that the expression of such visionary religious hope is not adequately understood if the response to it implies that the most important issue is whether or not or how certain we are of its realization.

One consequence of this is that unlike the view of hope which I characterized as 'popular' (basically a matter of fine and probably misguided feelings) hope focused by vision is hope that is discussable. One can give an account of why this is desirable, and of the importance of such a vision. Rather than simply either feeling 'cheerful' or not, as the case may be, one can examine, defend, moderate, develop the moral vision of such on society. One can question or underline such values. One can find new ways of expressing them. That is to say, the moral vision underlying such hopes (of which this is but one example) requires a full vocabulary and logic of critical and constructive reflection. It would even be possible to talk of an education into, or indeed out of hope.

None the less you may still have a nagging suspicion that the relation between such 'visions' and the empirical or practical world may be simply, as Franklin implied, one of distraction or ultimately delusion, and this leads us to the fourth point which I wish to make about religious hope founded upon vision. The relation between vision and reality can of course degenerate, but if healthy will have quite the opposite character. In the first place vision and its expression in hope helps redirect the minds of men and women from total preoccupation with this immanent world. It is comparable in important ways to the hope that those trapped in Plato's cave have for the clear light of day which provides perspective upon immanent preoccupations. In the second place, as with the Platonic forms the content of hope can provide a standard against which the particular and immanent may be measured. Thus conceived religious hope is a basis for the critical evaluation of our world, rather than a flight from it.

Joseph Godfrey draws an important distinction which underlies all that has gone before:

> Some hope is harmful and some not; some is curse and some blessing. I use 'sound' to refer to hope that is positively linked to human well-being.[11]

---

[11] Joseph Godfrey, op. cit., 2.

He goes on to point out that this allows a further distinction to be drawn between hopes which are and are not warranted. The key to the possibility of drawing such a distinction is to be found in the idea of hope based upon a vision of ultimate human well-being. This is not to claim that we can easily reach agreement on what counts as ultimate human well-being, but the latter is a discussable notion. We can paint pictures as those who believe in heaven or utopia have done over the ages. We can evaluate, defend and modify these pictures. Although not wholly determinative of them the empirical facts of the human condition gives a context and set of constraints for the elaboration of such a vision. *Ipso facto* the empirical realities of human life ought thus to be one of the formative elements of human hope if that hope is to be in any way warranted.

IV. Heavens and Utopias

For many the most distinctive object of religious hope, is the hope for heaven, and in this last main section of the lecture I propose to offer a few comments about the implications of this for our analysis of hope. The initial means of doing this will be to note certain comparisons between the role which the idea of heaven has had and the role which its secular counterpart, the idea of utopia has played.

Points of Comparison

(i) Both ideas have their location in the attempt to escape from what is transitory as being the final word about human life.

(ii) Both ideas have in the end to do with overcoming death, the death of the individual as the final word about human life.

(iii) Both ideas have then to do with fulfilment, individual and/or communal, and its possibilities. (NB: the ambiguity of 'possibility'.)

(iv) Conversely both ideas have to do with history, personal and communal, and how to write and interpret it. (Note that this alone shows that pre-occupation with 'heaven' is not *inevitably* life-denying or distracting. One's picture of this life, of human history *cannot* be contingently related to what one envisages as the possible fulfilment of this life. It will certainly lead to different accounts of what is of ultimate significance or value in this life, but that is a rather different charge from that of the irrelevance of such beliefs to how we live and decide here and now.)

(v) The relation of these ideas to history, however, is of a peculiar and subtle kind. Moltmann brings this out well in quoting Ernst Bloch:

The nerve of the true historical concept is and remains the new.[12]

[12] *Theology of Hope*, trans. J. W. Leitch (London: SCM Press, 1967), 263.

Bloch is of course one of the most important and influential writers on the concept of utopia. Moltmann is stressing the difference between a 'modern historiography' in which

everywhere a secular messianism becomes the dominating philosophical idea in the view of history (ibid., 262).

and earlier historiographies in which the dominant idea in the diagnosis of the human condition was a past golden age or pre-mortality which could at best be dimly recollected (e.g. Plato).

(vi) Lastly, and this is an important key to the role of these ideas, the concepts of utopia and heaven have to do with motivation and inspiration: this is recognized by two writers as different in character as St Paul, and the American philosopher Robert Nozick:

St Paul: If in this life only we have hope in Christ, we are of all men most miserable.[13]

Nozick: No state more extensive than the minimal state can be justified. But doesn't the idea, or ideal, of the minimal state lack lustre? Can it thrill the heart or inspire people to struggle or sacrifice? Would anyone man barricades under its banner? It seems pale and feeble in comparison with, to pick the polar extreme, the hopes and dreams of utopian theorists.[14]

Alternative Paths

Heaven—There are obviously different though not incompatible ways of trying to give sense to the idea of Heaven. The first is to focus upon our understanding of eschatology as of the 'last things' which will in the fullness of time, or at the end of the present age usher in the Kingdom of God. The second sense which has come to have a central place in theology since the time of C. H. Dodd, is to emphasize the "realized", or perhaps 'inaugurated' idea of eschatology which gives place to the Kingdom of God as, at least in principle, and in part, to be realized here and now.

In each case, however, there is a natural urge to try to give some *content* to the idea of heaven, whether of the life to come, or 'realizable' on earth. The question thus provoked is whether our concept of heaven does function in such a way as to require filling out? (i.e. on the basis of descriptive content)—and further, whether it can play its many roles *unless* it is so filled out? What certainly is clear is that Heaven will not be realized without the effective work of God.

[13] I Corinthians 15.19.
[14] *Anarchy, State and Utopia* (Oxford: Basil Blackwell, 1980), Ch. 10, 297.

> *Utopia*—Again there are basically two different ways in which this idea has been understood: the first is the idea of a state which we might envisage and in principle attempt to realize. The second is the idea of a changing progressive and processive developing utopia. (In so far as he has such a concept, Nozick's Utopia, or its 'framework' is of the latter sort.)

In his book, titled most significantly *The Perfectability of Man*, John Passmore brings out the distinction clearly by outlining the various classical views of Utopia, counter-balanced by those for example of B. F. Skinner and H. G. Wells:

> Once again we note the characteristic emphasis on change, novelty, improvement as opposed to the characteristic Graeco-Christian-Buddhist yearning for eternity, for a state of perfect rest in which change could only be a disruption to perfection. H. G. Wells had already drawn attention to this contrast in his *A Modern Utopia*, first published in 1905. The classical Utopias were all of them, he pointed out, 'perfect and static States', whereas 'the Modern Utopia must not be static but kinetic, must shape not as a permanent state but as a hopeful stage leading to a long ascent of stages'. Perfection is dead, long live perfectability.[15]

Although Marxism is often alleged to be utopian, Marx and Engels were dismissive of utopianism. There were many reasons for this, but central to it was the rejection of the utopian idea of being able to formulate a 'blueprint' for the future.

This is one strand of the Marxist insistence upon the poverty of a philosophy which contemplates rather than changes the world (even where the contemplation is of how it *should* be). Some later Marxists, however, have been happy to reinstate (albeit properly 'corrected') talk of utopia. The very radical nature of this is well caught by Kolakowski's characterization of Ernst Bloch:

> Bloch thus followed the Platonists in believing that things have a 'truth' of their own which does not coincide with their actual empirical existence but which can be discovered. In his view, however, this 'truth' is not actually in being anywhere, but can be made actual by the human will and human activity . . . Utopian philosophy is not eschatology in the sense of merely awaiting the *eschaton*, but is a way of attaining it; it is not a contemplation but an action, an act of the will rather than of reason. Everything we were promised by the Messianism of past ages, there is a possibility of actuating by our own

---

[15] *The Perfectability of Man*, 164.

power. There is no God to guarantee that we shall succeed: God himself is part of the Utopia, a finality that is still unrealized.[16]

There are thus certain critical points of similarity in the role which the ideas of heaven and utopia respectively can play and have played. Particularly important for our purposes is that there are two difficulties or uncertainties common to both.

The first is that the greater the detail, the fuller the translation of the hope *for* heaven, or utopia into the hope *that* x, y and z, not to mention A, B and C will come to be, then the greater the implausibility of the hope and the less likely it is to be widely shared.

The second difficulty consists in the dual alternative accounts in parallel in each case. On the one hand there is the account of heaven or utopia as a fixed picture of what might be—often popularly dismissed as pie in the sky—and on the other there is the radically different account characterized in Christian theology as realized eschatology. To this latter there is a secular alternative, as we see for example in the writings of Ernst Bloch.

My proposals here are twofold. On the one hand the picture of heaven in question, whether of a life to come, or of a realized eschatology, is richer and more potent if it continues to be a vision—in the sense outlined earlier in the lecture. That is to say it is not a matter of sketching out a picture which lends itself to the language of degrees of empirical probability.

On the other hand, the visionary picture can have vital and important links with empirical reality first by drawing a picture of human well-being based on that reality; and second by being a means of providing the degree of distance from that reality implied in critically evaluating it. In each of these senses the hope involved is an informed moral vision which we believe to be in at least some sense, possible. *Mutatis mutandis* this applies to the idea of utopia. The difference between the two is that the secular vision must ultimately believe that such a goal is achievable/possible through the efforts of men and women. The religious view is not bound to such a belief, and in many forms rejects it.

V. Conclusion

My conclusion is that we have travelled a long way from the initial witticism of Johnson and Priestley and in so doing have uncovered some of the dangers implicit in the presumed popular conception of hope.

The helpful questions raised by Day, Price and Harrison focused our attention upon the dual aspect of hope as involving desire and belief,

---

[16] L. Kolakowski, *Main Current of Marxism*, Vol. 3 (Oxford University Press, 1981), 423–424.

but as not being classifiable as one or the other. It was argued, however, that there are limitations in the general approach shared by these three empirically orientated English philosophers. The limitations were well exemplified by the realization that Mr Micawber, and his hope that something might turn up, exemplified effectively the conception of hope thus developed. Delightful as Micawber is as a character in fiction (rather than as a father or husband) such a summit to the achievement or exemplification of hope would not justify hope's place in the Pauline trinity of faith, hope and charity.

To see justification for this, with the initial help of Gabriel Marcel, I have sketched out an account of hope as the expression of vision—the vision of what might be which carries with it the redirection of our gaze from and the critical evaluation of the immanent finite world to which belong our various histories. It is however fundamentally grounded in that empirical world, for it is ultimately a proposal about what constitutes the ultimate well-being of men and women.

Christian Averroism, Fideism and the 'Two-fold Truth'

STUART BROWN

The man generally known as Averroes—Muhammad Ibn Ahmad (*c*. 1126–98)—was a Muslim scholar from southern Spain who came to be regarded as one of the great authorities on Aristotle's philosophy. Medieval and even later philosophers in the Scholastic tradition referred to him simply as 'the Commentator' just as they referred to Aristotle himself as 'the Philosopher'. Averroes' authority as an expositor was never wholly unchallenged and, in a purely historical context, the term 'Averroist' should strictly be reserved for those Aristotelians who followed the interpretations of Averroes rather than those of, say, Avicenna. Some of these interpretations, however, suggested beliefs that were inconsistent with acceptance of a Creator of the material world or with belief in a last judgment at which individual souls would be punished or rewarded for their life on earth. They suggested, rather, that the material world was eternal and that individual souls did not survive bodily death. This raised a general problem about what to say in the face of a conflict between faith and reason, between the teachings of the Church and the teachings of philosophy. Averroism became associated with a particular problem and with what was known as the 'two-fold truth', according to which it is possible to admit the conflict and continue to profess a religious faith without abandoning or abridging one's commitment to philosophy.

It is perhaps best to regard the two-fold truth as a problem rather than a theory. As such it clearly extends further than questions about who is the most reliable interpreter of Aristotle. For this reason Averroism came to be associated with other philosophers in the Aristotelian tradition. It was even to be associated, in the seventeenth century, with Modern philosophers who faced a similar problem and attempted, implicitly or explicitly, to find a similar way out of it. The problem can thus be seen as having a history stretching from the thirteenth century into the Modern period. Indeed, for those who do not think that philosophy can or should be neutral about the nature of the world, the problem is a contemporary one. It should even be of interest to those who think philosophy 'leaves everything as it is'. For, as I hope to bring out, it raises fundamental questions about the nature of belief.

The fact that Averroes himself was a Muslim should prepare us for the thought that it is to some extent an historical accident that the 'double-truth' has been specially persistent in the Christian tradition. It could arise for philosophers of any religious faith or even for philosophers with no religious faith at all. For instance, one of the problems that confronted Christian Averroists was how to reconcile a Christian commitment to free will with the fatalism that, on some interpretations of Aristotle, was taught as a philosophic truth. But even those who are not religious at all can perceive an uncomfortable tension between their outlook on people as moral agents and the attitude they may have as scientific determinists. Many of the difficulties raised by 'double truth' theories have to do with the nature of belief in general and not only with religious belief. And, in so far as they have to do with the nature of religious faith, they can often readily be transposed into contemporary problems about science and religion. There is, none the less, a case for taking some of the historical controversies as our starting-point, as I do in this paper.

To begin with, I outline and briefly document some controversies about Christian Averroism in their original, thirteenth-century context and then in the context of a Renaissance Aristotelian. I go on to pick out three issues that commonly feature in such controversies and discuss them in turn, drawing on some of the case material I have provided. In discussing these issues I aim to show their relevance to debates between some of the great figures of the so-called Modern period.

I

The 'double-truth' problem was one that confronted teachers in the early Faculties of Arts in the thirteenth century. They wanted to be able to expound the teachings of Aristotle for their own sake and without regard to the Christian religion. They wanted to acknowledge Aristotle's philosophy as the source of truth in so far as reason could aspire to it. At the same time it was not their intention, or so they claimed, to cast doubt on any of the truths of the Christian religion. Aristotle and the Church were, they held, two separate sources of truth.

For the most part, of course, this separation was unproblematic. But there were readings of Aristotle favoured by Averroes that yielded conclusions inconsistent with the teachings of the Church. According to his commentaries, for example, Aristotle's texts lend no support to belief in personal immortality. They suggest, rather, that individual souls after death will unite with a single 'active intellect'. Whatever the merits of this account as an interpretation of Aristotle, it cannot readily be squared with believing that we each have to account for our lives before the Seat of Judgment.

Christian Averroism, Fideism and the 'Two-fold Truth'

The Church authorities were inclined to regard the teaching of these Averroist philosophers with suspicion and concern and in the 1270s matters were brought to a head. Ecclesiastical 'condemnations' were directed against the Arts philosophers at Paris and Oxford. The Bishop of Paris, Steven Tempier, attacked the Averroists for saying that something could be 'true in philosophy, but not according to the Catholic faith, as if there were two truths, and as if in opposition to the truth of Holy Scripture there could be truth in the writings of these accursed Gentiles . . .'.[1] Among the 219 propositions banned by the 1277 Condemnation of Paris were, for example: 'That creation is impossible, although the contrary may be held as a matter of faith'. Or, to take another: 'That the natural philosopher as such ought to deny the creation of the world, because his opinion is based upon natural causes and reasons. The Christian, on the other hand, may deny the eternity of the world because his opinion is founded on supernatural causes.'[2] We do not know independently that this was what the Arts philosophers were telling their students. But these are the kinds of proposition that were plausibly attributed to them.

The Condemnations of the 1270s were by no means the end of Averroism. But they were the beginning of a long tradition of using the label 'Averroist' as a term of religious disapproval, which has only declined because the term itself has disappeared from common use. The label came to be used of philosophers who, though they professed to be Christians, were judged to be at bottom unbelievers because, where reason and faith conflicted, they followed the path of reason. Because Averroes was himself an infidel, from a Christian point of view, the label 'Averroist' was perhaps well-suited for conveying the implication that someone was not merely a disciple of Aristotle following a particular interpretation but an unbeliever.

There were no doubt philosophers against whom the charge of secret unbelief could fairly have been levelled, though the matter is more subtle and complex than has usually been allowed. But there must have been others who did not deserve the innuendoes of this label at all. Faced with a conflict between Christian faith and Aristotelian reason, one option (so to speak) was obviously to prefer reason. But there was equally obviously the other option, namely of preferring faith. Moreover, as well as those who did one thing or the other—who were clearly

---

[1] Quoted from J. Owen, *Evenings with the Skeptics, or free discussion on freethinkers* (London: Longmans, 1881), 22.

[2] Ibid., 23. A complete list of the condemned propositions is included as an appendix to P. Madonnet, *Siger de Brabant et L'Averroïsme Latin au XIIIme Siècle* (Louvain: Institut Supérieur de Philosophie de l'Université, 1911), 175–191.

rationalists or *fideists* in familiar senses of these terms, there were no doubt also many who never arrived at a clear resolution of their problem. They may not have deserved the patience of the Bishops of Paris and Oxford. But they and their problems are, as I hope to bring out, still worth the attention of other philosophers.

My intention in talking about 'Christian Averroism' is partly to signal my departure from the tradition of using the word 'Averroist' with its traditional innuendo of rationalist or unbeliever or philosophical heretic. Averroists may or may not have been led into religious deviation or unbelief in an attempt to resolve their intellectual problems. The 'two-fold truth' may or may not have been a subterfuge for some of its advocates. But Averroism, in so far as the 'two-fold truth' is integral to it, is above all a philosophical point of view and, if it is a deviation, it is above all a philosophical deviation.

It was of course a problem for Averroes himself, he being a professing Muslim. Averroes did indeed believe that the Koran and Aristotelian philosophy were quite separate sources of truth. Perhaps he was inclined to be a rationalist. Perhaps he was fortunate in not having to admit a real conflict between the teachings of the Koran, as he interpreted them, and those of Aristotelian philosophy. At all events Averroes did not say that there were some things taught by the Koran that were in conflict with the teachings of Aristotle but that somehow we ought to believe both. He wrote a treatise in Arabic on the problem that was, it should be said, not available to his admirers in the Christian world. In this treatise he wrote that 'we the Muslim community know definitely that demonstrative study does not lead to [conclusions] conflicting with what Scripture has given us; for truth does not oppose truth but accords with it and bears witness to it'.[3] If these remarks do justice to Averroes's thought, then it seems he was not himself an Averroist in the usually accepted sense. Averroes seems, on the contrary, to have been one of the harmonizers of faith and reason, who deny that the truths of faith could be at variance with those of reason.

He seems in this respect, therefore, actually to have agreed with one of the main claims later made by the anti-Averroists, including the most celebrated of the anti-Averroist Christian harmonizers, Thomas Aquinas. But whereas Averroes modified his understanding of the Koran so as to reconcile it with his Aristotelianism, Aquinas modified his Aristotelianism so as to reconcile it with his Christian faith. Aquinas produced a pamphlet in 1270 entitled *The Unity of the Intellect as against the Averroists*, in which he was particularly critical of this statement of the two-fold truth: 'Rationally I infer of necessity that

[3] G. F. Hourani (ed. and trans.), *Averroes on the Harmony of Religion and Philosophy* (London: Luzac, 1976), 50.

intelligence must be numerically one, but by faith I firmly hold the opposite'. Aquinas comments:

> This is tantamount to holding that belief can be about things whose contrary can be demonstrated. Since what can be so demonstrated is bound to be a necessary truth and its opposite false and impossible, the upshot would be that faith avows what is false and impossible. This is intolerable to our ears, for not even God could contrive such a situation.[4]

This pamphlet was directed against the Averroist philosophers at the University of Paris, one of whom was Siger of Brabant (*c.* 1240–84). Siger was under pressure from the Church authorities following the 1270 Condemnation by the Bishop. It may be, therefore, that his book on *The Intellective Soul*, which was published only two or three years later, represents a moderation of his earlier views. The book addresses the Averroist view that there are no individual human souls and that the human species shares a single intellective soul. Whether this view is philosophically defensible or represents a correct interpretation of Aristotle was a disputed point. In view of these difficulties Siger professed himself uncertain as to 'what should be held in the light of natural reason' and as to what 'the Philosopher' thought about the matter. 'In such doubt', he concluded, 'one must hold fast to the faith, which surpasses all human understanding.'[5]

This remark makes Siger sound like a fideist. But while there was later to be a considerable tradition of Christian fideism, married to scepticism about reason,[6] it is doubtful whether Siger anticipated such a generalized scepticism. That would have not been right for an Aristotelian philosopher. It is more likely that he was expressing a localized scepticism. He starts by doubting what it is reasonable to believe in a particular case. 'In such doubt'—where there is a conflict with what we are called upon to accept as part of the Christian religion—we should hold fast to the faith. That is what seems to be Siger's conclusion. Such a stance involves no compromise of the claims of reason for those cases where there is no doubt as to what it is reasonable to believe. Moreover it might just happen that there was such doubt in every case where a conflict was recognized between the requirements of faith and the deliverances of reason. It might just happen, therefore, that there was no actual conflict between what Siger was sure it was reasonable to

---

[4] Quoted from T. Golby (ed. and trans.), *St Thomas Aquinas: Philosophical Texts* (Oxford University Press, 1951), 30–31.

[5] Quoted from J. F. Wippel and A. B. Wolter (eds), *Medieval Philosophy from Augustine to Nicholas of Cusa* (New York: The Free Press, 1969), 365.

[6] See R. H. Popkin, *The History of Scepticism from Erasmus to Spinoza* (Berkeley: University of California Press, 1979), Ch. III.

believe—what, for that reason, he could not help believing—and what he held as a matter of faith. If this was the situation, we may be unhappy at the element of luck involved. Siger's declared position is not obviously untenable. We do not need to assume, though it may in fact have been the case, that he was disguising what he really thought.

Whether this was his true or a tactical position, it was not good enough for the authorities. Siger was summonsed to appear before the Inquisition and decided instead to flee Paris into obscurity. Averroism was effectively suppressed for a considerable period.

II

Averroist controversies were revived in the fifteenth and sixteenth centuries and lingered on even into the seventeenth century. The fifth Lateran Council of 1513 expressly attacked the two-fold truth and called on teachers of philosophy to justify the Christian doctrine in their lectures. One of those affected by this edict was Pietro Pomponazzi (1462–1525), an Italian who had an outstanding teaching career at Padua and Bologna, and who had not thought it appropriate to teach Christian doctrine in his lectures. Pomponazzi often disagreed with Averroist interpretations of Aristotle but his philosophical conclusions were often at variance with religious orthodoxy in respect of the same doctrines. This was true, for instance, of his treatise *On the Immortality of the Soul* (*De immortalitate animae*).

In this relatively long treatise, Pomponazzi argues the pros and cons of individual immortality, coming down time and again on the side of denying it. When readers reach his final chapter, they find Pomponazzi promising that what follows will be 'the final conclusion in this matter, which in my opinion must be maintained as beyond doubt'.[7] But what follows seems a curious *volte face*. Pomponazzi goes on to say that no 'natural reasons' can be found to clinch the argument one way or the other, that the immortality of the soul, like the 'eternity of the world', is therefore a 'neutral' problem, i.e. one that philosophy cannot determine. It is a matter on which 'famous men disagree with one another' and on which, therefore, we cannot, in the ordinary way of things, be certain. The question of immortality, he goes on to claim, 'can be made certain only through God'. It was something to be received as certain through faith.

The *De immortalitate animae* was found puzzling in Pomponazzi's own time, with some regarding it as heretical and others evidently

---

[7] E. Cassirer, P. O. Kristeller and J. H. Randall, Jr. (ed.), *The Renaissance Philosophy of Man* (Chicago University Press, 1948), 377.

content to take its concluding chapter at face value. It is difficult to believe, however, that Pomponazzi could be such a powerful advocate of the ephemeral nature of the soul in the earlier chapters without being convinced by his own arguments. Kant was later to put forward the idea that the immortality of the soul was a 'postulate' of pure practical reason.[8] And many others have wondered whether there could be any point in leading virtuous lives or any deterrent to living wicked lives if there was to be no reward and punishment in a life hereafter. This was one of the objections that Pomponazzi considered and to which he offered an impressive reply:

> . . . it must be known that reward and punishment have two meanings: one is essential and inseparable, the other accidental and separable. The essential reward of virtue is virtue itself, which makes man happy. For human nature possesses nothing greater than virtue itself, since it alone makes man secure and removed from every perturbation. For all things work together for him who loves the good: fearing nothing, hoping for nothing, but in prosperity and adversity ever the same, as is said in the end of *Ethica i*. And Plato says . . . 'To the good man neither alive nor dead can any evil happen'. But it is the opposite with vice. For the punishment of the vicious is vice itself, than which nothing can be more miserable, nothing more unhappy . . . Hence no vicious man is left unpunished, since vice itself is the punishment of the vicious man.[9]

Pomponazzi later rejects the suggestion that, if the soul is mortal, 'it would be vain to worship God, to honour the divine, to pour forth prayers to God', and so on. Indeed he even argues that belief in immortality, so far from being a spur to morality, may tend to corrupt it:

> . . . those who claim that the soul is mortal seem better to save the grounds of virtue than those who claim it to be immortal. For the hope of reward and the fear of punishment seem to suggest a certain servility, which is contrary to the grounds of virtue . . .[10]

Such passages as these have encouraged some of Pomponazzi's commentators to see him as strongly indebted to Stoicism.[11] Certainly he was not a pure Aristotelian or merely engaged in exposition. These passages are not merely exercises in scholastic virtuosity. They seem to be, rather, defences of what Pomponazzi actually believed.

[8] *Critique of Practical Reason*, II, ii, 4.
[9] Op. cit., 361–362.
[10] Op. cit., 375.
[11] For instance, J. H. Randall, Jr, in his introduction to the English translation. Op. cit., 274.

There is a further reason for thinking that this is indeed so. If we ask, why does it matter for a Christian whether a particular belief is true?, or, is a particular belief important or essential to Christian faith?, the answer we expect is one that will state the cost of rejecting it in terms of other beliefs which would also have to be rejected. If the belief is essential then to reject it would be to reject the whole system of Christian belief. This is the way one of the earliest of Christian theologians wrote about the resurrection of the dead: 'If there be no resurrection, then Christ was not raised; and if Christ was not raised, then our gospel is null and void, and so is your faith'.[12] These remarks may perhaps need further explanation for the uninstructed. But they clearly imply that the resurrection is essential to Christian belief. Moreover they are clearly stating a theological objection to those Corinthian Christians who were saying that there is no resurrection of the dead.

It is remarkable that it is just this pattern of theological argument that Pomponazzi considers amongst the objections to what appears to be his philosophical denial of immortality. If there were no immortality, it was objected, there would be no reward for the virtuous or punishment for the wicked: and if there is no such reward and punishment, then there is no just God ruling over the universe. The essence of the objection could be seen as that immortality is fundamental to Christian belief. And in that light the essence of Pomponazzi's reply is that it is not, or at any rate, that it is not fundamental in the respect given. The effect of this line of reply, were it accepted, would be to make belief in immortality more marginal. It may still remain a belief widely held by Christians, like the story of the three Magi who followed a star to Bethlehem when Jesus was born. But it would cease to matter so much whether or not professing Christians believe it.

In his concluding chapter, however, Pomponazzi seems to strike quite the opposite note. Pomponazzi there claims that, were a man to be in doubt about immortality, his actions would be uncertain.[13] He states, without explaining himself, that if a man did not believe in immortality he would despise eternal things and seek only after earthly things.[14] It is not at all obvious how this allegation could be made consistent with Pomponazzi's earlier claim that virtue is its own reward, indeed that belief in immortality provides no special motive 'to honour the divine'[15] in the sense in which that should be understood. For his earlier discus-

---

[12] *New English Bible* (Oxford University Press, 1961), I Corinthians 15:13–14.
[13] Op. cit., 377.
[14] Op. cit., 378.
[15] Op. cit., 374.

sion offers a way of giving a naturalistic interpretation to seeking only after eternal things and despising earthly things.

Like many other readers of his *Immortality of the Soul*, I find it difficult to avoid the conclusion that Pomponazzi was, in his final chapter, writing for the defenders of orthodoxy and hoping they would not read the earlier chapters too carefully. If he was merely pretending to believe in the immortality of the soul, he did not deceive everybody in his own time. The clergy of Venice almost certainly had information or had heard rumours about how Pomponazzi presented such subjects to his students in Padua. That might explain why they reacted so quickly against his book and persuaded the Doge, to whom it had been dedicated, to order that available copies of it be publicly burned. It should be added, however, that this was not how it seemed to the Pope's advisers when they examined Pomponazzi's book. The Pope refused to allow heresy proceedings to be taken further and a leading churchman saw to it that a memorial was erected to Pomponazzi when he died.

The ambiguities in Pomponazzi's position continued to intrigue later generations and the suspicion of Averroism hung about his posthumous reputation. Leibniz, writing nearly a hundred years later, was entirely on the side of Aquinas and Reformed Catholicism in rejecting the two-fold truth. His *Theodicy* has an important 'Preliminary Dissertation on the Conformity of Faith with Reason'. In this work Leibniz is writing in his 'popular' style, mixing serious philosophy with a kind of academic gossip, perhaps in imitation of Pierre Bayle. His account of the revived Averroist controversy is of some interest:

> . . . the Averroists . . . declared that man's soul is, according to philosophy, mortal, while they protested their acquiescence in Christian theology, which declares the soul's immortality. But this distinction was held suspect, and the divorce between faith and reason was strongly rejected by the prelates and the doctors of that time. It was condemned in the last Lateran Council under Leo X, when the *savants* were urged to work to remove the difficulties that appeared to set theology and philosophy at variance. The doctrine of their incompatibility continued to maintain itself *incognito*. Pomponazzi was suspected of it, though he declared himself otherwise; and that same sect of Averroists survived as a tradition . . .[16]

III

I have introduced these case materials partly to offer a background sketch of the Averroist tradition. But they will also provide me with an

---

[16] 'Preliminary Dissertation', Section 11, in C. I. Gerhardt (ed.), *G. W. Leibniz: Die Philosophischen Schriften*, Vol. VI (Berlin, 1885 reprinted Hildesheim: Olms, 1978), 56.

historical basis to which to relate my analysis of some of the issues involved in the controversies between the Averroists and their opponents. Here I identify and select three issues for discussion:

(1) There is a controversy about the nature of the necessity or impossibility there can be of holding a rational belief. Some Averroists claimed that one can hold something as a matter of faith even though it is impossible to believe it rationally. Aquinas, in the quotation given above, wants to stress that, on the contrary, not even God could confer faith in such circumstances. If it is impossible to believe something rationally, then, according to this anti-Averroist view, it is impossible to believe it at all and impossible therefore to believe it as a matter of faith.

(2) There is a controversy about the duality accepted by the Averroists. This might be put, on the one side, by saying that there are different ways of knowing that yield different and not necessarily compatible truths. But, since they are ways of knowing, we must accept as true certain pairs of propositions that are not consistent with one another. Against this there are gnomic-sounding utterances such as that 'truth is one' or Averroes' own statement that 'truth does not oppose truth but accords with it and bears witness to it'.[17]

(3) There is a controversy about the nature of faith, with the Averroists presenting it for the most part as non-rational, as quite different from rational belief, as not requiring the support of rational belief and indeed as, perhaps unlike other kinds of belief, a matter of what we resolve. Against such a fideistic account of religious belief there is that offered by Aquinas and others, for whom faith is to be harmonized with rational belief even though it may go beyond it.

Each of these controversies relates to a position that can be associated with Averroism, at least characteristically, if not universally. It is convenient to treat them separately, though there are points at which one debate runs naturally into or even turns upon another.

I consider first the claim—imputed to the Averroists and disputed by Aquinas—that although we may be compelled logically to conclude that there was no creation, or that there is a single intellective soul, or whatever, we may hold the contrary view 'as a matter of faith'. This first issue is connected with the third one in that it partly turns on the question whether faith is a species of ordinary belief or something quite different. But it also turns on how such modal terms as 'necessary' and 'impossible' are to be understood when used of belief. Aquinas seems to have wanted to say that if someone is rationally forced to one conclusion, nothing (not even God) could make it possible for that person to hold the opposite as a matter of faith. The Averroists, on the other

[17] See note 3 above.

hand, seem committed to denying the inference from 'X cannot believe p' to 'X does not believe p'.

The Averroists seem to be in a difficult position here, in so far as they appear to be denying a rational principle of interpretation without which we should be unable to make sense of systems of thought or rationally organized pieces of writing. To make sense of a piece of philosophical writing, for instance, we need to be able to assume that the author does not believe whatever is inconsistent with the conclusions offered or indeed whatever is declared to be true. That is why one is inclined to infer from a reading of Pomponazzi's treatise that he did not believe in immortality. Such a belief was not one it was possible for a philosopher with Pomponazzi's understanding of and commitment to Aristotle. If we then infer, however, that Pomponazzi did not believe in immortality and cannot have been sincere in his profession of such a belief, the Averroist may complain that we are making use of a principle that begs the question against Pomponazzi and those who subscribe to a 'two-fold truth'.

I think the Averroist would be right to make this complaint. For it is only *qua* Aristotelian philosopher that Pomponazzi was unable to believe in immortality and only *qua* philosopher that he was unable to make up his mind about it. *Qua* Christian, he could say, he was expected to believe it. So, according to his final chapter, he, Pomponazzi, did. Notice that the Averroist need not say that Pomponazzi believed one thing and held something quite different as a matter of faith. It makes sense for him to say that belief in immortality is impossible for an Aristotelian philosopher though it is quite possible for others—Platonists, for instance. He may say that it simply makes no sense to ask whether belief in immortality is possible *sans phrase*.

Aquinas, in the passage I quoted, makes much of the claim that the conclusion of a demonstration is a necessary truth. Here he seems to confuse the necessity which conclusions have as conclusions with the necessity propositions have if it would involve a contradiction to deny them. Yet there need be no controversy between the Averroist and his opponents about the absolute impossibility of believing a straightforward contradiction. The Averroist could then maintain that the duality between philosophy and religion is not of the straightforward sort.

This is not an unproblematic position for an Averroist to adopt. But it is not as straightforwardly incoherent as it might at first appear. Nor is it obvious that the words 'I cannot believe this, but I do . . .' could only be spoken in bad faith. These words only seem to express a straightforwardly incoherent position because we assume that, just as it follows that if I cannot run 100 metres in ten seconds I have not just done it, so if I cannot believe something then I do not believe it. But the logic of 'cannot believe' is different from 'cannot do'. If someone cannot do something then the question whether they ought not to do it does not arise.

An example may serve to illustrate this point. Suppose, in the Senior Common Room, Dr X catches Dr Y reading the horoscope section of the daily paper. She might say 'You cannot believe there is anything in astrology!' This utterance has the implication that, in the judgment of Dr X, Dr Y ought not to believe there is anything in astrology. It also, in some sense, implies that the utterer thinks Dr Y does believe, or is at least inclined to believe in astrology. But actually doing something is universally taken to be a sufficient refutation of the claim that one cannot do it. How then can Dr X have any basis for saying 'You cannot believe there is anything in astrology!'? Her basis is not what she knows about Dr Y in particular and especially not what she has just caught him doing. It lies in what may loosely be termed their common academic 'culture'. She may know perfectly well that in other cultures or sub-cultures astrologers hold positions of respect and credibility. (There is a financial astrologer in the City of London.) But she knows, or at any rate assumes, this is not so within orthodox scientific and therefore academic culture. Believing in astrology is, or so I am supposing, not proper for someone who is part of this culture. It is something therefore that, in this sense, Dr Y ought not to believe in. Dr X was at least implying this in haranguing him with the words 'You cannot believe there is anything in astrology!'

A good deal more needs to be said about this kind of example. It is intended only to be an example of a cultural duality and tension. My point in introducing it is to show how Averroism is not as obviously a pretended celebration of self-contradiction as Aquinas and other critics have made out. On this issue, I have been suggesting, Averroists may be able to stand their ground.

IV

A second focus for controversies between Averroists and their opponents relates to the duality claimed between how things are known philosophically and how they are known in religion. This duality was expressed in one of the claims attributed to the Averroists in the 1277 Condemnation of Paris: 'That the natural philosopher as such ought to deny the creation of the world, because his opinion is based upon natural causes and reasons. The Christian, on the other hand, may deny the eternity of the world, because his opinion is founded on supernatural causes.'[18] This duality might be couched in the language

[18] See note 2 above.

of the previous section by saying that the natural philosopher, *qua* natural philosopher, cannot believe in a creation. But it is possible, it may be said, to believe in a creation as a matter of faith, that being a gift of divine grace.

This raises questions about the possibility of fideism, the third issue I identified for discussion. But the idea that philosophy and theology are quite discrete forms of knowledge is particularly characteristic of Averroism. It has been opposed by those, such as Leibniz, who thought of their own philosophical enterprise in terms of harmonizing elements of truth that seemed to others to be at variance with one another. Leibniz objected to the false separation, as it seemed to him, of philosophical and religious truth that he detected in several of the leading Modern philosophers.

Descartes' treatment of free will may be given as an example. According to Descartes, it is both self-evident that we have free will and at the same time we know with certainty that everything is preordained by God.[19] But, he wrote, 'we can easily get ourselves into great difficulties if we attempt to reconcile this divine preordination with the freedom of our will, or attempt to grasp both these things at once'.

Leibniz's comment in one short paper was:

> . . . this is not satisfactory: for it is one thing for us not to understand something and quite another for us to understand its contradictory. So it is at least necessary to be able to answer those arguments that seem to suggest that freedom or the division of matter implies a contradiction.[20]

Descartes had written elsewhere that matter is divided *ad infinitum* but that this is something beyond our comprehension. Leibniz is pointing out that, on one analysis, there is a contradiction in the idea of an infinite division of matter. He is not suggesting that there is a contradiction in the idea of freedom itself but between belief in freedom and in divine preordination. His point is that such beliefs are *prima facie* indefensible and that the apparent contradictions need first to be removed.

Leibniz saw this meta-philosophical disagreement between his approach and that of Descartes as linked to the Averroist controversy. It is a disagreement that runs very deep and the side one takes will be affected by what one thinks the enterprise of philosophy is. My own

[19] *Principles of Philosophy*, Part I, 39–40. J. Cottingham, R. Stoothoff and D. Murdoch (trans.), *The Philosophical Writings of Descartes* (Cambridge University Press, 1985), I, 206.

[20] A. Foucher de Careil (ed.), *Nouvelles lettres et opuscules inédits de Leibniz* (Paris: Auguste Durand, 1857), 180.

predilections are on the side of Leibniz. But the idea that there are certain oppositions between statements that philosophy cannot resolve at the level at which it encounters them was to be supported by Kant. The 'critical philosophy' does not, for example, harmonize free will and causal determination in the way Leibniz sought to do, by incorporating both within a single metaphysical system.[21] What it claims to do, rather, is to make it possible to accept both of them by putting freedom forward as valid for things in themselves and causal necessitation as valid only for appearances. Viewed from the standpoint of Kant the anti-Averroist claim that 'truth is one', that metaphysics should seek to harmonize all truths, is a mark of the pre-critical philosophy.

I mention Kant only to indicate that this issue is a more complex one than the traditional opponents of Averroism believed. In this respect the Averroist controversy is still a live one, if not under that name.

V

The third and final issue between the Averroists and their opponents has to do with the relation or absence of it between faith and ordinary belief. According to the Averroists it is possible to have faith that something is so even though one has no reason whatever for believing that it is so and no inclination, in the ordinary sense, to believe it. Indeed some of them went further, as we have seen, and claimed that one could have faith that something is so even though it is impossible in the ordinary sense to believe it. Their opponents have tended to object that the profession of such a faith would be empty words. In his *New Essays*, for instance, Leibniz wrote that 'wise men have always looked askance at those who have maintained that there is no reason to trouble with reasons and proofs when it is a question of belief—which is indeed impossible unless "believe" signifies recite, or repeat and acquiesce in without taking any trouble over it'.[22] Such criticisms, however, tend to assume just the view of faith that Averroists reject, namely, that it is a species of ordinary belief. It is true enough that we cannot whimsically choose to hold beliefs in the ordinary sense without any basis in reasons. Were we to try to do so we would just be pretending to believe—going

[21] According to the Third Antinomy a strong argument can be mounted for both 'There is no freedom; everything takes place solely in accordance with laws of nature' and 'Causality in accordance with laws of nature is not the only causality from which the appearances of the world can one and all be derived' (*Critique of Pure Reason*, A 444/B 472).

[22] P. Remnant and J. Bennett (eds), *G. W. Leibniz: New Essays Concerning Human Understanding* (Cambridge University Press, 1981), 494.

through the motions, as Leibniz rightly implies. But the Averroist is not committed to encouraging such whimsicality.

However, the Averroist cannot be granted immunity from criticism just by virtue of insisting that faith is *sui generis*. On the contrary such an insistence brings problems of its own. By breaking the link with reasons and ordinary belief, the Averroist is left unable, for instance, to explain how faith is an epistemic state at all, how, that is to say, it is any sort of cousin of opinion, knowledge and so on, as is usually supposed. Having faith becomes, on such an account, a matter of banking on certain things being true or being resolved to act as if they were true. It is reduced to a dispositional state. People who like a flutter may bank on a particular outcome even though there is no reason whatever for expecting it, as commonly happens when people fill in the football pools. If this is what faith involves there is no difficulty about having it in the absence of any grounds. There is no reason why, if faith is understood in this way, Averroists might not bank on immortality even though, as philosophers, they were unable to find any basis for believing in it.

There is, however, a price to be paid for not conceiving of faith as an epistemic state. It is this: someone who believes something in the right way and turns out to have been right about it will be said to have known that it is true. But someone who merely banks on an event which just happens to come about would be counted as no more than lucky to have banked on the outcome and not as someone who knew what the outcome would be, not even as someone who was right about the outcome. If religious faith is a matter of banking on something being true then the same has to be said about those whose faith was, as things turned out, well placed. They cannot be credited with knowing or even being right just because they banked on the right outcome. And yet such a denial of religious knowledge is at variance with how faith is traditionally represented. Those who hold the true faith are traditionally credited with knowing, and certainly with being right about what they believe, though what they profess to know may be 'folly to the Greeks'. Faith, in short, is traditionally taken to be an epistemic state, bearing some relation to belief in the ordinary sense.

Such an argument is only likely to discourage half-hearted fideists. A thorough-going fideist may regard such an enforced repudiation of traditional accounts of faith as a virtually painless nettle to grasp. But, if not, there is another strategy available, one suggested by Pascal's wager. Pascal thought that, by banking on the truth of, say, Catholic Christianity, one would eventually come to believe it. A genuine epistemic state could be, on his account, the eventual but natural result of a decision. The belief would be induced by participation in all aspects of Catholic life. As Pascal puts it:

221

> You want to go to faith and you do not know the way? You want to cure yourself of faithlessness and you ask for the remedies? Learn from those who have been tied down like yourself and who now bet on their welfare. . . . Follow the way in which they have started. It consists in doing everything as if they believed, in taking holy water, in having masses said, and so on. That is just the way to bring you naturally to believe . . .[23]

There is no good reason to deny that belief can be induced in some such way. Banking on the truth of Catholic Christianity could lead 'naturally' to an epistemic state. Moreover a theologian might say that someone whose belief is sustained by the Catholic life did believe in the right way. Such a person could, supposing Catholic Christianity turned out to be true, be said to know it. The irony is, however, that modern Catholic theologians are unlikely to avail themselves of such a solution. Since the Catholic Reformation, as I have already indicated, that denomination has been officially against Averroism and indeed, though there was a quite separate tradition of Catholic fideism, it too is entirely contrary to the edict of the fifth Lateran Council. Pascal was a leading light of a deviant Catholic sect (the 'Jansenists') which was finally suppressed in the eighteenth century. Protestant theologians, amongst whom one might look with more hope of finding contemporary Averroists and fideists, are not likely to say that a belief sustained by going to church and otherwise living the Christian life is, by itself, sufficient. Genuine faith, they are likely to say, must arise from within us and cannot be produced by marking the externals of Christian life. So it may be that Protestant theologians, though they might be concerned with the problem, would not be attracted by my solution. On the other hand, as I have explained, Catholic theologians, though they might have liked my solution, are unlikely to be concerned about the problem. This is one example of the way in which theology puts constraints on the philosophy within Christianity. The account of faith that a philosopher produces may, perhaps through accidents of history, not be one that any particular tradition is likely to take up.

There is, however, another aspect of Pascal's wager that is more straightforwardly the concern of philosophy or what used to be called 'natural religion' and which has implications for fideism and Averroism. For, while Pascal rejects natural religion, he wants to suggest that the wager he recommends is one a rational gambler would adopt. The suggestion is that, while the *a priori* probabilities are even, the winnings for those who bet on Catholic Christianity are infinite bliss, if it is true,

---

[23] P. Sellier (ed.), *Pascal: Pensées—Nouvelle Edition établié pour la première fois d'après la copie de reférénce de Gilberte Pascal* (Paris: Mercure de France, 1976), 357.

and the loss is negligible, if it is false. Those who bet against Catholic Christianity, on the other hand, stand to make only a marginal gain if they are right and will have to face eternal misery if they are not.

Pascal's wager is an improvement on Pomponazzi's uncharacteristically lame defence of the need to accept immortality as a matter of faith. But Pascal's account seems to me to beg at least two important questions. In the first place it assumes that there are only two outcomes—Catholic Christianity being true and Catholic Christianity being false. But, from the point of view of *a priori* probabilities, Catholic Christianity should not be regarded as one side of a two-sided coin but as one side of an infinitely many-sided die. *A priori*, there is not just one chance but there are infinitely many chances of the wager not coming off. Moreover—and this is the second important question begged—the rational gambler will be aware that there may be infinitely valuable pay-offs and infinitely terrible penalties associated with many of the other religious betting options. But, if these considerations are brought into the reckoning, the wager loses its rational basis. There is, that is to say, no reason *a priori* for banking on one outcome rather than any other. Choosing one religion rather than another is turned by such a Pascalian fideism into sheer guesswork in which the chance of being right is infinitely small. Fideism, by this route, seems on reflection to lead to scepticism and scepticism to suspension of belief.

For the reasons I have given I doubt whether fideism is defensible and I am inclined to think that, on the contrary, faith has to involve beliefs of the kind that call for reasons. It is not just an ordinary kind of belief, since there is a virtue in faith being out of proportion to any evidence. Faith characteristically goes beyond reason and yet it is not wholly arational, still less is it irrational. In this I agree with Aquinas, Leibniz and other anti-Averroists and disagree, for example, with Wittgenstein's suggestion that religious belief is 'belief' in a different sense from ordinary belief.[24] Wittgenstein's name may seem a strange one to mention in connection with Averroism. But that is only because the label is associated with controversies of the distant past. On each of the issues I have discussed, Wittgenstein's later philosophy—for instance, his account of being forced to a conclusion and his account of language-games—offers more support to the Averroists than to their opponents. It would be wrong to pretend that there have been no significant changes between the earlier and the later forms of these controversies. But, if there has been any virtue in the way I have been revisiting the old Averroist controversies, it lies in linking the issues in earlier and later philosophies together.

[24] C. Barrett (ed.), *Wittgenstein: Lectures and Conversations on Aesthetics, Psychology and Religious Belief* (Oxford: Basil Blackwell, 1966), 53ff.

Does Philosophy 'Leave Everything as it is'? Even Theology?

RENFORD BAMBROUGH

Does *photography* leave everything as it is? Clearly not. It scalps Uncle George, as he stands at the church door, proudly, innocently, in the role of bride's father, and it decapitates his nephew James, who had until now been a head taller than any other member of the wedding group. It reduces to two dimensions, and to black and white, such solid three-dimensional objects as the Rocky Mountains and St Paul's Cathedral, such colourful scenes and sights as the Aurora Borealis and sunset in the desert.

Photography wreaks other changes, and of other kinds. It makes people self-conscious, and induces them to pose unnaturally. In its early days, when exposure times were longer, it did this to such effect that most of its subjects looked grim and pious and complacent. In more recent times it has over-reacted against the hypocrisies of its youth, and more often than not the camera is too ostentatiously candid.

In its search for news, photography tramples on the flower beds that separate it from the private grief on which it is expensively and con-scientiously intruding.

It has influenced landscape painting and portraiture, by imitation and by reaction. Some painters were moved by it to be 'photographic' in their representations; some portraits in oils have become cubist dia-grams or expressionist caricatures because there is no point in doing on canvas what a camera can do just as well or better on glass or celluloid.

All this is true. And yet it is also true that the camera changes nothing, even when we can at the same time say that it distorts and garbles and mangles the things to which it makes no difference.

Remarks on parallel lines might be made about many other activities and enquiries. Does archaeology leave everything as it is? It rifles tombs, breaks bones, enriches authors and broadcasters, and confers on them fame or popularity or obloquy or notoriety. Keynes said that any industrialist or Chancellor of the Exchequer who boasted that he was a practical man, and had no truck with airy-fairy theory, was bound to be the slave of some defunct economist. And he in his own way or ways made differences to Chancellors and company chairmen, to eco-nomies as well as to economists.

History is plausibly accused of changing the past (especially in the Soviet Union) and is acknowledged to change the present and the future when those who make laws and decisions and war and peace know or think they know what happened last time and why.

Even grammar is not altogether ineffective. When its norms too tidily articulate the structure of our speaking and writing they influence what it is their business only to report. Euclidean geometry, a byword for purity and impersonality, arose from land-measuring and had a hand in the construction of the Pyramids. (Does *surveying* leave everything as it is?)

Perhaps physics and chemistry do not change what they study; but they change many other things. They produce new compounds unknown to nature, and bombs and television.

It is not so clear now as many people have thought it was what Wittgenstein was doing when he said that philosophy leaves everything as it is (*Philosophical Investigations*, §124). It is unclear what *contrast* he had in mind, and what contrast his critics have had in mind, between philosophy and other things, or between Wittgenstein's conception of philosophy and alternative or rival conceptions. It is accordingly unclear how to account for the sense of shock that the critics evince and express when they read or hear Wittgenstein's remark; though it is partly accounted for, I am suggesting, by the failure of the critics to think what he might mean by it, bearing in mind as they do so that Wittgenstein, like the god whose oracle is in Delphi, *oute legei oute kruptei, alla sēmainei*: he neither utters nor hides his meaning, but indicates it by a sign.

This is close to another way of saying that the critics have not treated the remark *as* a *remark*—an *occasional* composition in a much misunderstood genre. A remark is made for a time and a season and an audience, and it is typically linked with and modified by other remarks of the same speaker or writer, but depends for much of its point on what is believed or thought by those to whom the remark is addressed, and by the bystanders who overhear it; including the critics whose sense of shock it is so easy and so tempting to evoke.

To help us with the understanding of Wittgenstein's remark we need to see or recollect its immediate surroundings in his text. When we do this we find that there is much emphasis on the contrast between empirical problems and the questions about 'the workings of our language' that are in the forefront of Wittgenstein's discussion. It is in 109 that he has declared that 'the problems are solved, not by giving new information, but by arranging what we have always known'. This thought is echoed in 127: 'The work of the philosopher consists in assembling reminders for a particular purpose', and in 128: 'If one tried to advance *theses* in philosophy, it would never be possible to debate them, because everyone would agree to them'. These observations are clarified and confirmed by 126, 129 and 130, where Wittgenstein says that nothing that is *hidden* needs to be brought to light by the philosopher: that philosophy deals with what is 'open to view, with what is possible *before* all new discoveries and inventions'; and that the study of language-games is not a preparation for 'a future regularization of language—as it were first approximations, ignoring friction and air resistance'. It is in 130, too, that Wittgenstein speaks of his language-games as *'objects of comparison'*; they are meant to illuminate the facts of our actual language by way of similarities and *dissimilarities*. (Compare 'I will teach you *differences'*.)

In the wider surroundings of the remark at 124—that philosophy leaves everything as it is—Wittgenstein is equally concerned to emphasize the differences between a philosophical enquiry and a scientific one. Some of his other individual remarks, whether on the neighbouring pages or in the wider context, are of course easy to misunderstand in the way that 124 has been misunderstood, but they do provide us with the materials for an account of the philosophical scene and of Wittgenstein's own part in it. In spite of proceeding by means of remarks, Wittgenstein offers what he himself is willing in one place to call 'fragments of a system' (p. 228).

In particular, he systematically distinguishes philosophy from science. When we have 'the method of science' before us, we philosophers are led into complete darkness (*Blue Book*, 18). Wittgenstein is so anxious not to confuse philosophical explanation with scientific explanation that he misleadingly suggests that there is no such thing as explanation in philosophy, but only description. The emphasis on description—on the philosopher as practitioner of a kind of 'natural history' (415, p. 230), helps us to rule out from the philosopher's procedures many of the modes of change and influence that science exercises, and which will be expected of philosophy by those scientists and philosophers who are apostles of 'scientific philosophy'.

The philosopher of mathematics, regarded as an observer of *what mathematicians do*, will leave mathematics as it is. And the philosopher with the wider concerns that Wittgenstein shows in the *Investigations* will leave *logic* as it is, including the vast area of logic that is outside Logic, and takes the form of description of our *practices* with words, of *what we do*.

The philosopher who operates in this way may be guilty of *distortion*, of misrepresentation of 'the workings of our language', but when his work is well done it does not distort; it 'leaves everything as it is'.

These last comments illustrate another difficulty that the reading of Wittgenstein's 'remarks' presents to those philosophers whose preferred modes of operation are 'logical' or 'scientific'. Though the remarks are assembled into patterns and sequences, each mints it own use of language, which may mislead us about the relation of one remark to another. A striking example is supplied by the relation between 124 and 129. In 124, just before he makes the remark that is the source of the title of this paper, Wittgenstein says: 'philosophy may in no way interfere with the actual use of language; it can in the end only describe it. For it cannot give it any foundation either.' On the next page, in 129, he writes:

> The aspects of things that are most important for us are hidden because of their simplicity and familiarity. (One is unable to notice something—because it is always before one's eyes.) The real foundations of his inquiry do not strike a man at all. Unless *that* fact has at some time struck him.—And this means: we fail to be struck by what, once seen, is most striking and most powerful.

The reference here to 'real foundations' is verbally in conflict with the dismissal in 124 of the idea that philosophy can give any foundation to our practice with language. There is no conflict of thought between the two passages. In one place Wittgenstein dismisses the opposition's view of the nature of the foundations of language by saying that there are no such foundations; in the other he equally effectively rejects their view of the nature of the foundations by preserving but reinterpreting the word 'foundation'. The same mechanism is employed in respect of the idea of what is *hidden*. In 129 it is acknowledged that something may be hidden by its extreme familiarity and *obviousness*, and here what is 'hidden' is what in 126 is described as 'open to view'. In 126, too, Wittgenstein says that 'what is hidden' is of no interest to us, while in 129, with its wider understanding of what is to count as 'hidden', it is what is hidden that we must most carefully attend to.

A good example of the same stylistic operation occurs in the *Remarks on the Foundations of Mathematics*. I once heard a paper devoted to the criticism of Wittgenstein's discussion of the idea of 'mathematical belief'. The author's insistence that Wittgenstein was deeply mistaken to argue against the coherent possibility of *believing* a mathematical proposition had to be checked by pointing out to him that Wittgenstein himself, on the next page, acknowledges that of course it is possible to believe a mathematical proposition (I, 106–112).

In each of these cases it is the wider use of the expression ('foundation', 'hidden', 'belief') that is the more ordinary, and hence in Wittgenstein's own terms the more correct; but the rhetorical narrowing serves its legitimate purpose, as it also does when Wittgenstein temporarily implies that only causal explanation ('something hypothetical') is explanation. There too he could have put the point in the more ordinary and correct alternative idiom, which explicitly recognizes the varieties of explanation, the fact that (to use one of Wittgenstein's own favourite idioms) 'there are many cases here'.

These examples establish another point about Wittgenstein's work that the shocked critics seem not to have noticed. The sense of shock is a reaction to what is taken to be a lazy and complacent conservatism. But Wittgenstein is not the relaxed or comfortable thinker against whom such a suspicion has any plausibility. His work is energetic, strenuous, dramatic; full of 'deep disquietudes', tension, conflict, high running seas of language, a perpetual struggle against the *bewitchment* of our intelligence by pictures that hold us *captive* in our fly-bottles. The notion that he is not *serious* enough or ambitious enough in his philosophical aspirations is reminiscent of the caption to Max Beerbohm's caricature of Matthew Arnold: 'Uncle Matthew, why are you never wholly serious?' His work is insistently *radical*, whatever may be said for the view that it is also in some sense or senses conservative. And he speaks in 133, two pages after the text in my title—of his striving to give philosophy *peace*, to escape from the power of the spells that bewitch us, from the obsessive entanglements in which we are embroiled by the original philosophical sin that we inherit along with language.

The sense of shock at Wittgenstein's remark may be more fully articulated by attending to some of the pictures of philosophy and its role that the remark appears to repudiate. Some of the critics, even when they are not Marxists, resonate to the rhetoric of another famous saying: 'The philosophers have endeavoured merely to understand the world; the point however is to change it'. Most of the critics are echoing older conceptions of philosophy as the queen of the sciences, or the handmaid of theology, or an under-labourer in an enterprise of reconstruction, whether of the world or of our conception of it. A more recent edition of the same dream is the desire for an ideal language, a *characteristica universalis*, a facility whose provision would allow philosophers, as Leibniz said, to respond to their mutual disagreements as mathematicians do, with the simple resolve: *calculemus*—let us do our *reckoning*.

Many of the critics are philosophically descended from Russell and from Popper, and are contemptuous of what they take to be the unscientific or non-scientific or anti-scientific tenor of Wittgenstein's thought; and of his untheoretical and anti-theoretical view of the role of the philosopher. Russell wanted philosophers to start with obvious premises and arrive at startling conclusions. Popper denies to philosophy any role of its own, and sees it as deriving its function from upheavals in science and society. They both think it all to the good that the philosopher, in their view of his purposes, should be as far as possible from 'the plain man'—just near enough to jolt him with firecrackers and blind him with science. Russell complained that Moore believed everything his nurse told him, and that Oxford philosophers did not know anything that had been discovered since the time of Homer.

But to preach these sermons on the text found in 124 is to be trapped in a simple confusion. Wittgenstein did not say that everything should be left as it is. He said only that *philosophy* leaves everything as it is. And among the everything that is to remain as it is is everything that makes for change, including revolutionary change, in society and in science. It is a small matter, but significant, that as near as 132 we find Wittgenstein conceding that there is a role for invented terminology. But such linguistic reforms are for scientific or practical purposes. It remains undesirable that Wittgenstein's remarks should have the effect on his followers of 'sowing a jargon'. The sowing of such a jargon, and the reaping of its fruits, would be—have been—cases of influence by a philosopher; not however an achievement of which a philosopher should be proud, any more than a photographer would or should be proud of scalping or decapitating a wedding guest—unless that happened to be his deliberate way of achieving his expressionist or surrealist caricature.

Does philosophy leave *everything* as it? Even *theology*? Consider first whether *theology* leaves everything as it is. (Some of those who complain about Wittgenstein's remark are theologians, and we should try to learn from them or understand for ourselves what contrast *they* have in mind.)

Theology surely does not change God. So theology leaves as it is the subject matter of theology. Like the philosophy described and practised by Wittgenstein, theology is concerned to describe things as they are, and to reject false accounts of the matter as false. The theologian's aim may be to change *ideas* about God. But it is equally open to Wittgenstein to change ideas about the things that it is according to him the business of philosophy to describe, and to understand, but not to change.

Wittgenstein is by implication saying that theology, or some theology, leaves everything as it is, when he speaks of 'theology as grammar'. He says this after remarking more generally that 'grammar tells us what kind of object anything is' (I, 373). This parenthetical phrase has sometimes been misunderstood and misapplied by theologians and philosophers who were determined to preserve 'the religious language game' from interference by philosophical critics. They have treated the remark as though it had been '*religion* as grammar'. It seems needless to ask 'Does *religion* leave everything as it is?' It so evidently does not leave things as they are: it changes minds and hearts and lives and churches and nations as well as ideas. It is only theology that is conceived as a grammatical investigation, and, as I have hinted, perhaps not all of theology.

The investigations that Wittgenstein calls 'grammatical' are at least closely akin to those that many philosophers would call epistemological, and epistemology is neutral between the conflicting theses whose 'logic' and whose modes of verification it examines and articulates. It is concerned with meaning rather than with truth, except for its concern with the truth of its own articulations.

The status of epistemology may be clarified by contrast with at least one use—the positivistic use—of the term 'metaphysics'. Ayer and his ancestors and descendants have used the word pejoratively. In their vocabulary, to repudiate a metaphysical thesis is not at the same time to endorse a metaphysical thesis, not even a negative one. There is another and better use in which a metaphysical thesis is any answer to a metaphysical question, and a metaphysical question, like any other question, allows as an answer the contradictory of any proposition that it allows as an answer. Similarly, the denial of an historical thesis is an historical thesis, the denial of a moral assertion is a moral assertion, and so on.

Description typically does leave things as they are, including the things that is describes. Wittgenstein's 'natural history' of our words and thoughts and practices leaves them as they are, just as other forms of natural history leave the birds and the flowers as they are. This point is not limited to the plain descriptions that Wittgenstein officially has in mind when he speaks of description and of natural history. The point applies equally to picturesque and paradoxical descriptions, to any form of representation of the character of anything: Uncle George's head, religious faith, positivist metaphysics, the workings of the Supreme Court or the structure of the nucleus.

Heraclitus leaves the river as it is when he says that you can't step into the same river twice. I leave the river and the mountain where they are if I add that a river is a fast moving mountain and that a mountain is a slow moving river. Wittgenstein leaves everything as it is when his mode of expression is less sober and less concrete and particular than it officially is, as when he says that every application of every word is arbitrary, or that games have nothing in common. A philosophical caricature, like a photographic caricature, or a pencil or oil caricature, leaves the sitter as he is even if it also distorts and disturbs him.

The remark we are considering—that philosophy leaves our actual use of language as it is—itself leaves our actual use of language as it is, and our actual philosophical practice as it is.

What would you *expect* philosophy to change? The critics of Wittgenstein's dictum do not answer that question explicitly, and their implicit answers are unconvincing. Their fear is of a deadening conservatism, of fixity in ideas and practice, of the placing of obstacles and opposition in the path of the scientific discoverers, social reformers and religious prophets. But what we would expect philosophy to change is ideas, and actions by way of ideas. And Wittgenstein's philosophy, even if there is excuse for calling it conservative, is as concerned as any other to change the ideas of those to whom it is addressed, and is with many readers and hearers as effective as any other philosophy in bringing about such changes. It is in a clear sense a *radical* philosophy, even if it is also in a good sense conservative. To bring people back to the recognition of the truths that their doctrines obscure may radically change their perspectives on life and thought and society, and this may be so when the truths that are obscured or implicitly or explicitly denied are familiar and widely recognized truths. Remember Wittgenstein's emphasis on *remembering*, on going 'back to the teaching', on resisting the imposition of 'requirements' (107), i.e. of *a priori* assumptions and artificial schemata which distort and oversimplify the actual complexities that it is the philosopher's business to describe, in order that he and his hearers may 'reject false accounts of the matter as false' (*PI*, 200).

What is needed to demonstrate this method and its results is a series of fully articulated examples from a wide range of enquiries and activities. One might consider whether *sociology* leaves everything as it is; and that would involve distinguishing logical from causal consequences in a number of contexts of social enquiry. Do opinion polls influence opinion, and if so how? Does the sociology of knowledge inhibit the search for knowledge? Is the sociology of knowledge itself a search for knowledge? Have religious convictions been weakened or otherwise affected by anthropological and psychoanalytic and historical and textual studies of the origins and development of religion and of particular religions? Here again it would be of prime importance to distinguish questions of the form 'Have people become less convinced of the truth of religious doctrines by reading and hearing the results of such enquiries?' from questions of the form 'Do the results of such enquiries show that what men thought to be good *grounds* for believing in religious doctrines are less good grounds than they were thought to be?'

By way of illustration of what I take to be the upshot of the present discussion I will take just one example, and take it from the realm of religion. I do so partly because that field is one of the main battle grounds over the meaning and validity of Wittgenstein's observation in 124, but partly and mainly because the example itself is of sufficient importance and difficulty to serve the purpose for which I invoke it.

One who asks 'Does philosophy leave *religion* as it is?'—note that we are now speaking of religion and not of theology—may be invited to think about the effect that various and conflicting philosophical accounts may have on our understanding of God's question to Job: 'Where wast thou when I laid the foundations of the earth?'

From the time of the writing of the book of Job to the present day, there have always been readers who have taken the account of the conversation between God and his servant Job in a way that one might call *literal*, and is sometimes called fundamentalist. The man Job is a person, and God is a person, and these two persons engage in a dialogue of which we have a divinely inspired record. In the course of the conversation God reminds Job that he is not a self-made person. He, God, made Job, and the world in which Job lives and suffers, and all that therein is, including his wife and his sons and his comforters. Job needs to be reminded sharply of his creator's power, and of his own human dependence, impermanence, insignificance.

The readers I now have in mind are not all 'fundamentalists'. Within their range there are widely differing degrees of literalness to be found. For example, many of them will not take quite literally God's reference to the *earth* (as opposed to heaven and earth, the world as a whole, the universe, or some other mode of expression of the whole frame and firmament of things). Many will be less than literal in their understanding of the notion that the earth or world has *foundations* in anything like the way that Job's house has foundations. But all the people I have in mind are serious and strict believers in *God*, in his personhood, in *his* independence and power and creatorhood and wisdom and compassion. They can be called theists and monotheists without benefit of 'reinterpretation' or 'reduction' or of too much stretching of the concept of *symbolism*, or *myth* or *imagery*. In so far as they would recognize the justice of any account of their beliefs that would centrally involve these interpretative concepts, they would regard the objects of the beliefs as infinitely transcending the mythical or symbolic means through which they are approached, and certainly not as deriving all their meaning and existence *from* those symbolic expressions.

The range of understanding of theology covered by this group is wide enough to include Luther and Milton, St Augustine and Newman, as well as the vast majority of Christian theologians in all ages and generations, and all the millions of simple believers in the Christian religion. To qualify as a simple believer, it is not necessary to be a prosaic and literal-minded believer, one who takes forty days and forty nights to be two days short of six weeks, or who forgives his brother exactly 490 times.

We might distinguish a second group of believers who would put more emphasis than the first group on the pictorial and analogical character of the formulations of their faith. In interpreting God's question to Job, these readers may not take the laying of 'the foundations of the earth' to be a datable divine action; they may interpret the temporal and spatial and physical language of the text as expressing ethical and metaphysical qualities and relations, whereby God's perfection and dignity and power are contrasted with the transitoriness and weakness of human beings and their words and works. Yet the members of this group will reasonably take themselves to be serious in their commitment to the absolute truths of their religion. They too regard themselves as engaged in a dialogue between God and man which is a real event or process and not the projection of human thoughts and feelings on to the world outside us. Many saints and divines throughout the centuries have given or would have given accounts of their faith that would place them in this group. It is probable that in the nineteenth and twentieth centuries most theologians, and most educated believers in general, have construed their beliefs in this second way.

The third group may be smaller, but is probably becoming more numerous. In the past its members have mainly been heretics and atheists and agnostics rather than professors (in either sense) of Christian belief. Now they include many who say that they subscribe to the doctrines they interpret, but a greater number who read the book of Job, and the Old and New Testaments generally, 'as literature'. To regard the scriptures in this light is not to cease to take them seriously, but it is to decline to give them unique and authoritative status. It is also to dispense with, or at least to regard as inessential, the doctrinal basis on which the authors of the Bible took themselves to be contributing to our understanding of the world and life. A brief positive account of the position of this group can take its starting point from some texts in the history of Greek literature and religion.

Homer and his heroes remark from time to time that the race of mortals is like the race of leaves, here today and gone tomorrow: *hoiē per phullōn geneē, toiē de kai andrōn*. The observation is sound, and expresses a truth that every human being knows but needs to be reminded of. The same thought is expressed in the gospels, where we are asked to consider the grass of the field which today is, and tomorrow is cast into the oven. A related thought is conveyed by Shakespeare's picture of 'man, dressed in a little brief authority'. And by God's question to Job. My third group of interpreters of biblical theology are those for whom all these sentences are independent but collaborative instruments of human thought on the human condition, all equally pictorial and not *committal* like the affirmations of the first two groups.

The scale of operations may be greatly increased without qualifying the contrasts. The *Oresteia* of Aeschylus may be used as a guide to some aspects of human life by an ancient Greek who also regards it as a historical record of relations between gods and men, and by a modern reader or critic for whom the mythology and theology are a medium, not a message. But the work still conveys to the modern reader much of what it conveyed to the Greek audience, and much of what the Bible has conveyed to a hundred generations of the race of mortals. We came late to the scene of the cosmic drama. As flies to wanton boys, so we are to the gods, who will shape our destinies however we rough-hew them. Not even the gods can change the past, or undo what they or we have done.

Our dependence and impermanence and fragility are well known to us, and we do not forget what we know well. Religion, like literature and philosophy, reminds us of what we know well and have not forgotten, because, as Mill said, we do not always fitly dwell upon the truths that are known to us. We often turn away from what is disturbing, and sometimes turn away from what is reassuring, and need to be helped back to a sense of proportion and perspective.

This sketch of a part of the place that religious beliefs play in many human lives is rough and unready. But if its three groups of believers and unbelievers are read as stages on a gradual slope, and not as steps on a staircase, they will serve to remind us of the internal variety and complexity that religious life shares with human life generally. It will thus help us to answer our question 'Does philosophy leave religion as it is?'

If the deficiencies of our sketchy description of religion were remedied, or if we had more than a sketch of Wittgenstein's own description of this aspect of our natural history, it would differ radically from its present form. It would note the varieties of use of religious texts and creeds and sentences and prayers and psalms and stories. That means that it would show the variety of the *users* of all these instruments, and of their purposes and practices and actions and emotions. In religion, as elsewhere, a Wittgensteinian description is a description of human beings and of the forms of human lives. It *notes* these phenomena, and rejects false accounts of the matter *as* false.

Does it leave everything as it is? It does: it presents what is there, ungarbled, unshaped by our desires or prejudices; it helps us to detect in ourselves and others the disposition to oversimplify the complex, to unify the diverse, to impose patterns and 'requirements' that the phenomena do not fit. It gives ethical as well as intellectual help, and the one via the other. In teaching us *differences*—that word is one of Wittgenstein's slogans—it helps us to see when our use of familiar words and practices has become hypocritical or merely conformist or merely radical, and has ceased to have the relation to their use by others in the past and present that it would need to preserve if we were accurately and honestly to be described as believing what we say we believe, valuing what we say we value.

Does it leave everything as it is? It does not: it clears minds, exposes fallacies, detects insincerities, provokes heresy-hunts. It does so by noting the variety of uses and of users of forms of words, by setting out parallels and differences between one assertion or practice and another, by reminding us of what we count as a prayer or a conversion or a sacrifice or a god. But this description of what it does is so like the description of it as not doing anything, as leaving everything as it is, that we should be reminded of our recognition that photography and archaeology and economics both do and do not leave things as they are. That is to say, we should be reminded of the variegated uses that can be given to the words 'It makes no difference' or 'It changes it out of all recognition' or 'Philosophy leaves everything as it is'.

When we react to the philosopher's description, to his natural history, our reactions themselves form part of the belief that the philosopher was describing. This is something we have already noted in noticing that what Wittgenstein's description leaves unchanged includes the machinery for changing things. Matthew Arnold said that Sophocles saw life steadily and saw it whole. Sophocles was not changed by Arnold's perception of the steadiness and wholeness of his fellow poet's vision. Life is not changed by the achievement of that vision itself, though lives may be changed by it; the life of Arnold, perhaps, or the life of Sophocles.

Chronological Chart

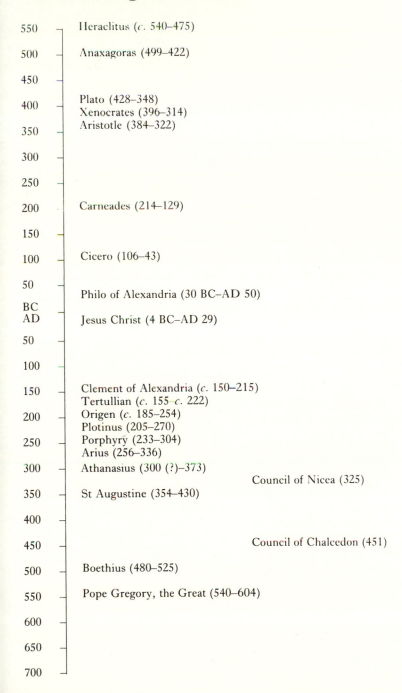

550	Heraclitus (*c.* 540–475)
500	Anaxagoras (499–422)
450	
400	Plato (428–348) Xenocrates (396–314)
350	Aristotle (384–322)
300	
250	
200	Carneades (214–129)
150	
100	Cicero (106–43)
50	
BC	Philo of Alexandria (30 BC–AD 50)
AD	Jesus Christ (4 BC–AD 29)
50	
100	
150	Clement of Alexandria (*c.* 150–215)
	Tertullian (*c.* 155–*c.* 222)
200	Origen (*c.* 185–254)
	Plotinus (205–270)
250	Porphyry (233–304)
	Arius (256–336)
300	Athanasius (300 (?)–373)
	Council of Nicea (325)
350	St Augustine (354–430)
400	
450	Council of Chalcedon (451)
500	Boethius (480–525)
550	Pope Gregory, the Great (540–604)
600	
650	
700	

237

Chronological Chart

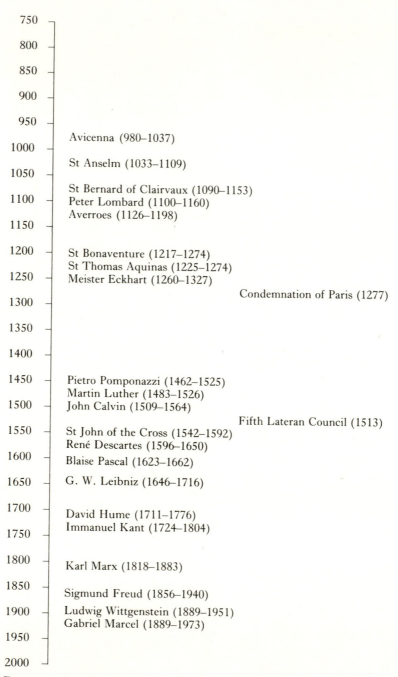

750	
800	
850	
900	
950	
1000	Avicenna (980–1037)
1050	St Anselm (1033–1109)
1100	St Bernard of Clairvaux (1090–1153) Peter Lombard (1100–1160) Averroes (1126–1198)
1150	
1200	St Bonaventure (1217–1274)
1250	St Thomas Aquinas (1225–1274) Meister Eckhart (1260–1327)
1300	Condemnation of Paris (1277)
1350	
1400	
1450	Pietro Pomponazzi (1462–1525)
1500	Martin Luther (1483–1526) John Calvin (1509–1564)
1550	Fifth Lateran Council (1513) St John of the Cross (1542–1592)
1600	René Descartes (1596–1650) Blaise Pascal (1623–1662)
1650	G. W. Leibniz (1646–1716)
1700	David Hume (1711–1776)
1750	Immanuel Kant (1724–1804)
1800	Karl Marx (1818–1883)
1850	Sigmund Freud (1856–1940)
1900	Ludwig Wittgenstein (1889–1951) Gabriel Marcel (1889–1973)
1950	
2000	

Dates are as in William L. Reese, *Dictionary of Philosophy and Religion* (New Jersey: Humanities Press, 1980)

Index of Names

Index of Names

Index of Names

Index of Subjects

Index of Subjects

RANDALL LIBRARY-UNCW

3 0490 0354804 /